W9-CDM-800

WITHDRAWN

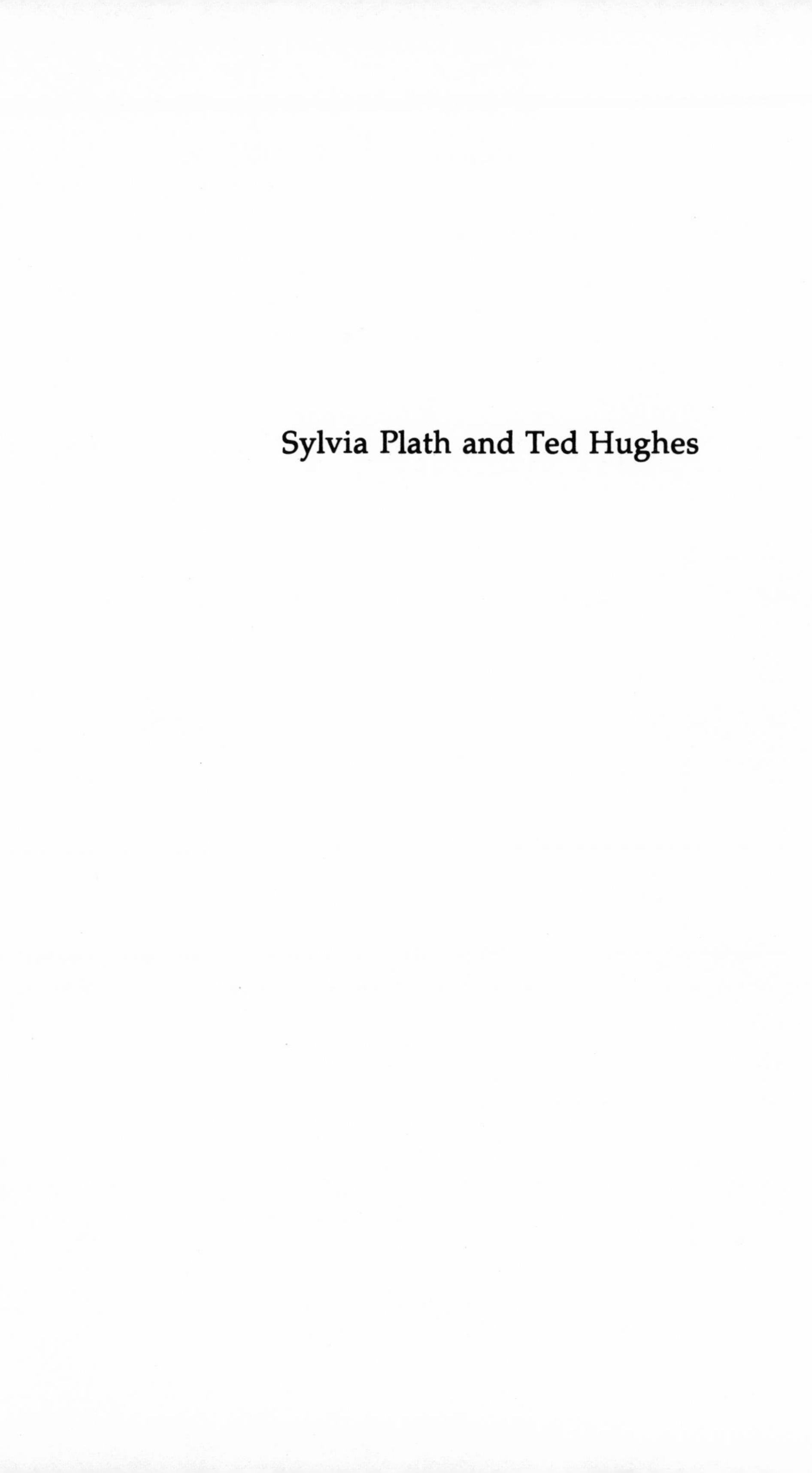

Sylvia Plath and Ted Hughes

University of Illinois Press *Urbana Chicago London*

SYLVIA PLATH AND TED HUGHES

Margaret Dickie Uroff

Second printing, 1980

Grateful acknowledgment is made to the following for permission to quote copyrighted materials:

Alfred A. Knopf, Inc.: "All the Dead Dears," "Hardcastle Crags," "The Manor Garden," "The Stones," and "Point Shirley," from *The Colossus and Other Poems* by Sylvia Plath (1962).

William Heinemann, Ltd.: "Black Rook in Rainy Weather," from *The Colossus and Other Poems* by Sylvia Plath (1960).

Harper & Row Publishers, Inc.: "Morning Song," "Nick and the Candlestick," "Cut," "Medusa," "Ariel," and "Years," from *Ariel* by Sylvia Plath (1966). "Wuthering Heights," "Maenad," "Insomniac," and "Witch Burning," from *Crossing the Water* by Sylvia Plath (1972). "Thalidomide" and "Purdah," from *Winter Trees* by Sylvia Plath (1972). "Wind," "Egg-Head," "The Martyrdom of Bishop Farrar," "Billet-Doux," "Parlour-Piece," "The Jaguar," "The Thought-Fox," and "The Hawk in the Rain," from *The Hawk in the Rain* by Ted Hughes (1957). "Mayday on Holderness," "Lupercalia," "Crow Hill," "November," "February," and "Thrushes," from *Lupercal* by Ted Hughes (1960). "Kreutzer Sonata," "The Howling of Wolves," "Stations," and "Karma," from *Wodwo* by Ted Hughes (1967). "Crow Hears Fate Knocking" from *Crow* by Ted Hughes (1971).

Library of Congress Cataloging in Publication Data

Uroff, Margaret Dickie.
Sylvia Plath and Ted Hughes.

Includes index.
1. Plath, Sylvia — Criticism and interpretation.
2. Hughes, Ted, 1930- — Criticism and interpretation. I. Title.
PS3566.L27Z94 821'.9'1409 79-74
ISBN 0-252-00734-4

To the memory of Margaret McKenzie Dickie
Edna Snyder Sweet
Hazel MacLeod Wills

Preface

The legends of Sylvia Plath and Ted Hughes are well known. She is the golden girl whose blaze toward suicide produced some powerful poems, and he is the explosive talent whose talking animals disrupted the calm of contemporary English poetry. They have been made to appear spectacular, as if their accomplishments erupted without sources or influences. Even the critical effort to get behind these legends and assess the poems has tended to regard the two writers as figures isolated from each other, responsive only to the inner compulsions of their independent spirits. That they are unusual and in some ways quite different poets cannot be denied, but such a view ignores the central fact of their careers: that they lived and worked together during a period of significant productivity. This book examines their poetic collaboration in order to see how it influenced their development.

To see their poems in the context in which they were written will not diminish the startling quality of these two poets' achievements, but it should provide the fullest and most accurate background against which to read them. Paradoxically, critics have regarded Plath and Hughes as unique poets and at the same time used them as convenient examples of new trends in American and English contemporary poetry. Plath's life and career have forced a comparison with Anne Sexton and John Berryman, whose confessional poetry and private misery seem to parallel her own. And Hughes has been discussed, along with Thom Gunn, George McBeth, John Wain, Peter Porter, and Anthony Thwaite, as a poet obsessed with themes of physical cruelty.[1] Their individual reputations have been established almost exclusively by classifying them along national lines: Plath, the American, and Hughes, the English poet. Such a division does not account for the actual circumstances of their lives: they lived and worked both in America and in England; they admit reading and being influenced by both American and English contemporaries; and, most significantly, they produced important portions of their major works as a result of their poetic association. This broader context demands consideration and may indeed explain certain anomalous aspects of their development, such as the ritualistic quality of Plath's late poems or the surrealism that surfaces in *Wodwo* and *Crow*.

Reading Plath and Hughes together might also help dispel the false magic of their reputations. The charge that they are killer poets loses its effectiveness when it is jointly applied. John Press's claim that Hughes "is a bruiser who pummels his readers with the harshest, most solid words in order to batter them into submission" is weakened when it is echoed by Elizabeth Hardwick, who says Plath's "work is brutal, like the smash of a fist; and sometimes it is also mean in its feeling."[2] Bruiser and brute they may well have been, but to a certain extent they encouraged this tone in each other. In some ways their poems appear to be charge and countercharge. Examining the development from Plath's early fastidious control to her late violent freedoms, along with Hughes's growth from rigid formalism to open form, we may see certain parallels in their careers and detect points at which they encourage each other by example and by criticism.

The hyperboles used to describe each poet will be tempered by a full examination of their working careers. Robert Lowell's contention that in her last poems Sylvia Plath "becomes something imaginary, newly, wildly and subtly created — hardly a person at all, or a woman, certainly not another 'poetess,' but one of those super-real, hypnotic, great, classical heroines," must be placed against the fact that this wild person was a woman, abandoned by her husband, who got up very early every morning to write before her children awakened.[3]

An exploration of her long apprenticeship to her craft, the several writing blocks through which she was helped and hindered by her poet-husband, and the ways in which she responded to his interests and success will suggest not only how she worked up to the accomplishment of her late work, but also how in these new and super-real creations she was returning to her earliest voice and concerns. The critical response to Hughes's *Crow* has likewise tended to polarize at the extremes of outrage or enthusiasm and has been aimed at denying or lavishing on him the status of a major poet. Even one of his most reasonable critics, Karl Miller, has said, "He can't, in fact, be said to favor atrocities. But he can be said to be fascinated by fear and fang, and this has been enough for criticism to imply, in its sanguinary way, that his fascination with such subjects is that of Count Dracula."[4] Again, an examination of Hughes's very slow development — the long poetic silence with which he responded to Plath's suicide, the radical shift in pose evident in *Wodwo*, the return in *Crow* to the beast fable as an escape from the personal turmoil he had suffered — suggests that, far from being a figure of control such as Count Dracula, Hughes was a poet who became painfully open to the terrors of his existence.

Although Hughes himself has insisted that Plath's poems were visitations from the spirit world, and that even his own poems often arrived without meditation or plan, a study of the actual stages through which they moved indicates that their poems were neither sudden nor unprepared creations. They were, rather, responses to certain shared experiences, as well as to various experiments. In the years during which they lived together, their devotion to their craft was uninterrupted. They learned from their own efforts as well as from each other, and the preparation for their later accomplishments was both thorough and demanding.

Finally, a consideration of Plath and Hughes together makes it difficult to assert baldly, as Hardwick has done, that in "Sylvia Plath's work and in her life the elements of pathology are so deeply rooted and so little resisted that one is disinclined to hope for general principles, sure origins, applications, or lessons."[5] Many of the elements in Plath's poetry that have been attributed to her emotional and mental disturbances have counterparts in Hughes's work, and may be linked more accurately to a common interest in the subconscious and the subrational that they explored together. When critics have examined this aspect of Hughes's poetry, they have generally described it as a philosophical view of the modern world. Yet this approach is no more illuminating than the pathological approach to Plath. We read Hughes not for his philosophy and Plath not for her pathology, but for the poetry that each produced. In this enterprise the crucial concern must be the poetic interests they nurtured. Plath called her own poems "Echoes travelling/ Off from the centre." My argument is that that center incorporated and enclosed Hughes as well.

In the process of writing this book, I have been greatly aided by comments and suggestions from Carol Kyle, Carol Neely, Cary Nelson, Elizabeth Shapiro, and Zohreh Sullivan.

— M. D. U.

Notes

[1] See Philip Hobsbaum, "The Temptations of Giant Despair," *Hudson Review*, XXV (Winter, 1972-73), 597-612, and Edward Lucie-Smith, "The Tortured Yearned as Well," *Critical Quarterly*, IV (Spring, 1962), 34-43.

[2] John Press, *Rule and Energy: Trends in British Poetry since the Second World War* (London: Oxford University Press, 1963), p. 182, and Elizabeth Hardwick, "On Sylvia Plath" (review of *The Bell Jar* and *Crossing the Water*), *New York Review of Books*, XVII, August 12, 1971, p. 3.

[3] Robert Lowell, "Foreword" for Sylvia Plath's *Ariel* (New York: Harper & Row, 1966), p. vii.

[4] Karl Miller, "Fear and Fang" (review of *Selected Poems, 1957-1967* and *The Iron Giant: A Story in Five Nights*), *New York Review of Books*, XXI, March 7, 1974, p. 3.

[5] Hardwick, "On Sylvia Plath," p. 3.

Contents

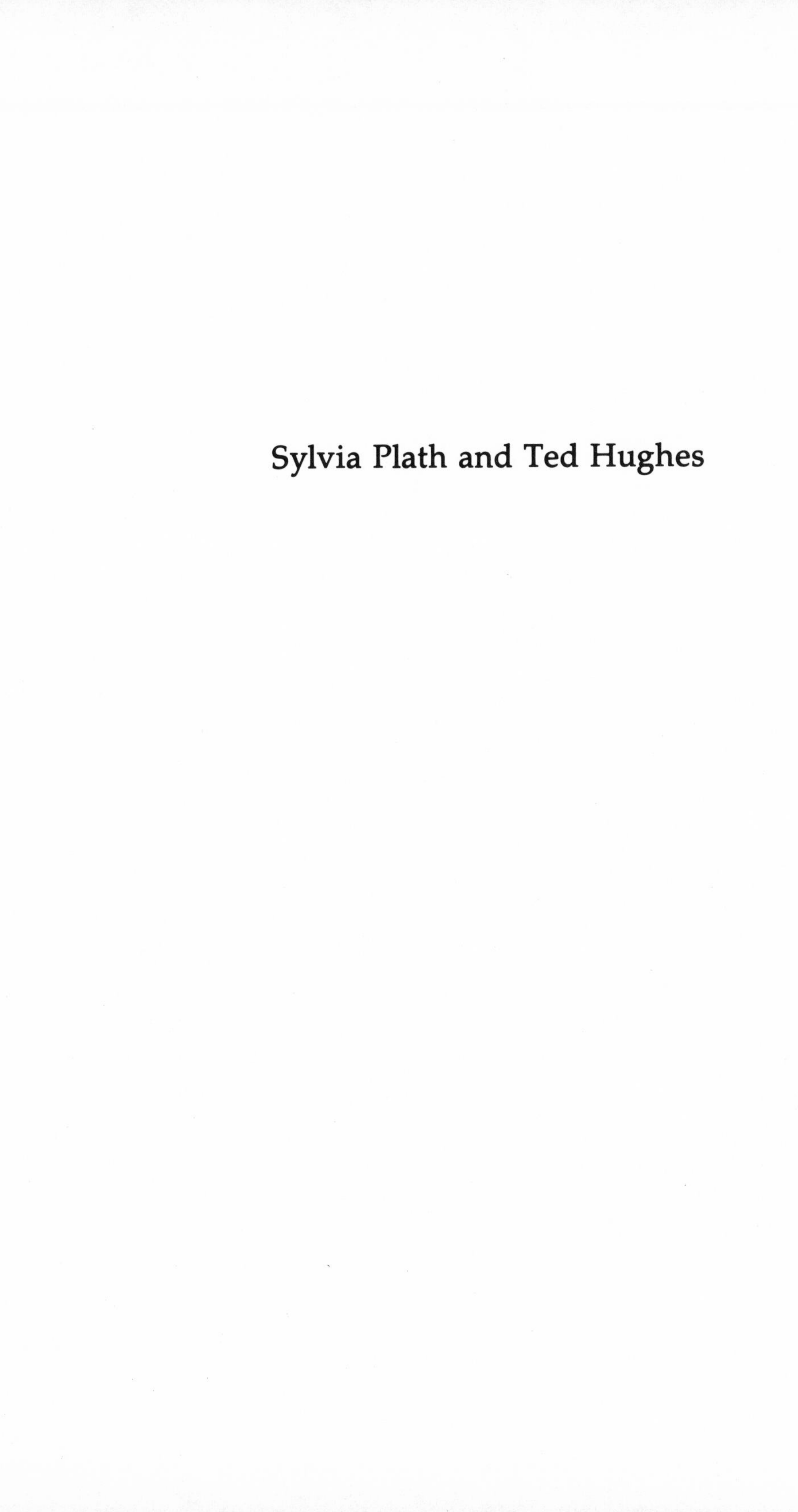

Sylvia Plath and Ted Hughes

ONE

Introduction

Two poets of comparable stature, Sylvia Plath and Ted Hughes, lived together during a crucial period in their creative lives. They read poems to each other and read each other's poems. They encouraged, criticized, and reacted to each other, and in the process wrote their own work. Certainly this close association cannot be discounted as a factor in their careers, although the hints of how they worked together (Hughes admitting that he suggested topics for poems to Plath, and Plath reporting their joint efforts to elicit subjects for poems from the Ouija board) are only minimally helpful.[1] To judge the importance of their creative relationship, the primary evidence is the work itself, and this study examines their poems in the context in which they were written.

A reading of the work of Plath and Hughes together would seem to be the most obvious approach to them, yet the usual critical strategy is to discuss Plath among American poets and Hughes among his English contemporaries. The distortions brought about by such treatment may be clearly illustrated. Plath has written a poem about the moors, "Wuthering Heights," in which she claims:

> There is no life higher than the grasstops
> Or the hearts of sheep, and the wind
> Pours by like destiny, bending
> Everything in one direction.
> I can feel it trying
> To funnel my heat away.

If I pay the roots of the heather
Too close attention, they will invite me
To whiten my bones among them.

One American critic places this poem in what she broadly terms a Romantic tradition, but actually defines only in its American phase. Joyce Carol Oates says, "Miss Plath is an identity reduced to desperate statements about her dilemma as a passive witness in a turbulent world. . . . There is never any integrating of the self and its experience, the self and its field of perception. Human consciousness, to Sylvia Plath, is always an intruder in the natural universe."[2] Such a self is said to be weak, submissive, indulging in regressive fantasies. Perhaps; but then how do we read Hughes's poem about the wind on the moors? "Wind" concludes with this image:

The house
Rang like some fine green goblet in the note
That any second would shatter it. Now deep
In chairs, in front of the great fire, we grip
Our hearts and cannot entertain book, thought,

Or each other. We watch the fire blazing,
And feel the roots of the house move, but sit on.

Here again we have a passive witness to a natural turbulence, a sense of fear, and a comparable split between the self and the world. Are we to assume, as Plath's critic would have it, that Hughes, too, is expressing the regressive fantasies of a weak and submissive ego? Or is it more accurate to view him as simply recording the terror inspired in the human observer by the immensity of the natural distances and the violence of the weather in his home country? An English critic comments on Hughes's poem:

This is a language uniquely fitted to express a "vital awareness of the continuum" outside human life, of the mystery embodied in the created universe. The mystery takes many forms. There is no mistaking it when it takes the form of a gale. . . .

Within the house, how can the occupants, their security gone, hearing those "wandering elementals" outside, continue with their civilized and complacent reading, thinking and conversation. . . .

They can only grip their hearts, hold desperately onto their integrity which is under siege. If the window gave and the wind came in, the whole charade of civilization would be swept away.

The wind is representative of all those natural forces we try to shut out of our lives, which, if let in on our sense would leave us blind, floundering or mad.[3]

Can Plath be considered a passive victim while Hughes, in a comparable situation, appears as a witness in control? Or are the two poets being judged by different standards? Behind the American and English critics are two different kinds of nature poetry. Although she places Plath at the end of a tradition and sees her as embodying its death throes, Oates is essentially concerned with that phase of Romanticism which, at its strongest point, stems from Ralph Waldo Emerson and claims that the poet's occupation is to convert the Not-Me into the Me or, to use more modern terms, to integrate the self and its field of perception. Emerson's transparent eyeball, Whitman's more boisterously celebrated inclusive self, as well as Stevens's ordering imagination stand behind Oates's reading of Plath's poems. In contrast, Keith Sagar locates himself and Hughes in an English tradition by assuming that the natural world really exists apart from the poet's imagining; that the powers of the world are in opposition to civilization rather than to self; that the poet's fears are real, not pathological. These assumptions derive from the nature poetry of Wordsworth, Blake, and Yeats.

To be sure, there are differences between Plath's "Wuthering Heights" and Hughes's "Wind," but they are probably not best defined as the difference between a desperate statement and a vital awareness. In fact, the intensity of Plath's fears may result from a heightened sense of the continuum outside human life, while Hughes's gripped heart may be considered a fairly desperate response. In the case of these two poems, splitting the poets along national lines encourages a distorted reading of Plath, who, as we shall see, was as interested as Hughes (and probably because of Hughes) in the mysterious forces embodied in the natural world. In other poems, however, national divisions are unfair to Hughes.

For example, English critics have reacted vehemently to the violence in his poetry, while American critics, more inured to violence, have been less shocked by Plath's use of it. Here again, it is worthwhile to examine what the two poets learned from each other and how their poems of violence are related.

Aside from setting the poems in a context and understanding that at times Plath wrote out of an English tradition and Hughes out of an American one — traditions they must have partly learned from each other — the value of reading Plath and Hughes together is to see a unique example of two important poets influencing each other. Hughes has warned, "This whole business of influence is mysterious. Sometimes it's just a few words that open up a whole prospect. They may occur anywhere. Then again the influences that really count are most likely not literary at all."[4] Certainly Hughes is right. Perhaps even the poet has forgotten how he came to write a certain poem, and clearly the critic can only guess. Despite this fact, in the poetry we can see shared interests that strengthened and directed their work. We can never know the few words that opened up new prospects for each, but we can see in the poems the prospects that were opened, the developments in technique, the experiments, the themes that they might have encouraged in each other. As the last phrase indicates, much of this book is speculative; but it is speculation based on a careful reading of the poems and a certain knowledge that the two poets knew each other's work intimately. Obviously Plath and Hughes were not the only contemporary influences on each other. They read widely in the work of their contemporaries and took what was useful from them. Without minimizing that wider context, this study will focus chiefly on the influences exerted between Plath and Hughes.

The direction of the study is provided by Hughes's comment that influences open new prospects. A reading of their work suggests that the two poets worked on each other in exactly this way. The full examination of their work in the following pages will confirm this suggestion; here we may point out only the general outline of their creative relationship. Each poet had quite specific interests and accomplishments, not only when the two first met, but also during their life together; however, this fact did not prevent each from taking or giving to the other. The most obvious example is Hughes's interest in animals, which quickly inspired Plath to write several animal or nature poems. In general, these poems are weak. Plath had caught Hughes's enthusiasm for nature without absorbing his intimacy with and feeling for animals; poems like "Faun" or "Watercolour of Grantchester Meadows" exude a fervency for the subject that exceeds her poetic possession of it. In other early poems, however, in which Plath takes Hughes's animals and uses them for her purpose — "The Shrike," for example, a love-hate poem and a subject on which she had written several early poems — she is more successful. By the time she wrote "Zoo Keeper's Wife" she had become completely familiar with Hughes's zoo and could use his animals for her own quite separate purposes (in this case, to criticize him). Later, when she wrote "Getting There," she had made Hughes's image of the "animal/ Insane for the destination,/ The bloodspot" entirely her own. The process also worked the other way. Hughes borrowed just as freely from Plath, and in somewhat the same way. His first efforts in her direction were fairly unsuccessful. For example, an early love poem such as "Parlour-Piece" may have been inspired by Plath, whom he had just met, but it also owes something to her own treatments of the subject. Then in "Incompatibilities" he masters the subject by giving a darker twist to the image of two lovers made one, and he comes to possess a new insight. Although he seems to retreat from this particular subject in the middle of his career, he returns to it in *Crow* with full force, and with a tone and style that owe much to Plath.

To suggest that their relationship worked in this way is to make very large claims for it, claims that might arouse the objection that such a symbiotic relationship would stifle rather than nurture development. It clearly did stifle certain tendencies: Plath's fastidious experimentations in sestinas and villanelles, for example, as well as Hughes's early exultation in gratuitous vulgarity. But it nurtured other interests. Their relationship may account for Plath's increased concern for the world outside the self and the study, and for Hughes's move toward surrealism. On balance, their association seems to have encouraged the strengths and the development of each poet, not because either poet served consistently as the teacher to the other, but because each was a voracious borrower. They saw and took what was helpful to them, as Hughes confirms in admitting that "you choose a subject because it serves, because you need it."[5] They had, of course, quite different needs, and perhaps for that reason they were particularly open to each other's work.

It is also clear that the two poets, living together and writing, frequently chose a subject not only because it would serve but also because it was close at hand. For example, Plath's "Sow" and Hughes's "View of a Pig" commemorate the same animal. These two occasional poems may not be very significant, but frequently the subjects close at hand opened new areas for each poet, and one was moved to a new stage of awareness by the work of the other. In calculating this kind of influence, the dates of the poems are crucial; often it is hard to pinpoint them. However, one example might serve to suggest the nature of this interchange. In the summer of 1957, Plath and Hughes spent a vacation at Cape Cod. There she wrote or was inspired to write "Mussel Hunter at Rock Harbour," in which, meeting fiddler crabs, she says she feels "shut out, for once, for all,/ Puzzling the passage of their/ Absolutely alien/ Order." She sees the husk of a fiddler crab which "Had an Oriental look,/ A samurai death mask done/ On a tiger tooth," and she concludes soberly, "this relic saved/ Face, to face the bald-faced sun." It is as if Hughes lifted that word, "relic," from Plath's poem and took it as the subject for quite different ruminations. In "Relic," published first in November, 1958, and written perhaps during the Cape Cod summer, Hughes also surveys the seaside waste. Dismissing Plath's concern for her status in the universe, he peers straight through the jawbone he finds to the natural cycle it represents, concluding, "Time in the sea eats its tail, thrives, casts these/ Indigestibles, the spars of purposes/ That failed far from the surface." These two examples seem to locate Plath and Hughes in the very divisions provided for them by Oates and Sagar: Plath the frightened alien, and Hughes the fearless observer. Yet, if we place these poems in the context in which they were written, we might consider that Plath is offering objections to Hughes's assertions, and that without his example she might not be out hunting for anything more than mussels.

Perhaps we could have had one poem of relics without the other, and in fact Hughes here employs an image which he would use again to suggest the strange fertility of nature. However, Hughes's shore poems begin at a time when Plath was also beginning to write a number of poems about the sea. The subject was essential for Plath, who said, "I sometimes think my vision of the sea is the clearest thing I own."[6] The point to be noted here is that she brings to her native landscape both her own clear vision and a strange sense of reserve about what she sees, as if she were trying to see through Hughes's eyes and simply did not succeed. Plath's feeling of being shut out from an alien natural world is not a new one in modern poetry, but her handling of it is unusual. Unlike Frost, who felt one had to be versed in country things not to think the phoebes wept for man's misfortune, Plath's speaker is not shielded from her puzzlement by either inside knowledge or tough skepticism. Her mussel hunter seems peculiarly open to nature, almost an anachronism among twentieth-century saunterers, and thus doubly shocked at the alien order she finds.

From what we know of Plath's early poems, we might assume that she would not send her characters into nature for any insights. That she does so here, and continues to do so in a number of poems that follow, suggests that she was attempting to broaden her range — and, even more than that, to include areas of exploration that Hughes's presence and poetry opened to her. It was Hughes, she has said, who first introduced her to nature.[7] That he claimed direct access to areas that puzzled her did not deter her from confronting them again and again in her poems. She seldom claimed to see what he could see, but neither did she cease looking. His own example may have encouraged her to turn to the landscape as a subject, and his particular interest not in the scenic qualities of the landscape but in the laws of nature it manifested may account for her concern with the order of the universe.

To be sure, a number of her sea poems center not on natural laws but on some private demon that rises out of the sea to threaten her; but along with these poems are others that explore the world outside her own psyche. These poems almost always express an uncertainty, and perhaps Plath's reservations on this subject account for the number of poems where Hughes returns to take a second glance at the natural world and to detail more concretely its attributes. His earliest poems of nature and animals simply point to an area beyond the human, which (from Plath's poetic point of view) was not sufficient evidence of its power. In later poems, such as "Ghost-Crabs" and "Second Glance at a Jaguar," he provides the needed evidence. Hughes says, "We go on writing poems because one poem never gets the whole account right. There is always something missed."[8] Plath's poems may have suggested to him what was missed.

Their poems are constant explorations and renewed elaborations of the insights their experiences offered. Their poems read as parts of a continuing debate about the nature of the universe, in which Plath's reservations and Hughes's assertions play against each other. Strangely enough, as Hughes developed he began to retreat from the confident insights of his early poems and to question the laws of the universe, to admit that the skylarks' song was to him "incomprehensibly both ways — / Joy! Help! Joy! Help!" In contrast, Plath casts off some of her early reservations, and in her later poems she associates herself with the very same natural order that had earlier shut her out, with the horse in "Ariel" and the queen bee in "Stings." She defines that order in terms Hughes uses in "Skylarks."

To claim that they worked over the same area in quite different ways need not minimize the extent to which each was engaged in the distinctly separate enterprise of recovering a genuine self — which was, as they understood it, the purpose of poetry. On the surface, the larger concerns of their careers seem far apart. Plath's interest in psychological states and extreme human experiences appears far removed from Hughes's concern with the non-human cosmos. Her movement backward in time to some particularly painful point in her psychic development and his movement outward in space toward the submerged life of the animal or the elemental have been considered totally different directions. Yet, what is Hughes's interest in animals but an attempt to express the submerged life in himself? And what is Plath's probing of the psyche but a search for the instinctual and elemental qualities of her nature? Hughes's animals may inhabit the world beyond the human, but as they come into his poems they are creatures made of words, carrying the burden of Hughes's vision, and what he sees in them is what he sees of his own deepest nature. Animals talk and think and dream only in poems, and when they do so, they express their own world only as it is refracted through the human eyes of the poet. At the same time, Plath's probing of her deeply buried pain may be less solipsistic than it has appeared. She has been accused of blowing up the tiniest personal experience into an event of universal significance — a criticism which assumes that her own experience was too abnormal to be generally meaningful, and that her poetry is only the case history of the pathological. But the very inflation of her experience in her poetry suggests, first, that she was searching beyond its private accidents for its larger meaning, and, further, that the impulse of her poetry is not confessional but visionary.

Even as they swerved away from each other in their choice of subjects, Plath and Hughes profited from a creative association which remained central, despite other influences. Perhaps nowhere is this situation clearer than in the remarkable poems of Plath's last months. Although these have been called confessional, actually Plath never confesses real experience in any detail. Her characters, called father or mother, are in fact highly ritualized figures. The realistic details that we find in other confessional poets such as Robert Lowell and Anne Sexton are largely absent from her work. In a sense, Plath does not confess anything here; rather, she vaunts her superior power, creating what Edward Butscher calls the mythology of the bitch goddess.[9] In its ritualistic quality, and especially in its ritual of creation and destruction, her late poetry is closer to Hughes's than to Lowell's and Sexton's. As we shall see, the speakers of "Lady Lazarus" and certainly of "Daddy" owe more to the defiant tone and incantatory rhythm of Hughes's "Hawk Roosting" than to the melancholic analysis of the man in Lowell's "Skunk Hour." To be sure, the rage of the killer woman in Plath's poems stems from a complex psychological situation that Hughes would claim has no counterpart in the hawk's mindless murderousness, however much the quality of that mindlessness must reflect the psyche of its creator. But she has been so brutalized by her experience that she is reduced almost to the level of the hawk. The violent energy that drives her wipes out her analytic powers, her humanistic scruples, until she rises at the end to the kill with the same instinctive fury that propels the hawk. To make this connection is not to claim that Plath modeled her women after Hughes's predatory animals, but only to suggest that, in addition to the psychological sources of the poem, literary sources should be considered. In creating the myth of the vengeful female who rises against her oppressors, Plath had available as an aid Hughes's own myth of enraged and captive energies, and his own image of the creative-destructive female.

Throughout his career, Hughes's imagination has been engaged by what he imagines to be violent energies in man and nature. In his efforts to describe these energies, to explore their connections, to explain their short circuits, Hughes has been drawn into submerged areas of the psyche. His knowledge of folklore and myth has encouraged him in this direction, but he has also been responsive to what he called Plath's extraordinary psychic gifts that made the world of her poetry "one of emblematic visionary events, mathematical symmetries, clairvoyance and metamorphoses."[10] Her contact with the spirit world was as intense as his own, and was frequently expressed in much more concrete and vivid terms. The depths she probed opened to her a dimension that corresponded to the underworld of Hughes's poems.

Hughes makes the connection between the powers within and the powers without in a number of poems, but nowhere more clearly than in "The Bull Moses." There, looking into the "byre's/ Blaze of darkness," he is abruptly struck with "a sudden shut-eyed look/ Backward into the head." In Plath's first collection of poems, the black man and dark spirits that rise up from the depths, as well as the thin people that hover on the fringes of her consciousness, are much more clearly defined than the presences Hughes can describe at first only as "Something more near/ Though deeper within darkness." As these spirits continue to inhabit Plath's poetry, they turn into surrealistic images under her gaze: in "Elm" the speaker says, "I am terrified by this dark thing/ That sleeps in me;/ All day I feel its soft, feathery turnings, its malignity." She admits finally, "I am incapable of more knowledge." While Hughes refuses such incapacity even when his experience appears to point to it, in his later poems he expands in the direction of Plath, toward surrealism. Even as early as "Mayday on Holderness," he sounds like Plath (in "Poem for a Birthday") when he talks about

> What a length of gut is growing and breathing —
> This mute eater, biting through the mind's
> Nursery floor, with eel and hyena and vulture,
> With creepy-crawly and the root,
> With the sea-worm, entering its birthright.

If Plath's surrealistic imagery served to express states at the extremities of consciousness, states which she could formulate in no other way, Hughes was also able to use such imagery to break through the rigidity of rational coherence to a deeper level of the imagination. He says that a poet "develops inwards into imagination and beyond that into spirit, using perhaps no more external material than before and maybe even less but deepening it and making it operate in the many different inner dimensions until it opens up perhaps the religious or holy basis of the whole thing."[11] That holy basis is something toward which Plath moved, and the stages of her own development may have helped Hughes as he developed inward toward what he was to define as an older and deeper area, the surrealism of folklore. Plath was not the only poet who could have pointed him in this direction, and perhaps Hughes did not need any help to break out of the rational and coherent structures of his early poems. Nevertheless, an exploration of the parallels in their work suggests that her efforts were useful to him.

The various ways in which their work developed along parallel lines are significant for a full understanding of their poetry; but, to conclude with a practical matter, perhaps they served each other best as publicists and editors. Although the evidence needed for a complete examination of this aspect of their relationship will not be available until their manuscripts are open to the public, we do have some indications of the importance of their joint roles in this area. Plath's letters attest to the fact that she acted as Hughes's first agent, typing and sending out his poems to magazines. Hughes had published very few poems before he met Plath, and she seems to have been the major force behind his earliest publication. As we might expect, she sent his poems to American as well as English magazines. Given the insulation of young American and English poets, he might not have sought the American audience for himself — and, significantly, it was a receptive one for him. The importance, to him, of his favorable American reception as a beginning poet who was going against the grain of the English poetic establishment cannot be measured, but it must have served as important encouragement early in his publishing career. Had Hughes not married Plath, he might have gone to Australia, where he was bound when he met her and changed his plans, and from Australia he would have had a much more difficult time establishing himself as a poet in either England or America.[12]

Conversely, Hughes played a major role in publishing Plath's poems after her death. If her reputation owes everything to *Ariel,* then it owes everything to Hughes, who offered this collection to the public. Had Plath lived, she would of course have continued to publish her poems, but whether she would have published *Ariel* in its present form (not to mention *Crossing the Water* and *Winter Trees*) is debatable. As we know from

Hughes, she was a tireless arranger and reviser of her first volume of poems, and she might have omitted several poems from *Ariel.* Critics have made much of the difference between *The Colossus* and *Ariel,* but no one has considered that the difference may be attributed to Hughes's editing of the second volume. His taste differed from Plath's. He liked "The Moon and the Yew Tree," which, he says, she regarded simply as an exercise; she might not have included that good poem.[13] Also, Hughes's role as editor of *Ariel* might be more critical than we now have evidence to judge. For example, Plath read such significant poems as "Lady Lazarus," "Fever 103°," and "Nick and the Candlestick" for the BBC on October 30, 1962, just three months before she died, in versions different from the ones that appear in *Ariel.* This fact suggests, first, that there were several versions of these poems, from which Hughes may have had to choose what he considered to be the last; and, further, that these poems may have been still in process, not in finished form. The long ending of "Nick and the Candlestick" in the BBC recording was published later as a separate poem by Hughes, a fact which opens the door for speculation that he has been a fairly energetic editor of Plath's poetry manuscripts. On these issues the evidence is too scanty to judge. It is important to note, however, that Hughes made available the poems on which Plath's reputation rests, repeating years later what she had done earlier for him.

This study, after an opening chapter on Plath's and Hughes's ideas about poetry, has a roughly chronological organization, dealing with stages in their developments and events in their lives that called forth certain poems. As this examination of their careers will reveal, the Muse visited each in turn. The organization of this survey will follow the Muse, focusing on Plath and then on Hughes in periods of extreme productivity. Moving from one poet to the other should suggest the extent to which each poet's work could serve the other and encourage certain directions and breakthroughs in each career.

Notes

[1] *Letters Home* by Sylvia Plath, selected and edited by Aurelia Schober Plath (New York: Harper & Row, 1975), p. 346. Also Ted Hughes, "Notes on the Chronological Order of Sylvia Plath's Poems," in *The Art of Sylvia Plath: A Symposium*, ed. Charles Newman (Bloomington: Indiana University Press, 1970), pp. 193-194.

[2] Joyce Carol Oates, "The Death Throes of Romanticism: The Poems of Sylvia Plath," *Southern Review*, IX (July, 1973), 512-513.

[3] Keith Sagar, *The Art of Ted Hughes* (Cambridge: Cambridge University Press, 1975), pp. 27-28.

[4] Ted Hughes, "Ted Hughes and Crow," an interview with Egbert Faas, *London Magazine*, X (January, 1971), 14.

[5] Ibid., p. 15.

[6] Sylvia Plath, "Ocean 1212-W," in *Writers on Themselves*, ed. Herbert Read (London: British Broadcasting Corporation, 1964), p. 102.

[7] Plath, *Letters Home*, pp. 234, 235.

[8] "Ted Hughes and Crow," p. 15.

[9] In his critical biography, Edward Butscher sketches the portrait of Plath as a bitch goddess. He says, "The 'bitch,' of course, is a familiar enough figure — a discontented, tense, frequently brilliant woman goaded into fury by her repressed or distorted status in a male society; and the 'goddess' conveys the opposite image, a more creative one, though it too represents an extreme." *Sylvia Plath: Method and Madness* (New York: Seabury Press, 1976), pp. xi-xii. While what Butscher has to say is based largely on interviews with acquaintances and friends, some of whom may be unreliable sources, this particular image of her is certainly insightful — even if it is dangerous to reduce a life to a single image, as Butscher has done.

[10] Newman, ed., *Art of Sylvia Plath*, p. 187.

[11] Hughes, "Ted Hughes and Crow," p. 15.

[12] For a brief reference to Hughes's plans, see Plath, *Letters Home*, p. 240.

[13] Newman, ed., *Art of Sylvia Plath*, pp. 193-194.

TWO

Home Territories

Both Sylvia Plath and Ted Hughes have written of that moment when they first discovered themselves as writers.[1] In essays prepared for a BBC production in which a number of writers talk about themselves, the two have traced the origins of the creative impulse to particular childhood experiences. In this they resemble the other authors in the series, who recognize (as did the ancients before them) that the Muses are daughters of Memory, and that creative energy springs from a particularly intense and early experience that splits the consciousness and divides the child from the illusion of unity between himself and his world. From the desire to return to that moment and simultaneously reexperience its intensity, and with the advantages of age and insight to heal its fateful divisiveness, the writer is born. But Plath's and Hughes's essays differ from those of the other writers as dreams differ from reminiscences. While the others recount particular events and people and locations that have commonplace existences and are heightened for us only because the authors insist that they were determining, Plath and Hughes evoke an intensity of feeling so stripped of the everyday that it has a mythic quality. Their essays are not autobiographical revelations, but explorations of the springs of creativity. Plath's American girlhood and Hughes's English boyhood, widely different though they were, nurtured sensibilities of such similar power, exuberance, and resolution that their details dwindle into insignificance, leaving not a particular story but the universal account of how the artist wrestles from experience his own creative existence. These essays were written late, after Plath and Hughes had discovered what they could do as poets; indeed, Plath's account was broadcast after her death. They may be read as clear indications of what the poets imagined were the directions of their poetry.

The essays are landscape pieces, evocations of the geography of their childhoods. Yet, despite the loving particularity with which the scenes are detailed, the interest is not directed toward nature. Rather, the focus is entirely on the child's recognition of the elements. As Hughes has said, landscapes are valuable to us not simply because of the presence of the elements, but for the encounter between the elemental things and the human feelings the landscapes inspire. The West Yorkshire landscape of Hughes's childhood aroused in him the darkening sense of being trapped under the evil eye of the wall of rock that hemmed in his valley, from which the only escape was to the desolate, eerie, but ultimately exultant moors on the northern horizon. Escape Hughes did; "the moors were the exciting destination," he says. There, in the "strange unearthly starkness" of the trees, Hughes felt "Something of the sky moving so close above them, of the bleak black wall of the laneside, the scruffy gorse-tufted bulge of hillside just beyond. Or perhaps it was simply the light, at once both gloomily purplish and incredibly clear, unnaturally clear, as if objects there had less protection than elsewhere, were more exposed to the radioactive dangers of space, more startled by their own existence." Hughes admits that returning home from these heights "was a descent into the pit, and after each visit I must have returned less and less of myself to the valley. This was where the division of body and soul, for me, began." What made the young boy so willing to entrust his soul to the moors, so anxious to leave part of himself elsewhere when he descended to town, was the conscious awareness that what he could not rescue of himself might be crushed by the gloomy weight of the rock that hung over his childhood. Of the rock he says,

> This was the *memento mundi* over my birth: my spiritual midwife at the time and my godfather ever since — or one of my godfathers.

From my first day, it watched. If it couldn't see me direct, a towering gloom over my pram, it watched me through a species of periscope: that is, by infiltrating the very light of my room with its particular shadow. From my home near the bottom of the south-facing slope of the valley, that cliff was both the curtain and backdrop to existence. All that happened, happened against it or under its supervision. At the same time, all that I imagined happening elsewhere, out in the world, the rock sealed from me, since in England the world seems to lie to the South.

Hughes never encountered the steep face of the rock, although one day when he was six he and his brother went up one side; there he experienced a "terrible piece of newness" as he looked down from the other end of the telescope, seeing his life and his house from a wholly unimagined angle. Although he says he felt an "alarming exhilaration," the visit did not free him from the rock's brooding influence or "tame the strangeness of our neighbor." He went on hating it, feeling it was alien.

At the top of the rock, his brother told him two stories which deepened his uneasiness about it. The first was of a wood pigeon shot in a tree, which then "set its wings and sailed out without a wing-beat stone dead into space to crash two miles away on the other side of the valley." The second was of a tramp who stirred while sleeping in the bracken on the rock's top and was shot for a fox, toppling over the slope. In fact, death is the central message of that rock: "You can't look at a precipice without thinking instantly what it would be like to fall down it, or jump down it." Everyone in the valley lived with that thought, but one of Hughes's ancestors, a farmer in the levels above the rock, "once when he was out shooting rabbits on that difficult near-vertical terrain below his farm, not quite in living memory, took the plunge that the whole valley dreams about and fell to his death down the sheer face."

Under this presence in a country where "Nothing ever quite escapes into happiness," Hughes awakened into consciousness:

If any word could be found engraved around my skull, just above the ears and eyebrows, it would probably be the word "horizon." Every thought I tried to send beyond the confines of that valley had to step over that high definite hurdle. In most places the earth develops away naturally in every direction, over roads and crowded gradients and confused vistas, but there it rose up suddenly to a cut empty upturned edge, high in the sky, and stopped. I supposed it somehow started again somewhere beyond, with difficulty. So the visible horizon was the magic circle, excluding and enclosing, into which our existence had been conjured, and everything in me gravitated towards it.

The human emotions that this landscape made Hughes conscious of are feelings not of fright but of gloom, oppression, constriction, and deathliness in the direction of the rock, contrasted with clarity, excitement, exposure, and exhilaration in the direction of the moors. Between these two sensations Hughes's childhood oscillated. The rock, the evil presence hovering over his birth, gradually and inexorably "pressed its shape and various moods" into his brain. But the moors, inescapable though they were, form the landscape of his conscious memories. Although he started his walks on the moors at a very early age, they were a willed destination, not a fate. In gravitating toward them, he moved toward freedom.

In his description Hughes attributes a mythic dimension to these two powerful elemental forces. The rock is a godfather, a monster, a death-beckoning demon, the representative of all that would restrict him and tie him to the heaviness of earth. In contrast, the "gentle female watery line" of the moors opens into illimitable space, "the unaccustomed weight of open sky" and, despite the ruined farms of the moors, a sense of immensity and endurance and vitality. Without the "evil eye" of the rock, Hughes might never have been driven to the moors; but without the moors he would never have been able to detach himself from the stone. Like the other people in Yorkshire, he would have remained "half-born from the earth," unable to escape the graves which are too close to the surface there.

He says the presence of the rock should have inured him to living in valleys, but in fact it made him hate them and rendered him uneasy and restless in even the slightest declivity. The rock, then, was the spirit of death that drove him to seek a larger life. In poem after poem he pays tribute to the tenaciousness of his native landscape; he never tries to wish it away or escape its factuality, but neither does he succumb to it. If he moves toward the horizon, he details every stubborn and impossible step of the way. It is this difficult struggle toward the horizon that is the subject of Hughes's poetry, rather than the visionary splendor of the seer who has reached the summit. His is not the long view that reduces the substantiality of the world, but the immediate, fierce, intense recognition of the irreducible elements. The direct battle with these elements interests him; to dwell only on the horizons is to deny the clash that, for this poet, proves his strength.

To move between rock and moor is to move between two inexorable elements, and if the moors were an escape from the oppression of the rock, they were not the route toward peace, security, and comfort. Unlike the rock, the moors did not impose themselves; instead, they surrounded and waited. They seemed to retreat as Hughes approached them, yet they were a part of everything he saw. In his account of his earliest memories he endows the landscape with a *genius loci,* and this tutelary and controlling spirit has a double aspect: masculine and feminine, restrictive and liberating, earthbound and skyborn, death-dealing and life-giving. It is not nature itself, but the elemental presence of the god allotted him by the place of his birth, that Hughes treats in his poetry.

Plath's landscape is predictably enough an American one, not landlocked but sea-bound. While Hughes's childhood vision is riveted to the rock, Plath's vista is the sea, and a particularly American version of that vast rhythmical force. If the wind is the "correspondent breeze" of English Romantic poets, the breathing, rasping, undulating sea is its American counterpart, first made memorable by Whitman's sudden recognition that "the sea whispered me." Although Whitman is not a poet with whom Plath shares much, his recollection that the old crone and ferocious mother of his seaside childhood nurtured the outsetting bard is close to Plath's own. Her essay in the collection to which Hughes contributed "The Rock" is entitled "Ocean 1212-W," and it seems to take up where Hughes leaves off:

> My childhood landscape was not land but the end of the land — the cold, salt, running hills of the Atlantic. I sometimes think my vision of the sea is the clearest thing I own. I pick it up, exile that I am, like the purple "lucky stones" I used to collect with a white ring all the way round, or the shell of a blue mussel with its rainbowy angel's fingernail interior; and in one wash of memory the colours deepen and gleam, the early world draws breath.

"Breath, that is the first thing," she continues, and to identify this first thing she leaps beyond her own breath and the breath of her mother to that "larger, farther, more serious, more weary" breath of the sea. It was not the wind that first stirred her creative impulse: "The motherly pulse of the sea made mock of such counterfeits. Like a deep woman, it hid a good deal; it had many faces, many delicate, terrible veils. It spoke of miracles and distances; if it could court, it could also kill." Again Plath's memories touch Whitman's, and Hart Crane's in "Voyages," as they identify the sea with a seductive, alluring, even comforting, but also destructive woman.

Just as the rock hovered over Hughes's pram, so the sea permeated Plath's infancy. "The breath of the sea, then. And then its lights. Was it some huge, radiant animal? Even with my eyes shut I could feel the glimmers off its bright mirrors spider over my lids. I lay in a watery cradle, and sea gleams found the chinks in the dark green window, blind, playing and dancing, or resting and trembling a little." She turned to the sea for consolation when her universe was split in two by the news that she would have a baby brother. Walking along the shore, she saw "coldly and soberly, the *separateness* of everything." Her self-consciousness arose from that early recognition that her "beautiful fusion with the things of the world was over." She says, "I felt the wall of my skin: I am I." If she felt cast out, she also felt newly cast. Having lost the world, she gained consciousness, and having lost her infant centrality, she sought "A sign of election and specialness." The sea, behind its veil perceiving her need, cast up in the form of driftwood a monkey of wood, a "totem," "a Sacred Baboon" which took its place in her house with her brother, whose advent was for her "the awful birthday of otherness."

But the sea was not always so benign. Plath's final memory of the sea is "of violence — a still, unhealthily yellow day in 1939, the sea molten, steely-slick, heaving at its leash like a broody animal, evil violets in its eye." Yet even this famous hurricane that ravaged the Massachusetts shoreline was a fascinating spectacle for her, "a monstrous speciality, a leviathan. Our world might be eaten, blown to bits." She and her brother could not be lured to bed; instead, they looked out the window where nothing could be seen, and listened to the "howl, jazzed up by the bangs, slams, groans and splinterings of objects tossed like crockery in a giant's quarrel. The house rocked on its root. It rocked and rocked and rocked its two small watchers to sleep." And finally her memory of the sea was intensified by her father's death and the ensuing move inland, "whereupon those nine first years of my life sealed themselves off like a ship in a bottle — beautiful, inaccessible, obsolete, a fine, white flying myth."

If her childhood was sealed off and compartmentalized in that way, its seaborne memories have been rendered accessible to her through a poetry that tirelessly seeks to pierce the veil and to find, in the otherness of the world, her special place. But Plath is also supremely aware that to probe the distances and miracles of which the sea is emblematic is a dangerous, if delicate, occupation. The wind may list where it will; but the sea's inexorable movement can overwhelm as well as sustain. Its savagery and its benignity are equally unpredictable. It can kill or court. Plath's early (although curiously cold and sober) awareness of the "*separateness* of everything" remained with her as a central part of her vision of the world. It accounts for the clarity, precision, and objectivity of her poetic imagery, and for the rigor with which she can detail her situation.

What is perhaps most interesting about these essays in which Hughes and Plath attempt to define themselves in terms of their childhood landscapes is not that they read as companion pieces, but that they were written by a man who actually spent his childhood in the coal-mining town of Mexborough and a woman who grew up in suburban Wellesley,

Massachusetts. Rural romps on rock, moor, or seaside rise up to block out any consideration of these urban or suburban locations where the two poets later began to write. They also omit any mention of the circumstances in which the poets developed: Plath's long academic preparation, for example, and Hughes's rebellion against Cambridge, the variety of odd jobs he pursued before he began his earliest productive period. Perhaps it is too much to ask for a full review of their poetic beginnings from these short essays, but one might note that what they have chosen to recall were, even in their childhood, memories of infancy: Hughes in his rock-burdened pram and Plath in her watery cradle. These essays are, in Plath's words, "a fine, white flying myth." Every poet has the right to offer his own myth of origins, although such a myth may be best understood by attempting to discover how it served its purpose.

By identifying himself as a poet formed by the powerful elemental forces of his native landscape, Hughes locates himself in the firm native line of Wordsworth, Yeats, Lawrence, Thomas, Graves, and at the same time he frees himself from the heavy weight of a literary tradition. Although he is neither a poet unschooled in the history of English poetry nor one whose work reveals no influences, he has insisted that English poetry since Shakespeare, and English culture in general, have been largely directed toward suppressing the instinctual life from which poetry springs. His desire to free himself from that tradition and to unburden himself of the repressive forces in modern civilization by stripping the industrial landscape of his native Yorkshire to its bare elements may be regarded as an attempt to restore in his own life and work the conditions where that instinctual energy may flourish. Man face to face with the elements may experience a primordial thrill and fear that, Hughes feels, is the basis of poetry. Of course, he shares this feeling with a long line of English poets going back as far as Wordsworth.

That Hughes takes such pains to elaborate his conviction that he was formed by his native landscape may be attributed also to the English poetic scene when he first started writing.

English poetry at that point was enjoying a period of conservative reaction that opposed the Romantic excesses of Thomas and placed a high value on everyday urban reality and conventional forms. As Hughes characterized this situation,

> One of the things those poets had in common I think was the post-war mood of having had enough . . . enough rhetoric, enough overweening push of any kind, enough of the dark gods, enough of the id, enough of the Angelic powers and the heroic efforts to make new worlds. They'd seen it all turn into death camps and atomic bombs. All they wanted was to get back into civvies and get home to the wife and kids and for the rest of their lives not a thing was going to interfere with a nice cigarette and a nice view of the park. . . . Now I came a bit later. I hadn't had enough. I was all for opening negotiations with whatever happened to be out there.[2]

Although Hughes identifies himself here clearly with the forces that grew up in opposition to the conservatives, his early poems were included in anthologies of both groups. He has been hard to place, partly because his early work does conform to certain conservative conventions of form and theme, and partly because he has been, if a poet of rural life, also a poet who has a university degree and who has spent most of his writing life in and around London. Although he has stood outside the battles of literary London, he has been a long-standing figure in the literary establishment, reviewing books, editing collections, writing film scripts, delivering talks on poetry for children on the BBC. In this context, the immense nostalgia for his home country shown in "The Rock" may be best understood.

Also feeding into "The Rock" were certain ideas about the source of poetry. Those ideas undoubtedly began forming at Cambridge, in Hughes's study of archaeology and anthropology, and have continued to develop into a strong interest in folklore and myth. In the early Sixties, his reviewing for *The Listener* reveals his convictions about the importance of primitive songs, folktales, and myths to the imaginative life. In a review of a collection of folktales, he praises modern collectors who have recognized the tales for what they are: "the cruelty and obscenity are vital evidence, the 'absurdity' is the mother and father of 'the rational,' which is not yet born, and the collectors, thank goodness, are men with shorthand or tape-recorders and no desire to put out a few charming fables in fine simple prose."[3] Of folksong he says, "We imagine primitives to possess some of the qualities of ideal poetry — full of zest, clairvoyantly sensitive, realistic, whole, natural and passionate; and so we might well look at their songs hopefully." He wonders if these "early stirrings of the poetic impulse might show something analogous to the gills in the human embryo, something as revealing of the inmost buried nature of the thing." And he concludes that, against these primitive songs, the "main body of civilized verse is a great deal duller."[4]

Hughes acknowledged his own attraction to mythic spirits in the title of his third volume of poetry, *Wodwo,* and its epigraph from *Sir Gawain and the Green Knight.* But his affinity for Sir Gawain is no mere literary fancy; the original dialect of Sir Gawain is the vanished, archaic dialect of Hughes's native Yorkshire. In an interview, Hughes commented on the importance of his West Yorkshire dialect: "Whatever other speech you grow into, presumably your dialect stays alive in a sort of inner freedom, a separate little self. . . . And in the case of the West Yorkshire dialect, of course, it connects you directly and in your most intimate self to middle English poetry."[5] Hughes talks of the importance of this native mythological tradition in a review of *Myth and Religion of the North,* a study of the worship of Odin and Thor:

> This particular mythology is much deeper in us, and truer to us, than the Graeco-Roman pantheons that came in with Christianity, and again with the Renaissance, severing us with the completeness of a political interdict from these other deities of our instinct and ancestral memory. It is as if we were to lose Macbeth and King Lear, and have to live on Timeon and Coriolanus; or as if a vocabulary drawn wholly from the Greek-Roman branch were to take over absolutely from our Anglo-Saxon-Norse-Celtic: there's no doubt which of these belongs to our blood. The combination of the two is our wealth, but in the realm of mythologies, the realm of management between our ordinary minds and our deepest life, we've had no chance to make a similar combination.[6]

In folktales and myths, he has found the basic experience of the poetic temperament to be the heroic quest. He discovers it as well in the variations of shamanism found all over the world. The shaman is the man who has a vision, undergoes a magical death, is dismembered by a demon, and is resurrected with new insides and a new body created for him by the spirits. His business is to guide some soul to the underworld, or bring back the sick man's lost soul, or deliver sacrifices to the dead, or ask spirits the reason for an epidemic or the whereabouts of the lost. In his flight and return he displays healing powers and provides clairvoyant information. In this way he brings up to our ordinary mind the revelations of our deepest instincts and spiritual insights. Like the shaman, the poet undergoes with phenomenal intensity the flight and return that will produce the practical results of a regeneration of spirit.[7]

Hughes's most elaborate exploration of the split between our everyday perceptions and the life that lies submerged beneath them is the introductory essay on Shakespeare for his collection of Shakespeare's work.[8] It is the central document in Hughes's thoughts about poetry, and although its focus is on Shakespeare's controlling fable, it illuminates the preoccupations of Hughes's own verse. Shakespeare's secret fable was, Hughes claims, the fable of his age; its taproot was a black and ugly sexual dilemma, a clash in which the repressive forces of reason, civilization, and morality on one side won a fatal victory over nature, violence, and sexuality. The public aspect of this struggle, political and theological, was between the radical Calvinists and the Reformed Church, at the head of which stood Elizabeth, the virgin queen — not so much a divinely sanctioned ruler as the Divinity Herself, the Queen of Catholic Christianity, the Queen of Heaven. Elizabeth tended to keep the Catholic feeling of the Church intact and predominant against the living opposition of the Puritans. Her position was complicated by the fact that the Queen of England was "already, automatically, the representative of the old goddess — the real deity of medieval England, the Celtic pre-Christian goddess, with her tail wound around those still very much alive pre-Christian and non-Christian worlds. That goddess had been naturalized into the old Catholicism as Mother Mary and Satan."

The significance of these complex and symbolic circumstances for Shakespeare was "the drastic way the Queen of Heaven, who was the goddess of Catholicism, who was the goddess of medieval and pre-Chistian England, who was the divinity of the throne, who was the goddess of natural law and of love, who was the goddess of all sensation and organic life — this overwhelmingly powerful, multiple, primeval being was dragged into court by the young Puritan Jehovah." As Hughes sees it, the struggle in Shakespeare's England was a clash between Dionysian impulses and a hardening intellectuality and morality.

This struggle shaped Shakespeare's fable and, in Hughes's view, is most clearly evident in his two long poems, *Venus and Adonis* and *The Rape of Lucrece*. While these poems may seem the obverse of each other — in the first the goddess of love rapes a Puritan youth, and in the second a lust-possessed king rapes a severely Puritan wife — they are deeply complementary. The boar that demolished Adonis is his own repressed lust, crazed and bestialized by being separated from his intelligence and denied. The Calvinist effort of Adonis to divide nature, and especially love, into abstract good and physical evil destroys him. Hughes says, "Nature's attempts to recombine, first in love, then in whatever rebuffed love turns into, and the Puritan determination that she shall not recombine under any circumstances, are the powerhouse and torture chamber of the Complete Works." Lust combines with the Puritan mind to produce a new being, the man of chaos who is the mouthpiece of poetry. "Each play," Hughes says, "represents an increasingly desperate effort to lift an increasingly ideal spirit of Lucrece from an increasingly infernal caldron of sexual evil." Shakespeare records the gradual defeat of Venus and the boar, although in his works he strives to measure the energy of Venus against the Puritan force that attempts to overthrow it.

Whether this fable is in fact the central fable in Shakespeare is open to question, but it is of extreme importance to Hughes, who took its rough outlines from Robert Graves's *White Goddess*. His criticism of the Puritan morality and abstracting and idealizing mind in Shakespeare's work and times has obvious relevance for his own work and times. If his scheme begins to sound vaguely reminiscent not only of Graves but also of Eliot, Hughes makes the connection clear when he says of the split he details: "To call that event a 'dissociation of sensibility' is an understatement."

Hughes is conscious of having inherited this dilemma, and his works are designed to confront it. From the dilemma he has made a parable that touches the basic issues of his time. As he defines them, these issues center on the violence that permeates twentieth-century life. Its force has been redoubled by the rationalist effort to simultaneously contain and deny it. The angry male god of the Puritans has been secularized and domesticated in the modern world as the ravaging intellect. The evil eye of the rock under which Hughes grew up made him conscious of the fury, the obduracy, the restrictive and death-dealing powers of that ferocious male god. The rock is a natural embodiment of the oppression and darkness that in human nature are identified as the Puritan denial. But for Hughes the rock is also an elemental presence, and in it he recognizes natural forces quite apart from human ones that bear down upon man with overwhelming strength and which no effort of intellect can deflect or control. The loving female god of pre-Christian and early Catholic England, so long suppressed by the Puritan Jehovah, is less evident in Hughes's poetry, although something of her fecundity, stark vitality, and endurance impressed itself upon him in his contact with the moors.

For Hughes, poetry is an attempt to move behind the abstracting and moralizing mind in order to find the vitality that has been submerged by it. This process is what Hughes calls thinking. He has described it for schoolchildren:

> There is the inner life, which is the world of final reality, the world of memory, emotion, imagination, intelligence, and natural common sense, and which goes on all the time, consciously or unconsciously,

> like the heart beat. There is also the thinking process by which we break into that inner life and capture answers and evidence to support the answers out of it. That process of raid, or persuasion, or ambush, or dogged hunting, or surrender, is the kind of thinking we have to learn and if we do not somehow learn it, then our minds lie in us like the fish in the pond of a man who cannot fish.[9]

Hughes himself admits that he learned this kind of thinking not at school, but while fishing. Watching the float on his fishing pole, his whole being rested — but with a kind of alertness for the twitch of the float, and with the full awareness of the fish below in the dark. He calls it "concentrated excitement" designed "to bring up some lovely solid thing like living metal from a world where nothing exists but those inevitable facts which raise life out of nothing and return it to nothing."

The condition of creativity is, for Hughes as for Wordsworth, a prepared receptivity. Hughes has said that the poet's only hope is to be "infinitely sensitive to what his gift is." He goes on to explain:

> His gift is an unobliging thing. He can study his art, experiment, and apply his mind and live as he pleases. But the moment of writing is too late for further improvements or adjustments. Certain memories, images, sounds, feelings, thoughts, and relationships between these, have for some reason become luminous at the core of his mind: it is in his attempt to bring them out, without impairment, into a comparatively dark world that he makes poems. At the moment of writing, the poetry is a combination, or a resultant, of all that he is, unimpeachable evidence of itself and, indirectly, of himself, and for the time of writing he can do nothing but accept it.[10]

The idea of poetry as a raid on the inner life is hardly new. Perhaps Hughes's formulation of it may be explained by the exigencies of reviewing, editing anthologies, answering interviews. Also in a period when English literary entrepreneurs were demanding a return to common sense, to common experience, and to a language that could be understood by the general reading public, and at a time when the leading English poet was Philip Larkin, whose work concentrates on the depressed character of actual contemporary life, Hughes's restatement of the idea that poetry is based on a mythic foundation was perhaps necessary. He had of course the superior examples of Eliot, Yeats, and Graves, and he drew generously on their insights; but he also had to refashion them to serve his own purpose. The boy who learned to be a poet while attending to his fishing pole is a homelier figure than the man who became a poet through the extinction of personality or the man who masked himself as a beggar, an aristocrat, a stylized character. But the fisher-poet is as much a literary pose as the impersonal artist. The rural boy had to read English literature before he became aware that the vanished archaic dialect of his native Yorkshire connects him to middle English poetry. As a self-portrait of such a boy, "The Rock" reveals how Hughes turned the repressions of his native environment into a poetic vocation. He did not discover himself in Yorkshire; he only discovered his need for imaginative nourishment. Not until he had studied anthropology and read folktales was Hughes able to identify a world that could sustain him and to make the connections between that mythic world and his own native landscape. If the rock hanging over his childhood fostered any feeling in him, it was the desire to escape; this desire never abated, even after he had left the gloomy rock far behind. He internalized the rock and the eerie moors, and he was constantly re-creating them in different forms: the repressive rationality of the Puritan in his essay on Shakespeare opposed to the pre-Christian goddess, the dullness of civilized verse opposed to the power of primitive songs, the world of everyday reality and the inner life. The strategy of much of his poetry is to break away from and defy the rational, the moral, the oppression of civilized life, which he sets up as a kind of darkened rock. "The Rock" suggests, more than anything else, his need to create an imaginative life in an environment that offered him none.

The usefulness of "Ocean 1212-W" is not so immediately apparent. Plath never posed as a rural poet, nor did she develop any lengthy statement about the importance of myths. If she had not actually read Hughes's essay before she wrote her own (and the way in which her first sentence seems to take up where he left off, matching the sea to his moors and rock, suggests that she had), she was indeed familiar with his affection for his home country and his interest in the Anglo-Saxon-Norse-Celtic mythology. The letters that first describe him to her mother are full of these two qualities: his intimacy with animals and nature, and his deep acquaintance with magic and the supernatural. He came with "pockets full of poems, fresh trout and horoscopes."[11] He became her teacher, opening to her a new vocabulary of woods and animals and earth. He read horoscopes, recounted his "marvelous colored dreams, about red foxes," and educated her daily by setting exercises of concentration and observation. She boasted, "When Ted and I begin living together we shall become a team better than Mr. and Mrs. Yeats — he being a competent astrologist, reading horoscopes, and me being a tarot-pack reader, and, when we have enough money, a crystal-gazer."

If Hughes introduced her to nature, she had made her own investigations into myths when she was at Smith, working on her senior thesis on the double in Dostoevsky. She wrote her mother from college,

> In connection with this [thesis] topic, I'm reading several stories by E. T. A. Hoffman[n]; *Dorian Gray*, by Oscar Wilde; Dr. Jekyll and Mr. Hyde; Poe's William Wilson; Freud, Frazer, Jung, and others — all fascinating stuff about the ego as symbolized in reflections (mirror and water), shadows, twins — dividing off and becoming an enemy, or omen of death, or a warning conscience, or a means by which one denies the power of death (e.g., by creating the idea of the soul as the deathless double of the mortal body).

Right here is the beginning of ideas that informed not only her poetry but "Ocean 1212-W." While Hughes claims to have brought her attention to Graves's *White Goddess*, her thesis reading had already prepared her to appreciate its subject.[12] And Hughes's gift of a tarot pack was made to a poet whose academic studies of T. S. Eliot had already made her aware of its significance.

If Hughes had any impact on Plath in this respect, it was to show her how research in myths could be used poetically. The exercises in concentration that he devised were followed, after the two were married, by meditations over the Ouija board in an effort to find poetic subjects. This activity (perhaps an example of what Hughes regarded as "thinking") produced the suggestion that she write a poem about Lorelei. She said, "This had never occurred to me consciously as a subject, and it seemed a good one: the Germanic legend background, the water images, the death-wish, and so on. So the next day I began a poem about them, and Pan [the name they gave the Ouija] was right; it is one of my favorites."[13]

By the time she came to write "Ocean 1212-W," Plath had absorbed Hughes's interest in nature, had reinforced her own concern with the supernatural, had learned the techniques he used to break into the inner life, and had begun to think of herself as a poet formed by a particular home country. Yet to use that phrase, "home country," is to understand immediately how foreign it is to an American writer. The Massachusetts coastline is not a home country in the same sense that Yorkshire is, nor, for all its history, does it have roots in an ancient mythology or a dialect that would put Plath in touch with an early poetic tradition. "Ocean 1212-W" was written for an English audience, and it seems to be an effort to prove that America has peculiar home territories that could inspire (as has the English landscape) its outsetting bards. Indeed, Plath claims that the English sea is in no way comparable to the particular place she remembers.

Like "The Rock," however, "Ocean 1212-W" reveals much about its creator. While Hughes's childhood oscillated between the evil eye of the rock and the gentle female line of the moors, Plath's clear vision was informed by the "motherly pulse of the sea" with its own dual aspect: its miracles and its violence, "heaving at its leash like a broody animal." If the rock is Hughes's *memento mundi,* the sea is Plath's. Hughes could locate the forbidding and repressive character (which he attributed to English Puritanism but which was also a part of his own psychic make-up) in the rock, and its release in the moors; Plath was equally able to project on the sea the psychic divisions between the forces that nourished and sustained and those that threatened and destroyed. Presiding over her landscape is the female figure that could court or kill. Plath talks of the "motherly pulse of the sea"; but the sea she envisions is a peculiar mother, both a nurturer, offering Plath a "totem" of her specialness, and a threat, a "monstrous speciality" whose breath is "more serious, more weary" than that of the life-affirming mother. She is also not a mother at all but a "deep woman" who "hid a good deal." In these ambivalent attributes Plath identifies the divisions in her own self-image. The need, evident in her poetry from the beginning, to repeat the tautology "I am I" stems from the real confusion about who that "I" is. Having been brought up by a single parent, Plath had to experience her mother performing the dual functions of nurturer and lawmaker, which she casts onto the sea in its motherly pulse and more serious breath. In addition, she divided the maternal image here (as in her poems) into the good or sweet — but often false — mother, versus the violent, even evil, but also true mother. Her poetry records the long search for that female identity that would confirm herself.

She had started out quite differently, Hughes informs us, writing her early poems "very slowly, Thesaurus open on her knee, in her large, strange handwriting, like a mosaic, where every letter stands separate within the work, a hieroglyph to itself. . . . Every poem grew complete from its own root, in that laborious inching way, as if she were working out a mathematical problem, chewing her lips, putting a thick dark ring of ink around each word that stirred for her on the page of the Thesaurus."[14] "Ocean 1212-W" fails to mention that Plath had spent most of her formative years not walking by the seaside, but at school or college, learning how to write poetry by reading poets, imitating their styles, experimenting in set forms, studying the thesaurus. Only after this long apprenticeship did she begin to improvise, to attempt to explore her inner life.

In a sense, Plath's development was fortunate in following the development of American poetry. She began writing under the influence of Auden when he was making a tour of American college campuses in the 1950's; of Wallace Stevens, whose academic reputation was at its peak when she was in college;

of Marianne Moore, whom she interviewed for *Mademoiselle*. She was ready for new influences when she read Lowell's *Life Studies*, and shortly after that Roethke's poems, and when she became acquainted with Anne Sexton in a seminar given by Lowell in 1958-59. These poets opened to her imaginative possibilities that Auden, Stevens, and Moore had denied. She claimed to have been very excited by "the new breakthrough that came with, say Robert Lowell's *Life Studies*, this intense breakthrough into very serious, very personal, emotional experience which I feel has been partly taboo."[15] Her receptivity to Lowell, Roethke, and Sexton had been in preparation for a long time in her reading, in the meditations she practiced with Hughes, and in his encouragement to break into her own inner experiences. Although she is frequently linked with these American poets as a confessional writer and has in fact written poems heavily influenced by Lowell and Roethke at least, she simply took from them the encouragement she needed to develop in her own way — a way which had been already clearly set. Hughes has accurately described her poems as "chapters in a mythology."[16] In this, they are unlike the openly autobiographical work of Lowell, Sexton, and Roethke.[17]

Nothing more clearly separates her from Lowell, for example, than her statement about the source of her poetry. She told an interviewer:

> I think my poems immediately come out of the sensuous and emotional experiences I have, but I must say I cannot sympathize with those cries from the heart that are informed by nothing except a needle or a knife, or whatever it is. I believe that one should be able to control and manipulate experiences, even the most terrifying, like madness, being tortured, this sort of experience, and one should be able to manipulate these experiences with an informed and intelligent mind. I think that personal experience is very important, but certainly it shouldn't be a kind of shut-box and mirror-looking, narcissistic experience. I believe it should be relevant to the larger things, the bigger things such as Hiroshima and Dachau and so on.[18]

When asked how he came to write confessional poetry, Lowell said that poets had become proficient in forms and needed to make a "breakthrough back into life." Plath's manipulation describes a breakthrough into a dimension other than the one Lowell has in mind. *Life Studies* is Lowell's effort to repossess his own life; its mode is properly confessional because in both the poems and the prose of that volume the suffering and victimizing speaker searches through his own pain in order to perceive some truth about the nature of his experience. Plath, in contrast, makes no such search in her poems. Her speakers are in touch with forces that would overwhelm them if they were not firmly controlled. As such, they are more like Hughes's shamans, disciplined and controlled to the task of entering the spirit world. Her poems are not cries from the heart that arise from personal suffering; rather, they are cries from a heart that has undergone torture and destruction in order to be re-created. The manipulative mind is the mind that engaged in meditations and invocations, and perhaps concentrations on the Ouija board, in order to summon the spirit world.

Although their purposes were different and their home territories widely separate, Plath and Hughes share a view of poetry as a raid on the inner life, a breakthrough into taboo territory. They seem to vie with each other to see who can make the most reckless raid and retrieve the most startling information. Their poems should be read together as raid and counter-raid, gathering intensity as they developed. Although Plath's poems have been seen as personal revelations and Hughes's poems have been regarded as confrontations with elemental powers, in fact, he has claimed to draw his poetry from memories, experiences that are luminous at the core of his mind, a connection with his private inner life that his critics have seldom been willing to make. For both these poets the inner life was full of terror, and in tapping that life they drew forth demons with a family resemblance. An examination of the first collection of each poet is perhaps the best way to understand how they came to work together.

Notes

[1] Plath, "Ocean 1212-W," and Hughes, "The Rock," in Read, ed., *Writers on Themselves*, pp. 102-110, 86-92. Subsequent quotations in the text are from these sources.

[2] Hughes, "Ted Hughes and Crow," pp. 10-11.

[3] Ted Hughes, review of *Folktales of Japan*, ed. Keigo Seki, and *Folktales of Israel*, ed. Dov Noy, *The Listener*, LXX (December 12, 1963), 999.

[4] Ted Hughes, review of *Primitive Song*, by C. M. Bowra, *The Listener*, LXVII (May 3, 1962), 781.

[5] "Ted Hughes and Crow," pp. 11-12.

[6] Ted Hughes, review of *Myths and Religions of the North*, by E. O. G. Turville-Petre, *The Listener*, LXXI (March 19, 1964), 484-485.

[7] Ted Hughes, review of *Shamanism* by Mircea Eliade and *The Sufis* by Idries Shah, *The Listener*, LXXII (October 29, 1964), 678.

[8] Ted Hughes, "Introduction," *With Fairest Flowers While Summer Lasts: Poems from Shakespeare* (New York: Doubleday, 1971), pp. v-xxiii. Subsequent quotations in the text are from this source.

[9] Ted Hughes, *Poetry Is* (New York: Doubleday, 1970) p. 53.

[10] Ted Hughes, "Context," *London Magazine*, n.s. I (February, 1962), 45.

[11] Plath, *Letters Home*, pp. 243-244. Subsequent quotations in the text are from this source.

[12] See Judith Kroll's book, *Chapters in a Mythology: The Poetry of Sylvia Plath* (New York: Harper & Row, 1976), for a complete treatment of the importance of *The White Goddess* in Plath's work.

[13] Plath, *Letters Home*, p. 346.

[14] Newman, ed., *Art of Sylvia Plath*, p. 188.

[15] Sylvia Plath, *The Poet Speaks*, ed. Peter Orr (London: Routledge & Kegan Paul, 1966), pp. 167-168.

[16] Newman, ed., *Art of Sylvia Plath*, p. 187.

[17] In her study of Robert Lowell, Marjorie Perloff makes a similar point from a different perspective. She characterizes Lowell's poetry as realistic or documentary or metonymic lyric which is at once highly personal and highly factual, a combination of Wordsworthian confessionalism and Chekhovian realism. In contrasting Lowell's "Waking in the Blue" to Plath's "Stones," Perloff says that the shift is one from "a world of concrete personalities and realistic events to one of pure being." She continues, "Sylvia Plath's 'I,' unlike Lowell's, is not subordinated to its attributes or surroundings. Rather, like the 'I' of Rimbaud . . . the self is projected outward; it seems to utter rather than to address anyone; it can recount only what is happening *now*, at this very moment." Finally she says, "The tensions in 'The Stones' is thus not between self and world as it is in Lowell . . . but between what Richard Howard has aptly called 'the lithic impulse — the desire to reduce the demands of life to the unquestioning acceptance of a stone — and the impulse to live on.' " See Perloff, *The Poetic Art of Robert Lowell* (Ithaca: Cornell University Press, 1973), pp. 181-183.

[18] Plath, *The Poet Speaks*, pp. 169-170.

THREE

The Hawk in the Rain

Ted Hughes has said that he started writing poetry at fifteen, when his first subjects were Zulus and the Wild West and sagas of involved warfare among African tribes, all in imitation of Kipling.[1] "Wild West," published in a magazine of the Mexborough Secondary School in June, 1946, shows Hughes already the master of preposterous violence. The poem is the tale of Carson McReared, who ran wild at twelve because a "teacher got him riled" and climaxed his career by getting "shot to hell" only after he had killed off "1,200 men on spirited horses." In rhymed couplets of thumping iambic pentameter, the young Hughes beats out his gory story of the fabulous McReared. Between 1946 and his first volume of poetry in 1957 Hughes published very little. Two poems included in *Poetry from Cambridge 1952-54* and never collected by Hughes are among the handful he published before his first volume. Karl Miller, the editor of the Cambridge anthology, has recalled that, when these poems came out, he was told by a don that this would never do.[2] Right at the start of his career, then, Hughes was seen as defying the conventions.

The first poem in the Cambridge anthology is "The Little Boys and the Seasons." It funnels the reactions to the seasons through the minds of boys who have newly awakened to the mysteries of sex, without quite losing a childish innocence; the poem has a kind of knowing naïveté and excitement about it. Of spring, the boys say, " 'What a bit of a girl,' " " 'To make my elder brother daft,/ Tossing her petticoats under the bushes. O we know,/ We know all about you.' " They will have nothing of her "tinny birds" or "soppy flowers"; but when she "cried a cloud" they all ran in. Nor are the boys too taken with summer, claiming " 'This one's not much either,/ She keeps my dad out till too late at night.' " The boys' awakening sexuality turns their eyes "Hot as fever with hostility" against the great woman who has made the pond "untidy with her underclothes." What they like better is the bullying autumn, "swearing/ At first so that the children could hardly believe it." He has the sun in his haversack "with hares/ Pheasants and singing birds all silent." When the parents warn them of the weather, the small boys only say, " 'Wait till his friend gets here.' " And the rough winter king is their favorite, overturning the horses, stamping up and down the fields, breaking up the sun for sabres. " 'Hurrah for the Jolly Roger,' " the boys shout, acclaiming the symbol of masculine triumph and conquest. Not exactly the traditional treatment of the seasons, it is remarkably faithful to the psychology of little boys — and, it must be admitted, to the psychology Hughes maintained into adulthood, with its disdain for the soppy sentimentality of spring and the dirty lethargy of a female summer, and at the same time its innocent excitement over feats of masculine prowess and daring.

"The Court-Tumbler and Satirist," the second uncollected poem in the Cambridge anthology, is a less interesting poem, although it moves closer to Hughes's central concerns in its distinction between the sexually active court-tumbler and the passive, self-important, rationalizing princes. In later poems Hughes castigates the man who hedges himself against experience; but here the princes' self-deception is too obvious. The princes' disdain for "how the blood of a true artist makes out" and the tumbler who "exercises to correct/ The court's stiff cock strut" depend too heavily on the shock of sexual references. However, here Hughes develops the distinction between the philistine (however courtly) rationalist and the artistic sensuous man, which he returns to treat in later poems.[3]

Another poem published before his first collected volume, "The Drowned Woman" (*Poetry*, LXXXIX [February, 1957],

296-297), tells the story of a "Millionly-whored" "thirty year old miss," who goes to the park to drown herself and find in "the mud bed of the lake" "her comforter." The contrast in this "park pastoral" between the children "catching armsful/ Of the untouched sun" and the "Fresh-floured and daubed 'whore' " who would "Ladder Jacob a leg" is the familiar contrast between innocence and experience, imaged as life and death. Although the whore could "statuesque and body a goddess" and pluck "men's eyes from happy homes," she watches the "garret death come" until she deliberately goes forth to seek it as her comforter. This poem reads as an interesting contrast to an early Plath poem, "Spinster," on the subject of a "park pastoral"; Plath's heroine refuses the "vulgar motley" of the springtime and returns home to lock herself into a virginal death.

One other early poem not included in *The Hawk in the Rain,* "Letter" (*New Statesman,* September 28, 1957), like the early "Law in the Country of the Cats," foretells Hughes's interest in violence, here depicted as a motiveless hatred between two men, one a store clerk and the other his customer. They "exchange in a flash a stunning headache blinklessly." Then the customer dreams that a meteorite crashed down on the shop and the clerk lurched at him "with unhuman shout — "

> But how changed! Your body seared black, your eyes
> Crazily, lidlessly staring,
> Frightening my hatred with your cries
> Pointing to the desolated horizon and the swinging skies.

Here Hughes seems to be moving toward the dream image of horror that informs his later poem. The shift from the shop counter to the desolate horizons is perhaps too abrupt for this short poem to bear, but Hughes does isolate the ferocity that he imagines can inform even our most trivial relationships.

Sex, lust, violence — these are the subjects that would not do in the Cambridge of the early Fifties, but they were (and remain) Hughes's poetic themes. Although before his first collection, *The Hawk in the Rain,* he published too few poems to provide us with a clear indication of how he worked up to the accomplishment of that volume, he seems to have had a kind of self-assurance from the beginning. Perhaps the advantage of growing up under the rock forced him to assert himself against the restrictive literary circles of Cambridge. It was very clear from the start what he opposed, and a number of poems in *The Hawk in the Rain* portray modern versions of the repressive Puritan. Not surprisingly, Hughes's targets are the intellectual, the churchman, the frigid woman, the poet cut off by his fame from the sources of his work.

The famous poet and the egghead in poems by those names have, each in different ways, learned to escape a direct confrontation with the "inner demon" that lives by "tankarding from tissue and follicle/ The vital fire, the spirit electrical," if indeed it is possible to tankard something electrical. Looking into the eye of the famous poet "For the spark, the effulgence," he finds "Nothing there/ But the haggard stony exhaustion of a near/ Finished variety artist." The poet has been "half-buried" by the world's insistence that he repeat the "pyrotechnics" of his youthful genius and by his accession to its demands in fruitless efforts to "concoct/ The old heroic bang from their money and praise." The famous poet has been turned into a monster by his own willingness to live outside the "fermenting of a yeasty heart" in the public gaze far from "the humiliation/ Of youth and obscurity," which kept him responsive to his inner demon. He has become "a lumbering obsolete/ Arsenal," a warehouse of ammunition he can no longer fire, a stegosaurus who has outlived his time.

The egghead, on the other hand, has never had in the first place what the famous poet has abandoned. He has resisted the evidence of the imagination, evidence which might have reduced him to forgetfulness or madness, but which would also have put him in touch with a world of mystery and power. With "wide-eyed deafnesses" the egghead leaves out

> A leaf's otherness,
> The whaled monstered sea-bottom, eagled peaks
> And stars that hang over hurtling endlessness,
> With manslaughtering shocks.

He lives instead

> By feats of torpor, by circumventing sleights
> Of stupefaction, juggleries of benumbing,
> By lucid sophistries of sight
>
> To a staturing "I am,"
> To the upthrust affirmative head of a man.
> Braggart-browed complacency.

This crafty but stupid intellectual affirms himself by denying the world's otherness. For Hughes, the only access to final reality is through the imagination, which awakens within us an awareness of our essential fragility in a world that is vital, destructive, awesome, and mysterious. And the solipsist who lives in his head and feeds off himself is fatally cut off from the world's manslaughtering jolts. His prudential caution makes him half-alive. A better defense against the shocks of experience, Hughes suggests, is (paradoxically) no defense at all: to dare "To be struck dead" by learning how to survive in an impossible world or by going under to "those champions/ Forgetfulness, madness." In elevating madness to championship, Hughes castigates the superbly controlled egghead, but he seems to forget that, if the life of the egghead lies within him like fish in the pond of a man who cannot fish, the depths of the madman's life are so accessible to him that he is unsteadied by his catch.

This poem, along with most others in the volume, is so serenely controlled that the egghead might have written it himself. In quatrains rhyming *abab*, the stanzas have a curious symmetry: a first line of two stresses, a longer second line with five stresses divided by a caesura, a four-stressed third line, and a two-stressed fourth line. The short opening and closing lines seem to enact the egghead's urge to limit experience that escapes him in the longer middle lines.

Like the egghead, the Reverend Skinner is also a life-denier; but his situation is more specifically sexual. Slapped on the cheek by the whore who prefers the devil to his black church, the Reverend Skinner takes the affront as a God-given punishment for his own pride and feels he should mortify the flesh by living on "dog-licks for ten years." But his self-flagellation does not purify him. Repugnance at his own sin only increases his awareness of evil in the world until finally even the heavens seem blackened with rot. "The Conversion of the Reverend Skinner" is to the devil's party, and he ends by blessing only what is defiled. His story has been told before, most notably by Yeats, but he belongs to Hughes's list of fools. His female counterpart in "Secretary" enjoys no such conversion. She "scuttles down the gauntlet of lust/ Like a clockwork mouse." Hughes boasts, "If I should touch her she would shriek and weeping/ Crawl off to nurse the terrible wound." At night, she tends to her father and brother and goes to bed early, "lies with buttocks tight,/ Hiding her lovely eyes until day break."

If it is easy to see what Hughes opposes, it is more difficult in his first volume to understand what he celebrates, not because he fails to identify his heroes — they are predictably the warrior, the martyr, the lover, the receptive poet — but because he enters into contradictions that he cannot adequately explain or reconcile. His problem is most clearly evident in the war poems that conclude *The Hawk in the Rain.* In "The Ancient Heroes and the Bomber Pilot," the modern pilot recalls "huge-chested braggarts" "restuffing their dear/ Fame with fresh sacks-full of heads," and concludes, "The grandeur of their wars humbles my thoughts." Perhaps; but it is not clear why. He celebrates their lustiness, how "They thinned down their fat fulsome blood in war," and suggests that by comparison the modern bomber pilot's destruction of whole cities is something less grand, and his heart, next to the large-hearted bloodthirsty ancient marauders, is "cold and small." The contrast does not work, and Hughes comes close to being himself the "timorous poet" of his own poem who "enlarges heroisms." Again in "Two Wise Generals" Hughes seems to elevate, over the "timid and aging" modern generals, "Black Douglas, bannered and trumpeted," "Letting the whole air flow breakneck with blood." The thrill of violence lives on even in the prisoner in "Invitation to the Dance" upon whose "sinews torturers had grown strong," who still dreams "That could he get upright he would dance and cry/ Shame on every shy or idle wretch." In these poems Hughes seems to resemble the onlookers at an air crash, whose position he scorns in "The Casualty." There "Sympathies/ Fasten to the blood like flies."

> The tears of their eyes
>
> Too tender to let break, start to the edge
> Of such horror close as mourners can,
> Greedy to share all that is undergone,
> Grimace, gasp, gesture of death.

It is not in the soldiers but in the martyr that Hughes comes closest to portraying a form of action he admires. "The Martyrdom of Bishop Farrar" suggests that violence can be purposeful, that suffering is action to those disciplined to it.[4] T. S. Eliot had made the point before in *Murder in the Cathedral*, and Hughes's poem owes a debt to Eliot. On being chained to the stake, Bishop Farrar told his followers (the headnote informs us), "If I flinch from the pain of the burning, believe not the doctrine that I have preached." So while Bloody Mary's men stoke the fire that burns the Bishop, boasting, " 'This is her sermon,' " Bishop Farrar's one wordless sermon blazes as his body "burned to get/ His words a bare honouring in their ears," and "The shrewd townsfolk pocketed them hot."

> His body's cold-kept miserdom of shrieks
> He gave uncounted, while out of his eyes,
> Out of his mouth, fire like a glory broke,
> And smoke burned his sermons into the skies.

Words that will burn the body and "be tongued with fire" are the only words that count for Hughes. They speak even to the "sullen-jowled watching Welsh townspeople" whose silence in the face of Farrar's burning did not disown him but confirmed him as their leader. Unlike the tearful bystanders in "The Casualty," these sullen, shrewd townspeople know the meaning of what they see. They are not themselves capable of such suffering, but they are capable, unlike modern observers, of responding fully to it. They are awed by the miracle, aware in their humble way that the familiar sermon has turned unfamiliar, that the dove has descended to them. For this kind of experience, faith is the first requisite. Hughes says, "the fire that struck here, come from Hell even,/ Kindled little heavens in his words." Such action is not possible in a secular world.

If ancient heroes and martyrs are gone, the lover remains the chief hero in the modern world of Hughes's poems. A significant proportion of the poems in *The Hawk in the Rain* deal with this subject, although many early poems embody an unreconciled contradiction between the man as possessor and the violent and destructive power of love as possession. And beneath this contradiction is an ambiguous fear and praise of women. "Fallgrief's Girl-Friends" is a careful hedging of love's possibilities by a man who settles for "a muck of a woman." Like Shakespeare's mistress whose eyes are nothing like the sun, this girl's looks "Were what a good friend would not comment on." This realistic lover will not be fooled by "the dream/ Where admiration's giddy mannequin/ Leads every sense to motley." Part of his boast is "Not that she had no equal, not that she was/ His before flesh was his or the world was." He claims that "What any woman born cannot but have,/ Has as much of the world as is worth more/ Than wit or lucky looks can make worth more." He will settle simply for sex and means to "stand naked/ Awake in the pitch dark where the animal runs." But his ending is a surprise:

> The chance changed him:
> He has found a woman with such wit and looks
> He can brag of her in every company.

Behind this braggart's pubside philosophy of muck is the fear that wit and looks in a woman "Were a ring disabling this pig-snout." He will take less, knowing that he is poor enough "To be more than bettered by a worst woman." But pride in his conquest ruins his realism, disables his pig-snout truth, and recasts him as a moonstruck lover. Fallgrief becomes the fall guy, although it is not clear how fully the poet behind the poem realizes that no man falls farther and looks more ridiculous in his unseating than the one who claims love cannot touch him.

Fallgrief's change is turned around in "The Dove Breeder,"

whose mild manners cause him to shriek when love strikes like a hawk into his dovecote, killing all his prized birds. Unlike the boastful Fallgrief, who had guarded against such a fate and was deceived, the dove breeder was taken unaware, yet now "rides the morning mist/ With a big-eyed hawk on his fist." This finicky dove breeder, who won prizes "With fantails or pouters," now has a bigger prize. However, here, as in "Fallgrief's Girl-Friends," the transformation that love has wrought is poorly prepared for. Hughes tells neither how Fallgrief chanced upon a woman of wit and lucky looks, nor how the wild dove breeder came into his conquest. They seem unlikely choices for such a visitation. Also, the final image of conquest does not grow out of the idea of love as a raid of the dovecote.

"Billet-Doux" concerns the male conqueror of the earlier poems. Now the woman is one who does not "sweeten smiles, peep, cough," but

> Who sees straight through bogeyman,
> The crammed cafes, the ten thousand
> Books packed end to end, even my gross bulk,
> To the fiery star coming for the eye itself,
> And while she can grabs of them what she can.

This clairvoyant demon has divested the man of his "twelve bright brass bands" so that, paradoxically, he now walks "naked as his breath" but "with his head high." Stripped yet proud, reduced yet exalted, this man claims:

> Love you I do not say I do or might either.
> I come to you enforcedly —
> Love's a spoiled appetite for some delicacy —
> I am driven to your bed and four walls
> From bottomlessly breaking night —

Love is for the sweet, smiling girls and for the doves who peep like them; but what he feels for this woman is a magnetic "desperation," "closer and harder than love." While Hughes elevates sexual attraction over mere romantic sentiment, sex is linked to danger. He wants the woman who sees right through him and grabs what she can; in fact, like the dove breeder, he will have the devourer. He chooses her, having looked far enough, he says; but it would appear that she has chosen him, or so bewitched him that he has no choice but to act out his desperation.

The "magniloquent truth" which Hughes claims he will tell us in this and the other poems seems to be the quite simple notion that love, or perhaps only a sexual encounter, will make even the muckiest man into a conqueror. In the process it will destroy his prizes, unsettle his swaggering, reduce him to nakedness; but its gifts appear greater than its destructiveness. In the end the men all walk the town with their heads held high. It is difficult to say how much of Hughes's sympathy rests with these characters. They are all stylized portraits of male prowess, and in some ways they appear ridiculous. Yet they share some of the qualities Hughes admires: they survive the onslaught of violent emotion without flinching; they are winners and survivors, bold and fearless. But if passion is a visitation from the spirit world that erupts so violently that life is transformed, then it is difficult to see in the cockiness of the dove breeder and Fallgrief a really appropriate reaction to it. They think they have conquered it. Only the man in "Billet-Doux," dispropertied but desperate, seems driven by love's fury, but then his naked pride seems ill earned. In these male characters Hughes is working toward a full expression of his understanding of the chaos of emotion; however, the stylization of his characters does not do full justice to his theme.

Missing from these early poems is the moment of coupling, the point at which love strikes. The violence, chaos, even murderousness of this moment strains beneath the surface of "Parlour-Piece," whose decorous lovers are rendered speechless as Hughes explains:

> With love so like fire they dared not
> Let it out into strawy small talk;
> With love so like a flood they dared not
> Let out a trickle lest the whole crack.

When he turns to the instant when the fire and flood are released, Hughes finds the metaphor for which he has been searching in these other poems. The change love wreaks is the impossible fusion of two into one. In this metaphor, the conquering man and the "muck of a woman" disappear, and with them vanish the contradictions they embodied. In the fusion of "Incompatibilities," the lovers are themselves obliterated, and desire, a "vicious separator," "Cold-chisels two selfs single as it welds hot/ Iron of their separates to one." It is a fury that "magnets," "furnaces," and "Hammer-blows" the two together until the division disappears. But even then it is not content:

> It dives into the opposite eyes,
> Plummets through blackouts of impassables
> For the star that lights the face.

Yet it leaves "Each, each second, lonelier and further/ Falling alone through the endless/ Without-world of the other."

The incompatibilities that Hughes recognizes in this poem are between a passion that fuses two to one and a more-than-physical need to find the star that lights the face, that "something other" which cannot be possessed and yet without which the lover now feels bereft. Having lost the single self yet "straining to follow down/ The maelstrom dark of the other," the light which will recompense the loss, each sees only endless emptiness. The union of man and woman is a moment of shared otherness in which the pair are joined violently, obliterated, and yet filled with a desire for the other who has disappeared. Against the fury of the emotion and the rush of language, the poem's quatrains are controlled by precise pararhyme that reflects its theme of dissonance.

The force that hammer-blows these two together is given a more sinister treatment in "A Modest Proposal," where Hughes says, "There is no better way to know us/ Than as two wolves, come separately to a wood." "Neither can make die/ The painful burning of the coal in its heart/ Till the other's body and the whole wood is its own." Their relationship is a contest for "a mad final satisfaction." The wolves are "even at a distance/ Distracted by the soft competing pulse/ Of the other." After every skirmish, each wolf "licks the rents in its hide," "the red smelting of hatred." The battle is, however, instantly interrupted when the great lord rides by from hunting, wearing an embroidered cloak and with two great-eyed greyhounds, the symbol of orderly conquest. The Swiftian title suggests that while the wolves may consume each other in the bloodthirstiness of their need, their violence can be stopped dead by the spectacle of a more elaborate, more stylized, more purely ritualized murderousness. If, as the poem's opening suggests, there is no better way to know lovers than as wolves, then there may be no better way to know love than as a hunt to the kill. Every day the lord's greyhounds "bring down the towering stag." The wolves are hunters, too; but the clash that engages them now is something more desperate than the cool control of the hunt. Driven by the heart's painful burning, the wolf is "warying to listen/ For the other's slavering rush," clamped in a life-or-death struggle to kill or be killed. The lord of the hunt counterpoints their fury. Although he is their antithesis — human, not animal; great, not small; controller, not controlled — he shares with them the lust for blood. The chaos and rage of their fight is the underside of his order and calm. Hughes's theme in "Incompatibilities" and "A Modest Proposal" derives from Yeats's theory of love as the violent fusion of opposites, although Hughes has given it a more desperate turn. For him, the fusion has fostered such a wild need for wholeness that the need is insatiable. The other becomes a competing pulse, not simply something else alive but something that threatens existence. It so maddens the wolf that nothing but its stoppage will insure him of his whole soul.

Love that welds two into one threatens the individual life with a discontent so deeply felt that existence itself is endangered. Love may come first as a promise of release from the imprisonment of "singularity," but it has bonds of its own. The lover in "Two Phases," now at liberty in his beloved's generous embrace, mourns his former state and the contentment of his solitude; nevertheless, like Caractacus, the captured British king of the Silures who would not bow down in his humiliation, the lover here is captured but proud. He will not admit his defeat to his conqueror. The first phase of love is when man feels his strength expanded by it, but the second phase makes man its slave, who

> Sweats his stint out,
> No better than a blind mole
> That burrows for its lot
> Of the flaming moon and sun
> Down some black hole.

Here, as in "Incompatibilities," love is not light but an opening into "The maelstrom dark of the other" — an abyss into which the lover plummets, straining as he falls.

The change in Hughes's treatment of love or passion between "Fallgrief's Girl-Friends" and "Incompatibilities" coincides with his marriage to Sylvia Plath. He actually met her at a party to celebrate the publication of *St. Botolph's Review,* a little magazine he founded with friends and in which he published "Fallgrief's Girl-Friends" and an even more misogynist poem, "Soliloquy of a Misanthrope." The transformation of the woman in his poems, from muck to one who sees through bogeymen, is matched by the transformation of the man from proud conqueror to proud conquered one.

Except perhaps for the woman with clairvoyant powers who can see straight through "the ten thousand/ Books packed end to end," Plath herself is not mentioned in these poems, which were probably written in the first year of their marriage. Still, her presence is everywhere felt in Hughes's elevation of women to predatory status equal with men. His early poems had not moved far from the views of "The Little Boys and the Seasons" in their hot fever of hostility toward women. One sees the tight-buttocked secretary, or the girl in "Macaw and Little Miss" who dreams of the warrior "Smashing and burning and rending towards her loin," or the Virgin Mary who "swallowed the honey of a parable" "Though that Jack Horner's hedge-scratched pig-splitting arm,/ Grubbing his get among your lilies, was a comet/ That plunged through the flowery whorl to your womb-root." From "Billet-Doux" on, however, the women are no longer passive victims or tamed hawks or frigid virgins; instead, they are equal partners, or occasionally superiors, in the overwhelming rush toward a "mad final satisfaction." Actually it is more accurate to say that women and men as separate entities disappear in these poems. Gone is the contradictory male possessed/possessor, and gone too is any occasion to detail the woman.

No "Ode to Sylvia" corresponds to Plath's "Ode to Ted," but it is not too much to claim that she is the force behind Hughes's general elevation of women in these later poems. "Bawdry Embraced," a poem not included in *The Hawk in the Rain* but dedicated to Plath, may be read as her tribute. In this poem Tailfever, a "bawdreur good," passes over "Great farmy whores," "tigery tarts," "All iced-wedding-cakey dolls," "the foxy slut," in favor of a "Born bawdriste." Even though "Heaven itself blazed in her bush," "Tailfever got her": "His palate picked out/ Of promiscuity's butchery/ Sweety Undercut." "From what dog's dish" she had come, "He questioned none: 'It is enough/ That she is and I am.' " Here is Hughes at his most sentimental, although he has masked his feeling in the bawdreur-bawdriste pose and in language that revels in vulgarity. He has not made clear why it is enough, or how heaven's blaze finds its way into promiscuity's butchery, or how the eating metaphor works between bawdreur and bawdriste. In fact, the stylization of the language on the one hand and its sexual slang on the other are totally inappropriate for the simplicity of the statement, although they reveal (as do some of his war poems) Hughes's early strategy of distancing feelings that are not quite fully developed. But "Bawdry Embraced" not only introduces the woman who will match the strutting Tailfever; it also focuses, after a tedious sexual history, on the moment that is "enough" even for such a predatory male as Tailfever. We know from other poems that this moment had its darker side, and was to grow even darker as Hughes returned to it later on; but at this point it triumphs. Plath also treated it in her poems of this time, where she also celebrates the fusion of two into one — a coincidence that suggests they were working together over common themes in these years and (in Hughes's case, at least) revising earlier positions.

Antedating the man possessed by passion in Hughes's poetry is the man possessed by another form of violence, which he confronts in animals. The earliest poem in *The Hawk in the Rain* is "The Jaguar," published first in a slightly different form in 1954. This poem, along with "The Thought-Fox" and "The Hawk in the Rain," introduces an important area of Hughes's imaginative world, although again in somewhat inchoate form. The situation of "The Jaguar" is the simple contrast between the animal and human, between the enraged freedom of the caged jaguar at the zoo and the fear and attraction of the trapped zoo crowd, between the violence in the animal and the violence that is submerged beneath rational control. Hughes's animals are even here both animals and spirits, creatures different from man and also representatives of something deeply embedded in human consciousness. Out of fear of their power, man has clamped the last wild animals into cages, but even there they continue to exert their magnetic force on the human imagination.

The zoo crowd is "mesmerized" by the "wildernesses of freedom" in the caged jaguar's stride. They stare "As a child at a dream," confronting in the jaguar something of the fury of the repressed spirit world. The stupefaction of the zoo-goers, hypnotized by the jaguar, testifies to their yearning for forces that may have been controlled in the modern world but cannot be denied. The last two stanzas of the poem published in *Poetry from Cambridge, 1952-1954* differ from the version in *The Hawk in the Rain* and make this point more explicitly. In the former the crowd at the zoo stares at the jaguar, which acts

> As if in a sudden frenzy: slavering jaw hanging,
> The crazed eye satisfied to be blind in fire,
> By the bang of blood in the brain deaf the ear.
> But what holds them, from corner to corner swinging,
>
> Swivelling the ball of his heel on the polished spot,
> Jerking his head up in surprise at the bars,
> Has not hesitated in the millions of years,
> And like life-prisoners they through bars stare out.

Hughes is no more explicit about what holds them, although he describes another caged animal as "a fugitive aristocrat/ From some thunderous mythological hierarchy" in "Macaw and Little Miss," where the macaw lashes out "in conflagration and frenzy" against its captivity. In that poem the animal embodies some sexual power, latent in "The Jaguar" as well, that the repressed little miss mistakenly thinks she can fondle and cajole until "his shriek shakes the house." Later Hughes described something of the jaguar's significance for him:

> A jaguar after all can be received in several different aspects . . . he is a beautiful, powerful nature spirit, he is a homicidal maniac, he is a supercharged piece of cosmic machinery, he is a symbol of man's baser nature shoved down into the id and growing cannibal murderous with deprivation, he is an ancient symbol of Dionysus since he is a leopard raised to the ninth power, he is a precise historical symbol to the bloody-minded Aztecs and so on. Or he is simply a demon . . . a lump of ectoplasm. A lump of astral energy.
>
> The symbol opens all these things . . . it is the reader's own nature that selects. The tradition is, that energy of this sort once invoked will destroy an impure nature and serve a pure one.[5]

Perhaps Hughes claims too much for his symbol here, as he admits later on in his comment. A symbol that stands for man's baser nature as well as for a beautiful nature spirit carries so much weight that it fails to serve either purpose adequately. Behind this explanation, however, and behind the poems as well, is Hughes's familiar belief that the modern world still suffers from the Puritan division of the spirit from the body, which made the body and all that was natural evil, so that all the natural energy contained and controlled by Catholicism was denied in Puritanism and became destructive. But that is only half the explanation, and accounts perhaps for the horror with which some critics of a latter-day Puritan persuasion receive his poems. The rest of the explanation is that the energy that was exemplified for the Puritans in the body is, in Hughes's view, a cosmic energy that operates quite outside the body and is in itself both creative and destructive. It must be controlled to be made creative, and modern man simply does not have the spiritual capacity for such control. The animals symbolize that energy to which man has responded (or failed to respond) throughout history.

One man, responsive to this energy, is the poet in "The Thought-Fox"; he has the inestimable gift of alertness to the fact that "Something else is alive," "Something more near/ Though deeper within darkness." This receptivity to the other, to "A widening deepening greenness,/ Brilliantly, concentratedly,/ Coming about its own business," allows the "sudden sharp hot stink of fox" to enter the "dark hole of the head." Although Hughes claims to have written this poem in a few minutes, its technical perfections suggest that either the visitations from the spirit world arrive in regularly alliterative rhymed quatrains, or that he worked over his initial inspiration carefully. The stresses are strictly controlled, the alliteration insistent, the rhyme and pararhyme fastidiously maintained. The entire poem, which reads as if it were casual speech, reveals upon analysis a rhythm that intensifies and loosens in a manner far from casual.

The opening line, with its alliterative stress ("I imagine this midnight moment's forest"), starts the poem with a sense of quickening expectation that is heightened by the second line's hint that "Something else is alive." The tension between the writer inside the room and the fox outside is maintained — both by the poet's deferral in identifying the something alive as a fox until the third stanza, and by the rhythm of the lines that slows to describe the writer's "blank page where my fingers move" and quickens, finally, when the fox enters the head. The fox's stealthy approach is described in lines of masterful suspension: "Cold, delicately as the dark snow,/ A fox's nose touches twig, leaf;" "now/ And again now, and now, and now." In the final tantalizingly sly movement of the fox and the equally wily waiting of the hunter, Hughes uses language that enacts the patience of the skilled capturer.

But what has he captured? Hughes says it is a fox and a spirit.[6] As one of the first animal poems he wrote, "The Thought-Fox" evokes a certain interest because it shows how he could combine his poetic craftsmanship with a realistic knowledge of how animals move. But the spirit he has summoned is less clear. Hughes's explanation of the poem insists that it is a real fox; however, a real fox that enters the head assumes some of the head's properties in its brilliant and concentrated purposes, just as the dark hole of the head corresponds to the fox's deeper darkness. As a result of his coming, "The page is printed"; the fox's "neat prints in the snow" become the neat words on the page. Concourse with the animal caused Hughes some difficulty in his poems because, while he was anxious to separate them from the human and the rational, they had to enter his poems through the medium of words and sometimes, as in the present case of the fox, with a concentration that veers toward the deliberateness of the rational. The counterpoint between the waiting poet and the arriving animal suggests that they are playing the same game. Part of the problem in "The Thought-Fox" is that the fox is so realistically detailed that his force as a separate entity is obliterated when he turns into the head. Furthermore, the spirit-fox has been described only as deeper darkness, deepening greenness — qualities too vague and general to describe with the same force as the realistic details what the fox as spirit represents.

The same evasion of just what the animal embodies is evident in "The Hawk in the Rain." There a man, slogging through a rainstorm and dragging his heels from "the swallowing of the earth's mouth," sees the hawk's "diamond point of will" "polestars/ The sea drowner's endurance" as he strains towards "the master-/ Fulcrum of violence where the hawk hangs still." The contrast seems simple, although Hughes's mention of the hawk's will makes the animal's pose slightly less effortless than the poem suggests. But just as the animal becomes established at the center of the universe in which man is a "dazed last-moment-counting" alien, the poet says that the hawk, too, will in his own time meet the weather:

> Coming the wrong way, suffers the air, hurled upside down,
> Fall from his eye, the ponderous shires crash on him,
> The horizon trap him; the round angelic eye
> Smashed, mix his heart's blood with the mire of the land.

The insistence on *him* (crash on him, trap him, mix his heart's blood) reveals the human revenge on the animal that seems to taunt his efforts, giving to "the round angelic eye" of the predator an ironic twist which reduces the hawk's mastery to mere chance. The hawk, too, is subject to "the habit of the dogged grave"; if he is not aware of it, it is only because his round eye circles a blank. The hawk hangs still at the master fulcrum of violence, not as the "diamond point of will" but as an instrument as vulnerable as man to its fury. The polarities shift in this poem; the center is not clear, and Hughes, recognizing what he had left out, returned to treat the hawk as well as the jaguar in later poems. At this point, he has simply indicated an area of violence and wilderness that he leaves undefined.

The technical virtuosity of this poem remains notable, however. The stress falls heavily on the key words, and the unaccentuated syllables work precisely with the meaning of the poem. The heavy alliteration of stress words in the first line and the elision of "swallowing" in the second perfectly enact the action they describe: "I drown in the drumming ploughland, I drag up/ Heel after heel from the swallowing of the earth's mouth." Just as in "The Thought-Fox," the rhythm intensifies here as the speaker's activity becomes more desperate, reaching its climax in the third stanza, where the five stresses are neatly proportioned.

Perhaps the craftsmanship, rather than the themes of these early animal poems, is most significant and most critically neglected. In fact, in this entire first volume of poems the technical achievement frequently outstrips Hughes's control of his subjects. He himself has praised a "utility general-purpose style" "that combines a colloquial prose readiness with poetic breadth, a ritual intensity and music of exceedingly high order with clear direct feeling, and yet in the end is nothing but casual speech."[7] But his own early style, far from casual speech, is highly literary in origins. Not only does *The Hawk in the Rain* show the heavy influence of Edwin Muir, Wilfred Owen, Dylan Thomas, and Gerard Manley Hopkins, but many of the poems are also experiments in traditional, not to say archaic, forms. Terza rima, ottava rima, elegiac quatrains, sprung rhythm, the chanson, syllabic verse — all are represented in this first volume. While it is true that contemporary English poets have been less interested in free verse than have their American counterparts, it is strange that Hughes, who had been so iconoclastic in themes, should show himself as a formal conservative, paying tribute to a tradition he claims is suffocating. The point is worth making especially when we place Hughes with Sylvia Plath, who also started out as an apprentice to traditional form and, with Hughes, moved as she developed toward a "utility general-purpose style." The stylistic contrast between the two poets is not so great: Hughes has his archaisms (the lover's plea in "Song"), his literary folk ballad ("Roarers in a Ring"), his strident colloquialisms ("Vampire") — in short, a formal stylization that often holds his subject at a distance.

This distancing is not merely a matter of the triumph of form over content; it is a strategy in the content itself. Despite Hughes's later claim that the poet must be receptive to his inner life, the inner life of *The Hawk in the Rain* is not clearly detailed. Obviously the egghead, the famous poet, and the Reverend Skinner all have no inner life; but what they miss is expressed in trite phrases ("the whale monstered sea-bottom"), in empty metaphors ("the fermenting of a yeasty heart"), in meaningless descriptions ("the quick ankles of whores"). Even when Hughes turns to the spirit world, he can find only abstractions ("dizzying blue apparition" or "deepening greenness" or "blackouts of impassables") to describe it. His language is marked by absence ("endless," "bottomless," "speechless," "helplessness"), by generalities ("wilderness of freedom," "the horrible angular black hatred," "contradictory permanent horrors"), by vagueness ("the horizons endure," "your dilemma-feebled spine," "a world wide with love"). The deficiency in the language suggests that Hughes had not yet found a means of expressing a full range of emotions.

The most successful poems in this volume are the poems of passionate fusion — hardly love poems, but the closest

Hughes comes to a violent emotion. Much remains beneath the surface of the poems, some of which, like Hughes's secretary, threaten to shriek if you touch them. When he speaks in a gentler voice, as he does in "The Horses" or "October Dawn," he veers into romantic reverie.

The distance of the language is reinforced by the distance of the characters. The number of stylized portraits (hags, vampires, drunks, ancient heroes, dead queens, celluloid photographs of soldiers) reveals the strategy of projection that Hughes devised to handle what are in some cases poorly defined areas of feeling. In part, these stock characters bring into the modern world an energy and violence that have no contemporary counterpart. For example, "Vampire" is entertained by hosts "almost glad he gate-crashed," marveling "where he gets his energy," until he leaves them "cold as a leaf," "heart scarcely moving," while "under the city's deepest stone/ This grinning sack is bursting with your blood." On the other hand, some of these projections serve simply to allow Hughes an expression of banal sentiments; for example, consider "Six Young Men," all killed in war, whose photograph reminds him of his own frailty until the horrors "shoulder out/ One's own body from its instant heat." The joining of the immediate instant heat with the impersonal pronoun demonstrates the general failure of the poem. Many of the poems in *The Hawk in the Rain* are marked by rigid categorizations (the zoo crowd/jaguar, the fox/poet, the hawk/man) that break down even as they are being established. Some poems end with a quick twist, a neat tie-up, a too easy conclusion. The massacre at the end of "Two Wise Generals" is unexplained, as is the great lord from hunting at the end of "A Modest Proposal." The ending of "The Horses" is a nineteenth-century convention: "In din of the crowded streets, going among the years, the faces,/ May I still meet my memory in so lonely a place." As Hughes developed, he worked out of these problems by learning how to be receptive to his inner voice, by developing a language that could handle feelings, and finally by dropping both the literary and the tough poses that marked these early failings.

Still, *The Hawk in the Rain* is an important first volume. The vehemence of its first English reviews suggests that Hughes was a new presence in the aridity of English poetry, although he was charged with his debt of English influences. *The Hawk in the Rain* won first prize in the 1956 poetry competition sponsored by the Poetry Center of the Young Men's and Young Women's Hebrew Association of New York, a contest which Plath urged him to enter. Hughes's American connections are worth noting, however, since they may account for some of the novelty in his nonetheless distinctively English poetic voice. He has claimed that, up to the age of twenty-five, he read no contemporary poets except Eliot, Thomas, and Auden; then, after writing nothing for about six years, he was inspired again by a Penguin book of American poets published in 1955. Among the poets who set him off, he lists John Crowe Ransom, Karl Shapiro, Richard Wilbur, W. S. Merwin, and Robert Lowell.[8] It appears at first to be a fairly eclectic group, and yet it is possible to discern in these poets certain qualities that would have been useful to Hughes. Their formal dexterity is one element. Beyond that, he would have been attracted in different ways to these quite divergent poets. Although he probably lacked sympathy for Ransom's traditionalism, he could recognize in Ransom's combination of archaisms and wit the pull of the past that he himself felt. Ransom's southern fundamentalism, his desire to restore to God the Thunder, has affinities with Hughes's own insistence on religious myth, although Hughes's arises from different cultural sources. Hughes has claimed that Ransom provided a model by helping him get his "words in focus." Shapiro's defense of ignorance and resistance to intellectuality in poetry, as well as his celebration of a Whitmanian cosmic consciousness, define poetry in the direction in which Hughes moves. Shapiro's advice to lower the standards and "Get off the Culture Wagon" would also be Hughes's own.

With Lowell, Wilbur, and Merwin, Hughes's connections are harder to trace. Lowell's confessional mode is not congenial to Hughes, and Hughes once described the style of *Lord Weary's Castle* as "lockjawed" and "tyrannous."[9] However, Lowell's willingness to engage madness and to revel in Dionysian forces might have attracted Hughes's admiration. Although Wilbur seems at the opposite pole from Lowell, his awareness that poetry needs periodic acquaintance with the threat of chaos is exactly the point that Hughes has made over and over again. The things of this world to which Wilbur is called share something of Hughes's factuality. In Merwin, a close friend, Hughes found another poet willing (as he was) to evoke demonic powers. Unlike the English poets of his generation, these American poets work in areas that appeal to Hughes. To say all this is not to suggest that the dominant influences in Hughes's poetry are American. He simply found in this country certain poets who were defining areas he considered important. This early discovery of American poets was also reinforced by the work and the shared concerns of Sylvia Plath.

Notes

[1] Hughes, "Ted Hughes and Crow," p. 13.

[2] Miller, "Fear and Fang," p. 3.

[3] The third poem by Hughes in the Cambridge anthology is an early version of his famous "The Jaguar," which will be discussed later.

[4] Hughes writes of Robert Ferrar, sixteenth-century bishop of St. Davids, who was condemned as a heretic and burned. He made good his assertion and did not cry out from pain when he was burned.

[5] Hughes, "Ted Hughes and Crow," pp. 8-9.

[6] Hughes, *Poetry Is*, p. 14.

[7] "Introduction," *Selected Poems of Keith Douglas*, ed. with an introduction by Ted Hughes (London: Faber & Faber, 1964), p. 14.

[8] Hughes, "Ted Hughes and Crow," p. 14.

[9] Ted Hughes, review of *Imitations* by Robert Lowell, *The Listener*, LXVIII (August 2, 1962), 185.

FOUR

Plath's Cambridge Manuscript

Unlike Hughes, Plath began publishing poems very early, although her first volume, *The Colossus,* did not appear until 1960, three years after *The Hawk in the Rain.* In 1957, when Hughes's book came out, she submitted a collection of forty-three poems as Part II of the English tripos at Cambridge University.[1] This manuscript, entitled "Two Lovers and a Beachcomber," contains poems written as early as 1951-52; some were published in *The Grecourt Review* and American periodicals before Plath came to England, and others were written in the first year of her marriage. Six of the Cambridge poems were included in the English edition of *The Colossus,* and, although Plath did not collect any more of these poems, she did offer them for publication in various English and American journals. The Cambridge manuscript thus serves as a valuable source for the study of Plath's development, and especially for an examination of Hughes's impact on her career.

The poems Plath wrote before she met Hughes in 1956 have two subjects, doomsday and love, frequently intertwined and conveyed in painstakingly ornate language and forms. Three villanelles, published first in the spring, 1953, issue of *The Grecourt Review,* indicate her proficiency in difficult set forms; her comment to her mother that "they are the best I've written yet"[2] suggests that at this point she measured her achievement in terms of formal accomplishment. (Admittedly, Plath always thought her most recent work was her best.) She may have been moved to try the villanelle by Dylan Thomas's "Do not go gentle into that good night," although "Doomsday," at least, is reminiscent of Archibald MacLeish's sonnet "The End of the World" (a poem echoed again in the early "Circus in Three Rings").

The idea in "Doomsday" started in the first line of "Sonnet," a poem Plath sent to her mother in November, 1951, with the following explanation: "It's supposed to be likening the mind to a collection of minute mechanisms, trivial and smooth-functioning when in operation, but absurd and disjointed when taken apart. . . . The 'idiot bird' is to further the analogy of clockwork, being the cuckoo in said mechanism."[3] The mind of the woman, broken in "Sonnet" so that neither "man nor demigod could put together/ The scraps of rusted reverie," has been generalized in "Doomsday" into the broken world, a version of Poe's "City in the Sea." "The streets crack through in havoc-split ravines,/ The doomstruck city crumbles block by block." The repeated lines, "The idiot bird leaps out and drunken leans" and "The hour is crowed in lunatic thirteens," lead not only to the unfortunate rhyme word "smithereens" but also to the pointless didacticism, "Too late to ask if end was worth the means."

The irony of using the tight villanelle form to write a poem about the break-up of world order apparently never occurred to Plath, since she wrote another villanelle on the same subject. "To Eva Descending the Stair" warns that "Clocks cry: stillness is a lie," directing this admonition to the woman unaware that "Red the unraveled rose sings in your hair." Despite the unfortunate echoings ("Blood springs eternal if the heart be burning") and the poeticisms ("Loud the immortal nightingales declare:/ Love flames forever if the flesh be yearning"), in the image of the ominous red rose Plath touches a central concern of her later poetry. She handles that image again, endowing it with some of the sinister qualities the color will assume in her later poetry, in "Circus in Three Rings," a poem probably written in 1953 and published in 1954. Performing in a tent "designed by a drunken god," she is "Daring as death and debonair" as she invades her "lion's den;/ a rose of jeopardy flames in my hair," "defending my perilous wounds with a chair/ while the gnawings of love begin."

More typical of her handling of love during this period is "Mad Girl's Love Song," where she combines, quite without reason, the end of the world ("The stars go waltzing out in blue and red,/ And arbitrary blackness gallops in") with the girl who "dreamed that you bewitched me into bed/ And sung me moon-struck, kissed me quite insane." Eve, "the elevator-girl ace," and Adam, "the arrogant matador," are the final pair of lovers in Plath's poems of this period; in "Dialogue en Route," they tell their romantic wishes to a "gargantuan galactic wink" overhead. Eve, with her desire for Dior gowns, Chanel, and filet mignon, is a typical Smith girl of the 1950's who has read her thesaurus so well that she can wish "venomous nematodes/ were bewitched to assiduous lovers,/ each one an inveterate gallant/ with Valentino's crack technical talent." The man is her Ivy League counterpart who wishes "O for ubiquitous free aphrodisiacs,/ and for pumpkins to purr into Cadillacs/ and voluptuous Venus to come/ waltzing up to me out of her cockleshell." She achieved what she attempted in this poem: a rollicking rhythm.[4] But Plath's Adam and Eve, who also desire to "corral the conundrum of space/ at its cryptic celestial origin," are probably less interesting for the rhythm of the sexains that enclose them than as one more treatment of an ominous conception of love and doom.

These poems were all written before Plath's first suicide attempt in 1953. The connection they establish between the end of the world, the chaos beneath a calm surface, and love as threatened by such a world, suggests that, beneath the polished surface of the villanelles, Plath was handling deeply repressed troubles. The general charge against Plath's early work is that she smothered her subjects in technique, and in these very early poems the surface polish does cover powerful fears. But while each poem may be read simply as an exercise in form, the persistence of a theme and the same peculiar combination of love and collapse point to an underlying obsession that makes these poems puzzling revelations. She told her mother that she wrote her villanelles to make herself feel better after she had broken her leg in a skiing accident: "Oh hell. Life is so difficult and tedious I could cry. But I won't; I'll just keep writing villanelles."

In the spring of 1953 Plath had turned from villanelles to imitations of Emily Dickinson, but her subject remained the same. "Admonition" centers on the dangers of dissection that might "cut the chord/ Articulating song" and ends with the familiar stopped clock-heart:

If you pluck out the heart
  To find what makes it move,
You'll halt the clock
  That syncopates our love.

Two more poems in Dickinson's style mark the connection between love and doom: "Parallax" regards love from two angles — "doom from above" or "all angelic reason"; "Verbal Calisthenics" talks of love as "Treading circus tightropes," admitting that "The brazen jackanapes/ Would fracture if he fell."[5] In retrospect, we can see that "To Eva Descending the Stair" was quite explicit: "Clocks cry: stillness is a lie." The solar schemes, "the ordered lunar motion," the galactic harmony, the universal clocks of these early poems are all projections of the mind, a system which functions when in operation but which is absurd when taken apart. The fissures, fractures, and crack-ups of these poems portend the fate Plath feared. The association between a mental crack-up and love is puzzling, since her letters do not reveal any deep emotional relationship with a particular man. In fact, men seem to be specimens, objects to be categorized rather than loved, at this point in her life. The editors who accepted these poems for publication in 1953 and 1954 may well have read some of them as expressing a fear of atomic destruction, rampant in those days — but, for Plath, the explosion was to hit much closer home.

In the summer of 1953 Plath attempted suicide. She spent the fall undergoing treatment at McLean Hospital, and in the spring she returned to Smith College. The experience was to form the basis of poems and of her novel, *The Bell Jar*, but she did not explore it for several years, nor did she write any poetry at all for a long period. On April 16, 1954, she sent her mother what she claimed was her first poem in a year. In that sonnet,

"Doom of Exiles," she talks of "returning from the vaulted domes/ Of our colossal sleep" to find an irrepressible image: "Each clock tick consecrates the death of strangers." "Green alleys where we reveled have become/ The infernal haunt of demon dangers," she prophesies. And, in a line that foretells the direction of her later poems, she says, "Backward we travelled to reclaim the day/ Before we fell, like Icarus, undone."[6] Altars in decay and "profane words scrawled black across the sun" are what she finds. The couplet draws back from these revelations: "Still, stubbornly we try to crack the nut/ In which the riddle of our race is shut." The positive crack here, placed against all the earlier ominous cracks in her poetry, as well as the clock tick, suggests that Plath was trying to turn her old language to new purposes. Traveling backward, she reclaimed a vocabulary by regeneration, assigning meanings that oppose her earlier attitudes. But "Doom of Exiles" is only minimally hopeful; it presents the image of separation from an earlier happiness that will become dominant in her later work.

Plath spent the following fall reading Freud, Jung, and Frazer for her thesis, and studying German. She had to translate and explicate a poem by Rilke; it interested her so much that she attempted to try a translation in verse, with rhyme and rhythm exactly like Rilke's.[7] The next group of poems that can be precisely dated comes from the early winter of 1955, when she wrote "Temper of Time." She claimed to feel "great advances in my poetry, the main one being a growing victory over word nuances and a superfluity of adjectives," and her line contracted, perhaps in reaction to Rilke's rhythm. She forestalled her mother's fear that "Temper of Time" might be too depressing by saying, "Understand that 'Temper of Time,' while ominous, is done tongue in cheek, after a collection of vivid metaphors of omen from the thesaurus, which I am rapidly wearing out. It is a kind of pun on the first page of the NY *Times*, which has news much like this every morning."[8] In fact, "Temper of Time" reads more like a dark version of early Plath than like a page of the New York *Times*. Like the other two poems she sent her mother at this time, it is written in short, rigidly regular lines. The "evil stars," "Black birds of omen," "hex on the cradle and/ Death in the pot" are out of folklore or the thesaurus, not out of the daily news. The other two poems, not included in the Cambridge manuscript, are "Apparel for April" and "Winter Words"; both enforce the same strict form, perhaps an influence from Auden as well as Rilke, but do not develop much beyond their titles. During this period Plath was writing five poems a week, and by April she was typing a manuscript of sixty poems, "a good bit of work to have produced in one semester."[9] It was in fact an accomplishment, although most of these poems do not appear in the Cambridge manuscript and may have been fairly weak.

The title poem of that manuscript, "Two Lovers and a Beachcomber by the Real Sea," was published in 1955 and must have been written during this period. In it we can hear clearly the voice of the later Plath.[10] The poem starts out in Wallace Stevens style: "Cold and final, the imagination/ shuts down its fabled summer house," but its final line is completely Plath.

> Water will run by rule; the actual sun
> will scrupulously rise and set;
> no little man lives in the exacting moon
> and that is that, is that, is that.

The dead end emphasis of the last line will be repeated throughout her later work: "You do not do, you do not do" of "Daddy," or "These are the isolate, slow faults/ That kill, that kill, that kill" of "Elm." "Two Lovers and a Beachcomber" is about the end of the season, the end of love, the realization that "We are not what we might be." The universe is diminished: Melville's "white whales are gone with the white ocean," and "Thoughts that found a maze of mermaid hair" "now fold their wings like bats and disappear/ into the attic of the skull." "No sea change decks the suntan shank of bone," she claims, borrowing from *The Tempest*, a central source for her later poems. But, the speaker says, "that is that, is that, is that."

Such acceptance of the universe was not to last long. In February, 1956, she met Ted Hughes. Plath immediately recognized him as "the only man I've met yet here who'd be strong enough to be equal with,"[11] and she even wrote a poem about him right after their meeting. "Pursuit" was, she explained to her mother,

> more in my old style, but larger, influenced a bit by Blake, I think (tiger, tiger). . . . It is, of course, a symbol of the terrible beauty of death, and the paradox that the more intensely one lives, the more one burns and consumes oneself; death, here, includes the concept of love, and is larger and richer than mere love, which is part of it. The quotation is from Racine's *Phedre*, where passion as destiny is magnificently expressed. . . . Another epigraph could have been from my beloved Yeats: "Whatever flames upon the night, Man's own resinous heart has fed."[12]

While the explanation outstrips the poem, Plath's identification of passion as destiny is a useful explication of the peculiar thrill this woman experiences from the panther who pursues her to the death. Although she admits in the second line that "One day I'll have my death of him," throughout the poem she describes him in exalted terms: "more lordly than the sun," "hauled by love/ On fluent haunches," "His ardor snares me, lights the trees," "His voice waylays me, spells a trance." His victims, "Kindled like torches for his joy,/ Charred and ravened women lie"; the speaker herself says, "Appalled by secret want, I rush/ From such assault of radiance." Even at the end when she is bolting the door, "Blood quickens" as she hears the panther's tread "Coming up and up the stairs." Here he is with rending teeth, bright claws, taut thighs, "Crying: blood, let blood be spilt;/ Meat must glut his mouth's raw wound," the demon lover. Although the woman runs from him, she seems to be always looking back to see that he "keeps my speed," filled with rapture, not fear. In discussing this poem and letters from this period, Judith Kroll has commented on the fascist sensibility in Plath's early glorification of Hughes, her desire to be controlled by an all-powerful figure of force.[13] Also part of the "terrible beauty of death" is the thrilling desire to be sexually consumed. Placed against poems written only a few years earlier, where love and death are juxtaposed and finally distanced, "Pursuit" reads as a torrent of sexual agony. The "black marauder" whose assault is "radiance," the panther who "Most soft, most suavely glides," the "lithe one" with "claws" — such images embody a complex tangle of sexual fear and desire, violence and gentleness, pain and joy that Plath could not separate. Although she flees from this beast and shuts her door on what she calls "that dark guilt," she is appalled by what is her own, as well as his, "secret want." His "starving body," his "need," are qualities she feeds and encourages, hurling her heart and squandering her blood in an ecstasy of submission, boasting that he "Compels a total sacrifice."

If Plath wrote this (as she said she did) shortly after meeting Hughes, the poem demonstrates the extent to which he magnetized her feelings. In the letter enclosing this poem, she talks of being "refined in the fires of pain and love" for a man named Richard, whose lack of the "athletic" physique she most admires "pales to nothing at the voice of his soul, which speaks to me in such words as the gods would envy." In Hughes she found an image of physical strength that matched her own, and in "Pursuit" she seems to have projected some of her intensity of pain and love for the frail Richard onto Hughes. Almost immediately she was to transfer to Hughes the god-like status of Richard, so that Hughes came to stand for the sought-after perfection of body and soul. How much the real man actually embodied the powers she cast upon him is beside the point; he entered her imagination as a symbol of superhuman force, and her first poetic treatment of him seems to borrow his own favorite predatory animal imagery. While she knew his poems before she met him and may well have modeled her panther on his jaguar, it would be several years before Hughes himself would write of an animal as ravenous as her panther. His early jaguar was caged, and not until *Lupercal* (1960) did Hughes release his animals from their bars. A more immediate source for her panther was probably the lion in "Circus in Three Rings." Still, "Pursuit" is important in the Plath-Hughes relationship because it demonstrates how deeply and immediately Hughes touched Plath's imagination, and how completely they shared a predatory concept of passion. The slavering wolves of Hughes's "Modest Proposal" may have come out of "Pursuit" as the two poets worked together to forge a new kind of love poetry. But while

Hughes's poems of this period concentrate on the passionate union of equally violent partners, many of Plath's poems celebrate the god-beast-man for whom submission by the woman is ecstasy.

Although her letters repeat her sense of joy in finding in Hughes a counterpart to herself, an equal in poetry and passion, Plath also exclaims, "To find such a man, to make him into the best man the world has seen: such a life work!"[14] A superior being, a counterpart of herself, a man to be made into the best man — these contradictory attributes betray the complicated psychology behind the poems. Only by being superior could he be a counterpart to this determined superwoman; only by being made over into the best man would he be desirable to this best woman. The submissive role masks a desire to be controlled that stems from the woman's fear of superiority. To conquer that fear she must create a superior man, and in the process she reasserts her control and superiority. The "life work" she mentions in her letter started in her poetic elevation of Hughes during the first months of their acquaintance.

Plath's letters reveal the remarkable creative energy unleashed when she first met Hughes. In the spring of 1956 they spent days together, reading, reciting, and memorizing poetry. She felt herself "living in the midst of a singing joy which is the best of Hopkins, Thomas, Chaucer, Shakespeare, Blake, Donne, and all the poets we love together." "I can't stop writing poems! They come better and better."[15] The subject of most of these poems is Hughes himself, the man and nature god and colossus she made him. In one poem she sent her mother, she celebrates (somewhat inappropriately) in the complex stanzas of the ode and in monosyllabic words the Whitmanian qualities of Hughes:

> For his least look, scent acres yield:
> each finger-furrowed field
> heaves forth stalk, leaf, fruit-nubbed emerald;
> bright grain sprung so rarely
> he hauls to his will early;
> at his hand's staunch hest, birds build.

Ringdoves roost well within his wood,
shirr songs to suit which mood
he saunters in; how but most glad
could be this adam's woman
when all earth his words do summon
leaps to laud such man's blood![16]

In "Song," her heart is "a green-tipped leaf/ kindled by such rare seizing/ into an ardent blazing." "The Glutton" takes up the eating metaphor developed in "Pursuit." The man is "hunger-strung, hard to slake," and the woman, more explicitly than the woman of the earlier poem, feels "That all merit's in being meat/ Seasoned how he'd most approve."

Plath was the first to comment on the male image she was presenting here. In "Soliloquy of the Solipsist" she concludes,

I
Know you appear
Vivid at my side,
Denying you sprang out of my head,
Claiming you feel
Love fiery enough to prove flesh real,
Though it's quite clear
All your beauty, all your wit, is a gift, my dear,
From me.

Here is the female-god-creator who is never far beneath the surface of the sacrificial woman.

The identities are joined for a moment in "Wreath for a Bridal," where she develops the idea of lovers fusing into one — the same concept that Hughes had used or was to use in "Incompatibilities." She and her lover are "pure paragons of constance," "Whose stark act all coming double luck joins." While Hughes's lovers are driven by an animalistic fury, Plath's pair seem to accept innocently and willingly their union as they "seek single state from that dual battle." An almost pastoral gaiety surrounds their love-making in "that luck-rooted mead of clover/ Where, bedded like angels, two burn in one fever." From this pact that is made once only comes a new life:

From this holy day on, all pollen blown
Shall strew broadcast so fair a seed on wind
That every breath, thus teeming, set the land
Sprouting fruit, flowers, children most fair in legion
To slay spawn of dragon's teeth: speaking this promise,
Let flesh be knit, and each step hence go famous.

This poem passes over the fears of "Pursuit," the submission of "The Glutton," to celebrate the sex act as "wedlock wrought within love's proper chapel," and the life that it promises will fructify the earth.

Even when Plath gives the subject a darker treatment, as in "Epitaph for Fire and Flower," she remains on the surface of love's cruelty and pain. At the poem's opening, a knowing voice declares that, despite love's pain, nothing will keep "These two most perishable lovers from the touch/ That will kindle angels' envy, scorch and drop/ Their fond hearts charred as any match." Her tone switches to disdain as she exclaims over "what an age of glass/ These lovers prophesy to lock embrace/ Secure." The foolish lovers think they can "conquer cinder's kingdom," but their very desire "Blackens flesh to bone and devours them." Images of quartz, stone, diamonds, rock, fossil describe the lovers' efforts to make their passion permanent, while all the time the "passing dazzle" and "instant flare" of the devouring fire make a mockery of their hopes. Love's fire here burns right through the lovers' bones, destroying not only their dreams of immortality but also the most solid substance of their mortality. Consumed by love, these lovers do not survive to know the ultimate pain, as Hughes describes it, of unbearable loneliness when each discovers his inexorable solitude.

Pure paragons of constance, Plath's poetic lovers did not remain for long, nor did the poetic woman find eternal merit in being meat seasoned to her man's taste. In "The Shrike," when "royal dreams beckon this man" "From his earth-wife's side," she becomes the eater, waiting in rage for his return "When her shrike-face/ Leans to peck open those locked lids, to eat" "And with red beak/ Spike and suck out/ Last blood-drop of the truant heart." In "Vanity Fair" she is the witch who knows that "Each vain girl's driven/ To believe beyond heart's flare/ No fire is, nor in any book proof" "So she wills all to the black king." The witch concludes, "The worst sloven/ Vies with best queen over/ Right to blaze as satan's wife." "Monologue at 3 A.M." returns to the idea that it is better that "every fiber crack/ And fury make head,/ Blood drenching vivid/ Couch" than "to sit mute" "wrenched from/ My one kingdom." And "Complaint of the Crazed Queen" celebrates the "giant" "With hands like derricks,/ Looks fierce and black as rooks," who romped through the queen's dainty acres "And used her gentle doves with manners rude." Unlike Hughes's dove breeder, whose experience this woman seems to copy, the queen is the conquered, not the conqueror; she is then abandoned, doomed to trek "in blood through sun and squall." The same giant stalks in "The Snowman on the Moor," a poem which is explicit about the dangers of smart women. The woman runs to the moors after a fight with her unruly man, and there she meets a "sky-high" figure with "ladies' skulls dangling from his spike-studded belt." These skulls "clacked their guilt:/ 'Our wit made fools/ Of kings, unmanned kings' sons: our masteries/ Amused court halls:/ For that brag, we barnacle these iron thighs.' " The woman is humbled and returns "brimful of gentle talk."

The darkest poem in this collection is "Aerialist," where Plath returns to the image of the acrobat from her early "Verbal Calisthenics" and develops its ominous qualities by introducing the predatory male who dictates her performance. Although she is "Cat-clever" despite her maestro's "whip crack and roar," "lunge and menace," she concludes her act only to discover "Tiger-tamer and grinning clown" "bowling black balls at her" to "shatter to atoms/ Her nine so slippery lives." The poem looks forward to "Lady Lazarus." The woman here escapes, but now, "as penalty for her skill," she must walk in dread "Lest, out of spite, the whole/ Elaborate scaffold of sky overhead/ Fall racketing finale on her luck." Penalty for her skill is the price Plath's persona feared she would have to pay, and, as we see from this familiar image of the falling sky, it is a fear deeply rooted in her poetry. Rousing spite, angels' envy, for her luck, she felt threatened paradoxically because she was so strong, adroit, skilled, artful. Here she fears not simply the black balls trapping her, because if she should escape them there is always the further danger of the sky falling in. In this image Plath draws upon her earliest formulation of doom. The sexual imagery ("coming correct," "Hung/ In dead center of her act," the "menace/ Of every pendulum") deepens the fears of this performance and makes her daytime "dread" a mixture of joy and guilt.

The queen, the defiant woman, and the aerialist are brought low by monsters of force that they themselves seem to have created, but the thrill of the woman in "Pursuit" and "The Glutton" has turned to fear and misery. The towering male figure that Plath created in her early poems looms larger and larger in her imagination as she develops. The allegory of the crazed queen and the humbled woman presents, in very simple terms, the dangers of erecting such a powerful image. At best, she could turn on this figure and deride him. In "Letter to a Purist" she says, using an image that will reappear in her father imagery later, "That grandiose colossus who/ Stood astride/ The envious assaults of sea" "Has nothing on you/ O my love." She continues,

> O my great idiot, who
> With one foot
> Caught (as it were) in the muck-trap
> Of skin and bone,
> Dithers with the other way out
> In preposterous provinces of the mad cap
> Cloud-cuckoo,
> Agawp at the impeccable moon.

The cuckoo and the colossus coincide here; the image of doom from her poetic past is fused to the image of doom that will blacken her later poems. Here the colossus can dither with a symbol of Plath's deepest fear of breakdown and endure the assaults of the element that threatened to overpower her; she derides this psychic strength by praising it. Much later she was to use the same tone, in "Zoo Keeper's Wife," to describe the man's stupid invulnerability to worries that terrified her.

In these poems of love-hate, Hughes's poetic presence is strong. The claws, beaks, blood, and marauders come straight out of his poems, but they are more ominous and directly threatening in hers. The welding of two into one, the conquering male, the woman dreaming of violent assault, the sexual imagery, as well as a whole vocabulary of doves, rooks, squalls, and owl-hours are gifts from Hughes. Even the enjambment of words, the crowded syntactical arrangement of the lines resembles Hughes as well as Hopkins and Thomas. Hughes had freed her from the villanelle and sonnet, opening to her his own strongly stressed style, although, as we have seen, she had been moving in this direction since "Temper of Time." He had also confirmed in her the importance of certain of his favorite poets. If Plath sometimes sounds like Hughes, it is because they both sound like Yeats. Her crazy women, witches, and spirits belonged originally to Yeats. Queens, kings, monsters abound in her poems of this period as another borrowing through Hughes from Yeats. George Steiner claims to see the strong influence of John Crowe Ransom (a poet Hughes admired, as I have mentioned) in Plath's archaism and rhetoric of violence.[17] In this discussion I have maintained that Plath was influenced by Hughes, and at this point in their careers that seems to have been the case. But Hughes himself was then working on poems for *The Hawk in the Rain,* and he may also have been influenced by Plath's poems, especially by her treatment of passion. The predatory woman of "The Shrike" may have inspired "Billet-Doux," or the panther, "A Modest Proposal."

Hughes's influence certainly exerted itself in Plath's nature poems during this period. She had not shown a particular interest in nature in her early work, but it was to assume more importance in her poems as she developed. Here what she has to say either is heavily indebted to Hughes or is a poetic answer to one of his poems. "Spinster" and "Two Sisters of Persephone," both poems Plath included in *The Colossus,* are drawn from Hughes's "Secretary." Plath places the title characters in natural settings. The spinster, afflicted by spring, "a burgeoning/ Unruly enough to pitch her five queenly wits/ Into vulgar motley," barricades herself in a house where "no mere insurgent man could hope to break/ With curse, fist, threat/ Or love, either." The language is Hughes's (a direct quotation from "Fallgrief's Girl-Friends"), as is the animus against the frightened woman, although the setting is Plath's own. Nature is associated with the man in this poem, just as it was in Plath's experience at the time. She makes the connection more explicitly in "Two Sisters of Persephone," where the bitter, "wry virgin" is the intellectual sister who "works problems on/ A mathematical machine" in a dark room, while the other sister lies "Lulled/ Near a bed of poppies," "their red silk flare/ Of petalled blood/ Burns open to sun's blade." The poppies and blood are to reappear in her late poems, but here they are images of fertility as the woman copies them to "Freely become sun's bride." The disdain for the intellectual woman evident in these poems may well reflect Plath's growing disenchantment with academic life during her Cambridge years, and the elevation of the natural woman may reveal her own new sense of herself as Hughes's sun-bride; but certainly these are attitudes Hughes shared, and perhaps encouraged. Interestingly, the frightened spinster and the intellectual sister, castigated here in Hughes's style, are prototypes of the worrier and the thinking women who surface not only in the later poems, but also in other poems of this same period.

Perhaps the poems that most clearly connect and distinguish Plath and Hughes at this time are "Black Rook in Rainy Weather" and "The Hawk in the Rain." It is not simply the rain that unites these poems, although even the weather hits each poet in a different way: Hughes's "rain hacks my head to the bone," while Plath's rain is "desultory weather" in a "dull, ruinous landscape." Hughes captures the feeling of the rainstorm which Plath can only generalize. As poems about nature walks, the works demonstrate what the two poets were looking for and what they found. As we have seen, Hughes's tramp is a battle of human endurance against the murderous force of the elements; he finds that the hawk appears to mock his efforts. The energy of the poem is directed toward conveying the desperation of the man against nature, and against the hawk who nonetheless "polestars" his efforts.

The rook in Plath's poem, arranging and rearranging its feathers, seems like the fastidious spinster in comparison with Hughes's hawk. It is an object set out on the landscape for no particular purpose, because Plath's real desire is "some backtalk/ From the mute sky." Neither rook nor sky speaks, but the walker is very wordy, full of parenthetical phrases ("Although, I admit, I desire," "At any rate, I now walk"), concerned not with the actual landscape but with her own thoughts. She finally reattaches these thoughts to the landscape by saying,

> I only know that a rook
> Ordering its black feathers can so shine
> As to seize my senses, haul
> My eyelids up, and grant
>
> A brief respite from fear
> Of total neutrality.

The rook, then, is just a ploy, a common bird which serves only as the focus of a vision. No master-fulcrum of violence in this landscape will ever compare to "that rare, random descent" of radiance that hallows "an interval/ Otherwise inconsequent." This poem may also be compared to "The Thought-Fox," in which Hughes embodies his poetic inspiration in the fox's sly approach; what in Hughes comes through the fox is foisted unnaturally onto Plath's rook. On the other hand, Hughes is no more specific than Plath about what the hawk or fox represents. "Black Rook in Rainy Weather" may, however, be an attempt to answer Hughes's hawk poem. "Miracles occur," she suggests hopefully. The fear of total neutrality can be relieved by poetic vision, Plath claims, against Hughes's conviction that nature is anti-human.

Plath's early nature poetry is in fact a strange concoction of Hughes and Wallace Stevens. "November Graveyard" borrows Hughes's language (an echo of Yeats) to claim, "Here's honest rot/ To unpick the elaborate heart, pare bone" and then switches instantly to Stevens in the next line, "Free of the fictive vein." She concludes with the injunction: "At the essential landscape stare, stare,/ Till your eyes foist a vision dazzling on the wind." In "On the Difficulty of Conjuring Up a Dryad," she again combines Stevens and Hughes. First, Stevens: "The vaunting mind/ Snubs impromptu spiels of wind/ And wrestles to impose/ Its own order on what is." Then Hughes: " 'I shall compose a crisis/ To stun sky black out, drive gibbering mad/ Trout, cock, ram/ That bulk so calm/ On my jealous stare,/ Self-sufficient as they are.' "

The strategy of her nature poetry is set out in "On the Plethora of Dryads," where she starts to starve her fancy down "To discover that metaphysical Tree" and discovers instead Hughes's "miraculous art." She says that "Before I might blind sense/ To see with the spotless soul," she was "ravished" by each particular quirk. "No visionary lightnings" descend here:

> Instead, a wanton fit,
> Dragged each dazzled sense apart
> Surfeiting eye, ear, taste, touch, smell.

Thus snared, she rides "earth's burning carousel" and is doomed to "watch sluttish dryads" in every tree. This poem is an autobiographical sketch of her imaginative activity with Hughes, and it is not entirely clear without reference to their joint nature jaunts. Hughes, who "Haunched like a faun" and turns into the goat-man in "Metamorphoses," lived, in Plath's heightened imagination, in a world of spirits. She, on the other hand, was always wrongly attempting to impose the mind's order on nature. Vaunting mind and blinding sense, as the language suggests, are vain efforts. Starving her "fancy" — a curious word choice in this context, since what she is talking about is the imagination — she seeks a vision like the one she had in "Black Rook in Rainy Weather." Here, however, she is overtaken by a "fit"; it comes neither from above nor through the spotless soul, but by way of the surfeited senses. It is not a temporary visitation, but a permanent change: for her now "no chaste tree but suffers blotch" of the seductive dryads. She could not always work this miracle, as she records in "On the Difficulty of Conjuring Up a Dryad"; there "no hocus-pocus of green angels/ Damasks with dazzle the threadbare eye" and no Daphne can be concocted, although she is aware that "In dream-propertied fall some moon-eyed,/ Star-luck sleight-of-hand man" (Hughes described in Stevens's words) can accomplish what her own "beggared brain" fails to do.

If she had trouble conjuring up a dryad or problems once she had, the spirit in "The Lady and the Earthenware Head" remained "Steadfast and evil-starred," "Refusing to diminish/ By one jot its basilisk-look of love." In this poem about a model clay head that she attempts to junk, she cannot rid herself of its evil charm. In this connection one should recall Plath's comments on the double, made when she was writing her thesis. Here is the double as enemy, an omen of death. She must keep the head safe in order to be safe herself. If she throws it in the ash heap, she fears some rough boys will maltreat it and "waken the sly nerve up/ That knits to each original its coarse copy." Thrown into a "dark tarn," it "Lewdly" beckons her, and her courage wavers "as one who drowns." The "antique hag-head" haunts her. There is no need here to conjure up its spirit. Leering, beckoning, ogling, this head, a model of her own, seems to have no intellect but is a sinister, seductive, even sexual image that she must protect in order to protect herself. Although she resolves to launch it in a tree, the head refuses to become a dryad; it remains "shrined on her shelf," an indoor demon. The same evil spirit stalks her in "Dream with Clam-Diggers," where she returns to the landscape of her childhood, "that far innocence," only to find that

> Clam-diggers rose up out of dark slime at her offense,
> Grim as gargoyles from years spent squatting at sea's border
> In wait amid snarled weed and wrack of wave
> To trap this wayward girl at her first move of love,
> Now with stake and pitchfork they advance, flint eyes fixed on
> murder.

The difference between fauns and dryads on the one hand, and basilisks and gargoyles on the other, measures the distance between the poems Plath wrote in an effort to concoct Hughes's nature spirits and the poems she wrote about her own native spirit world. In this latter category she struck closer to the area of Hughes's animal poems than in her evocations of mythical spirits. The murderous clam-diggers and the evil-starred head are predators in the style of Hughes's hawk and fox, although where Hughes locates his evil vision in animals, Plath identifies it with her own head or dreams, thus endowing it with a more terrifying presence. At this point Hughes always remains at a safe distance from his animals; they are placed high in a tree or behind bars, and even when they enter his head they come from some other realm, a thought-fox that is both fox and spirit. He does not make the immediate connection between animal darkness and human darkness until his poems in *Lupercal,* nor do his animals turn on human beings until later. In *The Hawk in the Rain,* Hughes's human characters are mesmerized but safe from evil spirits. The abstractions he uses to describe his animal spirits are another form of distancing which contrasts to Plath's more immediate details in "Dream with Clam-Diggers" and "The Lady and the Earthenware Head." Plath's poems are not fully realized (the clam-diggers' revenge seems motiveless, and the model head-head connection is blurred); still, they are, as psychic explorations, more particular, more intense, more ominous, and more psychologically complex than Hughes's poems. The connection between love and death, between attraction and repulsion established in the subtle rendering of the spirits she evokes is fuller than Hughes's presentations.

The poem in which Plath is most specific about her spirit world is "All the Dead Dears." There she focuses not on nature, but on the skeletons of a woman, a mouse, and a shrew, all from the fourth century A.D.; she discovered them in the archaeological museum at Cambridge. These three bear "Dry witness/ To the gross eating game" that she would wink at if she did not hear "Stars grinding, crumb by crumb,/ Our own grist down to its bony face." She identifies the threat with mother and father, not nurturers, but life-takers:

> Mother, grandmother, greatgrandmother
> Reach hag hands to haul me in,
> And an image looms under the fishpond surface
> Where the daft father went down
> With orange duck-feet winnowing his hair.

In the Cambridge version of this poem (which was revised for *The Colossus*), the father was more explicitly described and associated with the god-man figure that Hughes assumes. These "long gone darlings" threaten to domesticate themselves in the speaker's mind, "Between tick/ And tack of the clock," the old smooth-running mechanism that can be easily rendered useless. They will not be satisfied until she goes "Deadlocked with them." The eating metaphor of Plath's early love poems and the embrace of death that encloses love are tangled here into an elaborate plot, one that Plath was to spend her life exploring.

The Cambridge manuscript won no poetry prize, nor did it even earn Plath a first at Cambridge. She was to work it over for three years, deleting most of the poems, before she finally had a volume that would be accepted for publication. Since Plath worked on that collection while Hughes was collecting *The Hawk in the Rain*, it demonstrates her progress at this point and may be compared to Hughes's book only as it reveals her accomplishments and interests of this period. In this manuscript her development may be traced: from the undergraduate villanelles, to the exercises in rhythm and pared language which she engaged in after her suicide attempt, to the romantic celebration of Hughes which shaded into a darker look at love's dangers and the imagination's difficulties, and finally to the threatening spirits and demons she detailed in free form.

In general, "Two Lovers and a Beachcomber" is a much less distanced collection than *The Hawk in the Rain*. Despite Plath's gift at ventriloquism and her ability to speak through the language and forms of other poets, despite her fascination with set forms and verbal calisthenics, these poems reveal both an obsession with certain troubling themes and a perilous understanding of their complexity. The stock characters of Hughes's poems are generally absent from Plath's, where everyone but the spinster, Persephone's sister, and the faun is an identity seen from within. Plath sometimes copies the rigid categories of Hughes, as in "The Death of Myth-Making" or "Natural History," where she talks allegorically of Reason, Commonsense and the Monarch Mind; but generally her characters are fluid, shifting, threatened. Even Eva in the early villanelle is a character posed on a stairway that is about to collapse.

In fact, fear of collapse is the theme that unites these poems from"Doomsday" to "All the Dead Dears." Unlike the stalwart ancient heroes of Hughes or the fearless poet entertaining the thought-fox, Plath's characters are always threatened. Hughes's themes of sex, lust, and violence concern Plath in this manuscript, but, while he celebrates their force and power, Plath recoils from their dangers. Only in "Wreath for a Bridal" is Plath's speaker confident, although she sometimes approximates the bravado of Hughes's speakers in the love-hate poems she wrote when she first knew him. Those are poses that did not serve her well. "Spinster" and "Two Sisters of Persephone" to the contrary, the speaker in Plath's poems is most typically the worried or thoughtful woman. In fact, sometimes she is too thoughtful, and such poems as "Black Rook in Rainy Weather," "On the Plethora of Dryads," and "On the Difficulty of Conjuring Up a Dryad" are rather loose examples of thinking in poetic lines, simply ruminating on the problem of imaginative vision. At her best, Plath's thinking speakers are extremely sensitive to particularities. Although she makes fun of the paranoid woman in "Miss Drake Proceeds to Supper" (the character is "No novice/ In those elaborate rituals/ Which allay the malice/ Of knotted table and crooked chair"), the typical Plath speaker has the same painful openness and heightened awareness of dangers. Miss Drake can see "in the nick of time/ How perilous needles grain the floor-boards," and the same clairvoyance turns a skeleton into hag hands which haul the viewer into the coffin, or the earthernware head into a basilisk. Miss Drake is mad; the speaker in many of Plath's darker poems is possessed of a terrifying vision. Perhaps what most separates Plath's poems from Hughes's is her psychological penetration. She handles feelings and intolerably heightened fears even in these early poems, and, once beyond her undergraduate days, she begins to explore complicated psychological states. If her speakers are more threatened than Hughes's, it may be because they are more sensitive and more aware of dangers.

Her poems are not without obvious shortcomings. She usurps the language of other poets; she shamelessly copies rhythms and styles; she frequently lapses into dullness or borrowed archaic language (Ransom's "bruit," Hughes's "luck-rooted mead of clover"); she veers between an arch literary style and prosaic emptiness. Her imitations of Dickinson suggest that her fine ear and facility with words placed her always in danger of plagiarizing, and much later Plath was still borrowing the techniques of any poet she expecially liked. The hazards of these abilities for a young poet are evident in this manuscript. But, in the poems written at Cambridge especially, she demonstrates that she was beginning to find her own voice and her own complicated subject matter. In this respect, at least, *The Colossus* marks only a slight advance over this earlier manuscript. The breakthrough into her inner life, especially into her feeling that it was dangerous to be an artful woman, was the central insight of her career, and she had already discovered it in the poems of the Cambridge manuscript.

Notes

[1] Most of the poems in this manuscript have been published. For their source, check Cameron Northouse and Thomas P. Walsh, *Sylvia Plath and Anne Sexton: A Reference Guide* (Boston: G. K. Hall, 1974).

[2] Plath, *Letters Home,* p. 103.

[3] Ibid., p. 82.

[4] Ibid., p. 108.

[5] Ibid., pp. 110, 111.

[6] Ibid., p. 136.

[7] Ibid., p. 149

[8] Ibid., pp. 156, 157.

[9] Ibid., pp. 164, 172.

[10] A. Alvarez points out this fact in "Sylvia Plath: The Cambridge Collection," *Cambridge Review,* XC (February 7, 1969), 247.

[11] Plath, *Letters Home,* p. 221.

[12] Ibid., pp. 222-223.

[13] Kroll, *Chapters in a Mythology,* p. 249.

[14] Plath, *Letters Home,* p. 252.

[15] Ibid., p. 235.

[16] Ibid., p. 238.

[17] George Steiner, "In Extremis," *Cambridge Review,* XC (February 7, 1969), 249.

FIVE

The Colossus and *Lupercal*

Plath's first volume of poems, *The Colossus,* and Hughes's second, *Lupercal,* were published in 1960. Most of these poems were written after their marriage in 1956 and during a three-year period of hectic activity, difficult decisions, and two transatlantic moves. For Plath especially it was a time of turmoil. She and Hughes returned to America in June, 1957, and after a summer of writing she began what she might have assumed would be a permanent teaching career at Smith. Although she started with enthusiasm, she discovered that teaching left her with no energy for writing, and, against opposition from her mentors at Smith and with some hesitation on her own part, she decided to give up teaching and devote herself entirely to writing. Hughes, who had taught for the second semester at the University of Massachusetts, had also had a trying year; first he had been unable to locate a job, and then he had felt isolated in America. In June, 1958, with the savings accumulated from their teaching posts, they rented a small apartment in Beacon Hill and began a year of study and writing. Plath also worked part-time at Massachusetts General Hospital and audited Robert Lowell's poetry course at Boston University, but it was not a period of great poetic productivity for her. By the end of the academic year, the Hugheses had decided to move to England, where their first child would be born. But, before going, they spent the summer on a cross-country camping tour of the United States and two months of the fall at Yaddo, where Plath was able to produce a number of the poems in *The Colossus.*

Although Hughes had his dry periods during these years, he was able to work more steadily than Plath, for two reasons: he did not have to agonize over the decision to give up teaching, since he had never seriously contemplated it as a career; and he had already found his poetic voice in the poems of his first volume. *Lupercal* continues the concerns and themes of *The Hawk in the Rain,* and while it is more polished than his first book and contains two or three of his most famous poems, it is the consolidation of his early achievement, not a new departure. A. Alvarez met the two poets after they had returned to England; he says, "This was Ted's time. He was on the edge of a considerable reputation. . . . God alone knew how far he was eventually going, but in one essential way he had arrived. . . . He was in command. In those days Sylvia seemed effaced; the poet taking a back seat to the young mother and housewife."[1]

Alvarez is certainly right about Hughes, who was enjoying the satisfactions of his accomplishment while he was suffering the dangers of repetition implicit in those satisfactions, but his view of Plath (curiously enough, a view shared by Robert Lowell) is not entirely accurate. Behind the effaced appearance was a poet relentlessly experimenting, trying to expand and develop her range, struggling with her craft in an atmosphere that was not entirely congenial to her needs. For a working poet, close contact with other poets is always significant; but in this particular context it had its hazards as well as its rewards. In some sense, the roles of Hughes and Plath had reversed from their first year together, when she had been the scholarship-holder and public person. Now he was the one who was asked to give poetry readings, whose work was recognized by other poets, who won a Guggenheim fellowship and the Somerset Maugham Award for his book. He became the prize winner and she the less public partner.

At a time when Plath felt she was ready to publish a first volume of poems and desperately needed the kind of recognition that publication involves, she not only was unable to find a publisher but also had to live with the fact of Hughes's success. She remained extremely pleased with Hughes's achievement, but it made her own creative difficulties during this period more intense. Although in the long run this time of upheaval and discouragement allowed her to break free of what she accurately called her "old rigidity and glassy glossiness," its immediate results — the poems in *The Colossus* — frequently take as their subject imaginative failure. They also reveal that failure at points where Plath was unable to fully realize her subject. They demonstrate her desire to move toward new areas of experience in her poetry, but they show, too, the many false starts she made. From Hughes's success she had learned what kind of poem was acclaimed, and part of her struggle in these years was to fit her own concerns and tone into that model or to explain the difficulty of such an effort. In the end, her attempts to deal with the non-human world, to incorporate the dimension of myth and magic into her intensely private vision, did enrich her poetry, but the process was long and difficult.

The two poets were at different stages in their careers during the three years when they worked in close creative cooperation to produce *Lupercal* and *The Colossus:* Hughes had arrived, but Plath was still floundering. If Hughes's success affected Plath, her experimentation and trials were useful to him. He had learned how to write a publishable poem, and the temptation (to which he fell prey in a number of poems in *Lupercal*) was to repeat that poem. His early success had spoiled him for new developments. Plath's efforts to explore and expand during this period provided him with certain possibilities that he might not otherwise have considered. He recognized, long before the reviewers, the self-exploration and visionary qualities of her early poems, and he was particularly impressed with the dark dream world that she plumbed, calling her "a lucky fisherman" of her inner life at this time. Although his own poems do not reveal the same kind of luck, he was moved to attempt the surrealistic vision of Plath in such poems as "Mayday on Holderness" and "Fire-Eater." Not entirely successful, these poems nonetheless reveal the direction his poetry was to take when he made his next significant advance in *Wodwo* some seven years later. He also began to use figures from literature and myth in his poetry at this time, perhaps following Plath's example. Of Plath's "Eye-Mote," a poem of this period, he has said, "The mention of Oedipus, and the Greek Tragedians' figures elsewhere, may seem literary, but if one can take her dream life as evidence, those personalities were deeply involved in her affairs."[2] This lesson was not lost on Hughes, who included in *Lupercal* his own versions of Telemachus, Cleopatra, Lupercalia, and Mozart. These are only a few examples of the multiple cross-currents between *Lupercal* and *The Colossus.* Because Plath and Hughes wrote the poems in these volumes during a very brief span of time, and under close mutual scrutiny, an examination of them in this context should enhance our understanding of individual poems, and of the general creative development of the two poets.

Perhaps no poems more clearly indicate the poets' psychic and creative situations than the title poems of their two volumes. "Lupercalia" is Hughes's prayer for life and celebration of fertility; "The Colossus" is Plath's admission of defeat and analysis of her own impotence. They are key poems, not only because they characterize their authors at this point in their careers, but because they reveal the strengths and weaknesses of each poet and the extent to which they interacted creatively. Both poems turn to mythology for their subjects. Hughes writes about the ritual of the fertility god, Lupercus; rubbed with the blood and milk of sacrificial goats and dogs, young athletes ran through the streets, striking barren women with whips of goatskin in order to fertilize them. The four parts of his poem constitute a narrative of this rite. Plath transfers elements from the myths and rituals of the dying god to the colossus figure and elaborates them with references to Greek tragedy to make her poem a complicated, often enigmatic, study of her own failure.[3] Her poem is more ambitious than Hughes's because she was attempting to do more than restate an old story, and, although it is not fully successful, "The Colossus" does show how Plath possesses poetically mythical and classical images. "Lupercalia" is a more distanced and controlled use of myth, and in the final analysis the poem is thin, despite the exuberance of its subject. We hear echoes of early poems: the dog "good enough/ To double with a bitch as poor" from "Fallgrief's Girl-Friends"; "It held man's reasonable ways/ Between its teeth" from "Hawk Roosting"; the image of the barren woman from "Secretary," or the black goat from "Meeting." Because its characters — the dog, the woman, the goat — seem to be from other poems, they fall together uneasily in this context. Without some outside knowledge of the ritual of the Lupercalia, a reader might have difficulty putting the poem together. The "old spark of the blood-heat," the stink "of a rank thriving" do not enliven this poem, which must end in a direct statement of its appeal: "Maker of the world" "Touch this frozen one." Hughes obviously found the ritual of the Lupercalia an important means of contacting the powers that control the life force. The intercession of the goat and the dog, as evidence of an animal vitality, would be especially appealing to him. His testimony in other poems where the animal is caged or repressed suggests that he felt it necessary to make the connections ritualized in "Lupercalia," but in this poem, at least, he does no more than point toward an ancient ceremony. Still, his poem has a consistency of tone that Plath's lacks.

Plath selects the ancient role of the female who mourns the dying god, or the heroine who tends the idol, and brings it into her poem as felt experience. In fact, it is so fully felt that its classical and mythical references become entangled in a confusion of meaning. The colossus is a statue, a father, a mythical being; he is a ruined idol, "pithy and historical as the Roman Forum," and at the same time a figure whose great lips utter "Mule-bray, pig-grunt and bawdy cackles," an echo of Hughes's language. The persona in the poem crawls over him, squats in his ear, eats her lunch there — intimate activities that hardly seem the rites of a priestess. The colossus himself is both a stone idol with "immense skull-plates" and "fluted bones and acanthine hair," and at the same time a natural wilderness covered with "weedy acres" and "A hill of black cypress." Much remains beneath the surface in this poem, and much on the surface appears confusing.

The fact that the statue is addressed at one point as "father" has caused most critics to link this poem with Plath's own father and her poetic treatment of him; but nothing in this poem demands that single interpretation. Perhaps the colossus is not the actual father but the creative father, a suggestion reinforced by the fact that the spirit of the Ouija board from which Plath and Hughes received hints of subjects for poems claimed that his family god, *Kolossus,* gave him most of his information.[4] The colossus, then, may be Plath's private god of poetry, the muse which she would have to make masculine in order to worship and marry. The concentration of mouth imagery to describe the colossus also points to his identification as a speaker or poet. The persona has labored thirty years "To dredge the silt from your throat," although, she admits, "I am none the wiser." She suggests, "Perhaps you consider yourself an oracle,/ Mouthpiece of the dead, or of some god or other." In the end, she says, "The sun rises under the pillar of your tongue." No messages came from the throat, the mouthpiece, the tongue of this figure; this god is silent, yet the speaker feels bound to serve him. The sense of servitude and of the impossible task of such service reflects the creative exhaustion Plath felt during this period. Her statement at the end that "My hours are married to shadow" may be an admission that she is married, in fact, to darkness and creative silence, rather than to the god of poetry who could fertilize her. Her fears also center on the catastrophe that produced the crumbling of the idol: "It would take more than a lightning-stroke/ To create such a ruin." This admission, enigmatic if the statue is her father or a dying god, recalls Plath's early poetic concerns about creative paralysis and the sense of a collapsing order.

"The Colossus" and "Lupercalia," while different, are not unrelated poems. They both concern service rituals: the fertilizing of the women and the tending of the idol. If the woman is "perfect;/ But flung from the wheel of the living" while the colossus is in ruins, both figures suffer a similar fate that must be reversed: "The past killed in her, the future plucked out." The "Maker of the world" in both poems is a power compounded of animal vitality (Plath's "Mule-bray" and Hughes's "Stink of goat") and superhuman energy, and the object of both poems is to restore this power. That Plath's image is a stone (if pithy) statue, while Hughes's image is a compound of the dog's "anarchy of mindless pride," the goats' "eyes' golden element," and the maker of the world, would seem to establish these poems as polar opposties. Also, Plath's sense that she will never be freed from her impossible task of restoration clashes directly with Hughes's confidence that "Nothing mortal falters" the "poise" of his "racers." He dismisses Plath's concern easily: "The dead are indifferent underground./ Little the live may learn from them — / A sort of hair and bone wisdom,/ A worn witchcraft accoutrement/ Of proverbs." As if echoing his image, Plath is dismayed that her statue's "fluted bones and acanthine hair are littered/ In their old anarchy to the horizon-line." Hair and bone wisdom quickly canceled, hair and bone anarchy seriously feared, these images define each poet's stance. In some ways they speak across the poems to each other and reveal a private argument: the wisdom Plath fails to find is canceled out in Hughes's poem, and the anarchy Hughes celebrates is the subject of Plath's concern. At the same time, these images place the two poets in sexual roles defined by mythology: the female worshipper and attendant, mourning and helpless; the male celebrant and racer, active and assured. In other poems each poet wrote during this period, when they turned frequently to the same subject, these identities are reconfirmed, although, as we shall see, each poet had a wide range of poetic moods. In these poems, however, the identities served to cover Hughes's early confidence and Plath's temporary creative uncertainty.

A subject that dominates *Lupercal* and *The Colossus* and places the two poets in apparently distinctive positions is the landscape. Plath marked attention to landscape as a new departure in her work, admitting to her brother that she had cast off her old interests and was "well on the way to writing about the real world, its animals, people, and scenery."[5] But Hughes, too, began to write landscape poems during this period. Plath's earliest nature poems had been concerned with conjuring up dryads; now she turned to particular locations and to the sensations they aroused in her. The depth or immensity of the landscape and the intensity of its weather conditions are her subjects as well as Hughes's. A heightened awareness of the overwhelming power of the landscape frequently reduces Plath's speakers to a sense of their own vulnerability. In contrast, the wind, the rain, the pounding sea, and the heaving hills excite Hughes's imagination with their strange strength. They re-ignite in him what he has termed "the ancient instincts and feelings in which most of our body lives," "prehistoric feelings" that are deadened by civilization. Wild surroundings evoke those sensations which refresh and renew the spirit, he claims in his comments to schoolchildren about nature poems.[6] But this renewal jolts rather than sustains Hughes's human observer, who feels himself as vulnerable to the elements as do Plath's personae.

Plath's earliest landscape poems treat foreign territory and focus on its strangeness. That fact must be taken into account when one assesses these poems, which form a contrast to poems she wrote on native American scenes. "Watercolour of Grantchester Meadows," a poem of her Cambridge years with details drawn directly from a punting expedition with Hughes in the early spring of 1956, is a poem of gushing enthusiasm about the English countryside, infused with the sentimentality of the typical American tourist. Here in this "country on a nursery plate," in meadows of "benign/ Arcadian green," even that ominous sign, the "blood-berried hawthorn," "hides its spines with white." The entire scene is bathed in "a moony indolence" until the very last lines, when Plath reminds herself that "in such mild air/ The owl shall stoop from his turret, the rat cry out." The "spring lambs," the "tame cygnets," "Spotted cows," droll water rat, and the entire pastoral scene so carefully pictured are swept away in the threat of the last line, a threat which will dominate her later nature poems. But the stylized landscape of this poem establishes a kind of distance from such threats. Quite another distance is the subject of "Departure," a memory of the Spanish fishing village of Benidorm, where the Hugheses spent the summer of 1956. Here the poet attacks nature's penury and the sea's brutal, endless beating. The vacationers have run out of money, and "nature, sensing this, compounds her bitters." The brutal sea will return to Plath's poetry as a more ominous image; here its indifference protects her from its full force: "Ungifted, ungrieved, our leavetaking."

The "leaden slag of the world" of Benidorm serves as the opening image of "Hardcastle Crags," a poem about Hughes's home country, a narrow valley in the Pennines in West Yorkshire which they visited at this time. Here, "Flintlike, her feet struck/ Such a racket of echoes from the steely street." Even when she reaches the fields where the "incessant seethe of grasses" "as a moon-bound sea/ Moves on its roots," she finds "'no family-featured ghost," but "The long wind, paring her person down/ To a pinch of flame." "All the night gave her, in return" for "the beat/ Of her heart was the humped indifferent iron/ Of its hills." She concludes with an image from Hughes:

> The whole landscape
> Loomed absolute as the antique world was
> Once, in its earliest sway of lymph and sap,
> Unaltered by eyes.

But for her it was "Enough to snuff the quick/ Of her small heat out."

When Hughes takes the same scene for his subject in "Pennines in April," he uses a similar image of the country as a sea; but for him the "hills heaving/ Out of the east," "rolling westward through the locked land," are "barrellings of strength." Yet his conclusion that the hills "surf upwards/ In a still, fiery air, hauling the imagination,/ Carrying the larks upward" draws on Plath's observation in "Black Rook in Rainy Weather" that a rook "can so shine/ As to seize my senses, haul/ My eyelids up." In Plath's poem the momentary shining provides a respite from the fear of total neutrality, and, while Hughes does not emphasize the fear, he expresses the same need to see in nature a force that would sustain his imagination. Plath fears in "Hardcastle Crags" and the later but similar "Wuthering Heights" that her heat will be snuffed out by the immensity of the landscape; that feeling is an intensification of her fear in "Black Rook in Rainy Weather" that she lives in an indifferent universe, and it derives from her sense that the whole landscape is "absolute," so strong that "the weight/ Of stones and hills of stones could break/ Her down to mere quartz grit." For Hughes, this weight itself can be reduced to insubstantiality, as the heaving masses become "Landscapes gliding blue as water."

Hughes gives the subject a broader treatment in "Crow Hill," another poem about the moors, where he acknowledges the threats of the landscape. In this poem, "The farms are oozing craters in/ Sheer sides under the sodden moors," and he claims the rain will "shake/ Dreams beneath sleep it cannot break." But Hughes wastes little concern on those shaken ones; he is rather realistic about the living conditions on the moors: "Between the weather and the rock/ Farmers make a little heat." For him, the endurance of the animals is more remarkable:

> Cows that sway a bony back,
> Pigs upon delicate feet
> Hold off the sky, trample the strength
> That shall level these hills at length.

And more remarkable still is not man, but the maker of the universe:

> What humbles these hills has raised
> The arrogance of blood and bone,
> And thrown the hawk upon the wind,
> And lit the fox in the dripping ground.

Holding off the sky, trampling the strength of the earth, the animals seem more successful than man at resisting the weight of the elements that threaten Plath's speakers, although in "November" Hughes pictures a tramp who seems to rival the animals in his ability to withstand the "welding cold" of a rainstorm. The speaker, watching the tramp in a ditch, says, "I thought what strong trust/ Slept in him — as the trickling furrows slept,/ And the thorn-roots in their grip on darkness."

The speaker has no such trust, runs for shelter, and in the gamekeeper's gibbet sees even greater evidence of animal vitality:

> Some still had their shape,
> Had their pride with it; hung, chins on chests,
> Patient to outwait these worst days that beat
> Their crowns bare and dripped from their feet.

The tramp and the animals share a stupid patience, of course: the tramp in danger of dying from exposure, the animals already dead but still gripping life. The vitality and trust in the life force that they share remain admirable, in Hughes's view, although poems such as "Crow Hill" and "November," as well as the early "The Hawk in the Rain," suggest also that a trust in such a life force is life-threatening even to those "Buttoned from the blowing mist" who "Walk the ridges of ruined stone." The fears that Plath expressed about the moors are natural ones, and if Hughes does not choose to dwell on them, he nevertheless acknowledges their reality — in the man tramping through the storm in "The Hawk in the Rain" or running for shelter in "November," or in the farmers' "little heat" in "Crow Hill."

In considering Plath's poems about the moors, we must keep in mind the extent to which they are efforts to convey realistically the extremities of the weather there. As such, they are a new subject for her and a new poetic perspective. They also parallel Hughes's treatment of this landscape, although he thrills to the dangers that frighten her. It is also useful to remember that the moors were Hughes's home territory, whereas for Plath they were a strange country that she might never have treated had she not known Hughes. She had been led to the "antique world" "in its earliest sway of lymph and sap" by Hughes, who found there a fantasy home which did not comfort her.

When she moved away from the moors and attempted to probe the landscape of her psyche by dealing not with the land but with a more familiar locale, the sea, she translated Hughes's affirmation of the powers she encountered into a more ambiguous reaction. "Lorelei" was written at a time when she also was exploring a new interest in her Austrian-German background and ocean childhood, which, she said, "is probably the foundation of my consciousness."[7] This probing into her own memory through legend starts with a brief mention of Gothic "massive castle turrets," then turns quickly to a confrontation with underwater "shapes" that "float/ Up towards me, troubling the face/ Of quiet." They sing "Of a world more full and clear/ Than can be" and "lay siege," "Deranging by harmony/ Beyond the mundane order." Although the speaker clearly recognizes that these voices "lodge/ On the pitched reefs of nightmare" and their "ice-hearted calling" is "Drunkenness of the great depths," she relents in the end, claims to see in them "great goddesses of peace," and prays, "Stone, stone, ferry me down there."

Another poem of this period, "Full Fathom Five," deals with the same complex of knowledge, fears, and eventual passivity. Here it is not the sirens but another sea shape, "Old man," the "old myth of origins/ Unimaginable," that surfaces. Although the speaker claims that this figure is "to be steered clear/ Of, not fathomed," that his "dangers are many," that he is "Inscrutable,/ Below shoulders not once/ Seen by any man who kept his head," still she relents in the end and pleads, "Father, this thick air is murderous./ I would breathe water."

These two poems follow the psychic pattern of "The Colossus": the depiction of a grand harmony beyond the mundane order that is deranged or the old myth of origins (the old man with his "spread hair" and "grained face" recalls the colossus) that the speaker knows is inscrutable, the fears this figure engenders, the fatal attachment to it beyond these fears, and the final surrender to it. The "Sisters" and "Father" of her dream life may promise her a world more full and clear; but they live beyond mundane order, in a world inscrutable, unimaginable, unfathomable. This world is for her ultimately attractive but frightening, since she must sacrifice to it all that is safe, imagined, ordered. She relents in the end because, she says in "Full Fathom Five," "I walk dry on your kingdom's border/ Exiled to no good." Here again, as in "The Colossus," she places herself in the secondary role: serving, being seduced, accepting the other's "godhood." As the hearer of the Lorelei's song, as the abandoned daughter, as the attendant to the idol, the Plath speaker must adopt a passive role; in these mythic situations she has no alternative. That Plath continues to put her speakers in these roles suggests, of course, their fascination for her. Hughes says that "one can see that in these poems for the first time she accepts the invitation of her inner world"; but he also admits that they "coincided with a decision, made with great difficulty and against great tactical opposition from individuals she regarded as her benefactors, to leave teaching and throw herself on writing for a few years."[8] Most readings of these poems center on what they reveal about her feelings toward her father, but they should also be considered in light of Plath's real turmoil over her teaching career and her writing. In some sense, the passivity they express and the death wish they embody may derive from the career struggle that had exhausted her, temporarily making it difficult to write. Her decision to (in Hughes's terms) "throw herself on writing," however hard won, was, like the desire to be ferried to the depths or to breathe water, a submersion of her public and acclaimed teaching self into her private and unrecognized writing self. The father and sisters were the spirits of an underworld which she feared, with good reason, might destroy her.

It is useful to consider "Lorelei" and "Full Fathom Five" in the context of the poems Hughes was writing during this period. To date Plath's poems have been read exclusively as the first explorations of her suicidal impulse and the troubled relationship with her father, when actually they were written at a time when both Plath and Hughes were attempting to probe depths that they identified with the world of magic, legend, folklore, and nature — a world that had dangerous aspects. Hughes's poems have never attracted the autobiographical and psychological readings that fascinate Plath's critics, because he deals with animal spirits rather than with fathers or sisters; but he, too, was beginning to explore life submerged beneath the mundane order, and he finds there the same attraction and treachery, fatal powers that must be confronted.

In "Pike," Hughes looks into the water at what appears to be an actual fish: "Pike, three inches long, perfect/ Pike in all parts, green tigering the gold." Instantly it turns, under Hughes's poetic gaze, into an ominous image: "Killers from the egg," "silhouette/ Of submarine delicacy and horror," "A life subdued to its instrument." Hughes develops this image by recounting, again with startling factuality, the grim story of how three small pike that he kept in a tank fed on each other until there was one left "With a sag belly and the grin it was born with." In the manner of good fisherman's tales, one such story calls up another and, maintaining his devotion to facts ("Two, six pounds each, over two feet long"), he records the example of two dead fish which he found on the ground, "One jammed past its gills down the other's gullet." At this point, the momentum of the tale carries us easily into another reality, the pond where the speaker fishes. It "Had outlasted every visible stone/ Of the monastery that planted them." "Stilled legendary depth:/ It was as deep as England. It held/ Pike too immense to stir." The man "dared not cast/ But silently cast and fished/ With the hair frozen on my head." He listens, horrified, to the owls hushing the woods "Frail on my ear against the dream/ Darkness beneath night's darkness had freed,/ That rose slowly towards me, watching." If he does not give in to this darkness, as Plath's persona does, this man is as mesmerized by it. He cannot move beyond its powers. The legendary depths of which fishing for such pike makes him aware bring him into contact with a submerged life that thrills as it horrifies.

The boy in "The Bull Moses" gets another look at this depth. While the boy swings on the byre's half-door, shouting and waving at the bull, the bull swings at a fly but pays no attention to the boy, who realizes that he himself "Was nothing to him; nothing of our light/ Found any reflection in him." Leaning over the door, the boy sees "Blaze of darkness" — not nothing, but a darkness permeated with "the warm weight of his breathing,/ The ammoniac reek of his litter, the hotly-tongued/ Mash of his cud." The boy recognizes that, in this animal vitality, "Something come up there onto the brink of the gulf." It is a recognition not only of an energy that is totally non-human, but of something in himself that corresponds to it. A look into the byre is "a sudden shut-eyed look/ Backward into the head." This glimpse is only momentary; the bull seems as cut off from this depth as the boy who puzzles over the bull's docility in his captivity, "as if he knew nothing/ Of the ages and continents of his fathers." The bull follows the farmer to the pond each night and comes strolling gently back, "the fetch/ Of the distance drew nothing to momentum/ In the locked black of his powers." Still not content with this apparent acquiescence of the bull, the boy imagines "some beheld future/ Founding in his quiet."

The darkness that the fishing man and the boy evoke rises from their confrontation with the pike and the bull, but it does not inhere in the animal world. It belongs to an undefined dream world: "dream/ Darkness," something from the gulf, not between man and the animal, but between rational man and terrors submerged in his head. It inspires not only fear but also fascination as both man and boy conjure its power. It attaches them to some ancient time, legendary depths, ages of the bull's fathers when perhaps their dreams were founded. As such, it relates to Plath's legendary darkness, "The old myth of origins." It should be noted that Plath's night in "Lorelei," like Hughes's in "Pike," is also beneath night's darkness, "Black beneath bland mirror-sheen."

In a poem Hughes wrote when Plath was writing "Lorelei" — in fact, a poem suggested to him by the Ouija board that provided Plath's subject — he explores this legendary depth by meditating on the otter, a "water body, neither fish nor beast." This real animal, its features carefully detailed ("webbed feet and long ruddering tail" and "round head"), brings into Hughes's poem the "legend of himself." This legend, like that of other animals in Hughes's imagination, involves the otter's dispropertied nature: "Of neither water nor land. Seeking/ Some world lost when first he dived, that he cannot come at since," he crosses the sea "Like a king in hiding. Crying to the old shape of the starlit land" throughout the night. But the otter's legend may be also that of man who seeks his own lost world, finding it sometimes in the dream of darkness, or in the "Drunkenness of the great depths," or in Plath's realization that she is exiled to no good on the land.

It is the poet, after all, who identifies the otter's cries and searchings, and with this identification endows the animal with human longings. The otter of Part I of the poem is a creature seeking its own element; in Part II he is the hunted. Just as he cannot find his lost world, so his hunters cannot find him when he hides "In double robbery and concealment — / From water that nourishes and drowns, and from land/ That gave him his length and the mouth of the hound." He is nourished by killing "Big trout muscle" at the depths where "Blood is the belly of logic." This double-featured creature, hunted and hunter, lost yet safe, breathing air "tainted and necessary," nourished and drowned by water, is more than mere animal. His cries are Hughes's own, and, like the dreams of the man in "Pike" and the boy in "The Bull Moses," the otter "Wanders, cries;/ Gallops along land he no longer belongs to." In Part II, when the otter hides from his hunters, Hughes observes, "So the self under the eye lies,/ Attendant and withdrawn." Again the otter provides an analogy for man, who seeks his true self in a world that, opening a gulf between himself and his dreams, makes those dreams terrifying. Although the otter appears now to belong to a world governed by killer instinct, his legendary existence "before wars or burials, in spite of hounds and vermin-poles," attaches him to a world which was lost when man and his predatory habits appeared to hunt the animal — in other words, to Eden. In his present status, while he has adopted man's hunting instincts, he also shares man's condition: a nature fatally divided against itself, hopelessly searching for the land to which he belongs.

These poems and others like them in *Lupercal* can serve to place Plath's poems of this period in the larger perspective of interests she shared with Hughes. While Plath was exploring her own inner life, she was also expanding her knowledge of myths and legends, and at the same time reading books on fiddler crabs, meteorites, animals, birds, wildflowers, and the submarine life of Rachel Carson's *Sea Around Us*. These interests coalesced in such poems as "Lorelei" and "Full Fathom Five," which reveal a new depth in her awareness of the connection between her dream world and the worlds of legend and nature. Hughes's own interest in the "delicacy and horror" of the submarine life, his poetic explorations of the origins of this life, and his concern with a spirit world reinforced and directed her development. Specifically, his fascination with the darkness beneath night's darkness and his contention in a number of poems that such darkness could not be evaded may account for Plath's relinquishment to these powers at the end of "Lorelei" and "Full Fathom Five." To be sure, his own poetic personae remain always distanced from this darkness; but, their attention riveted to it, they remain still completely within its power.

In other poems Hughes began to explore the dark spirits that haunt the world. While he typically identified them with animals and not with the dead father and goddesses of Plath's poems, he deals with the same shifting spirits that rise in Plath's work. As he pursues them and they escape, he projects onto them more extreme attributes than Plath imagined at this point. His animals frequently rise from the dead to seek revenge on the living, as do Plath's spirits. The stoat in "Strawberry Hill" comes like a vampire out of the Gothic past nourished by Hugh Walpole. Killed and nailed to the door, this stoat's "red unmanageable life" is sustained by eating the dead ("sucked that age like an egg") and "Emerges, thirsting, in far Asia, in Brixton," as threatening as ever. The red life, turned deadly and now not even trivialized by the artificial tricks of a Walpole, has become the principle of death in "February," in a world that still cannot use legend, fairy tale, or photographs to control its violent fury. The wolf-spirit stalks the world long after the last wolf has been killed in Britain. Hughes deals with the magic belief that man can be transformed into wolves by focusing on the wolf's need:

> These feet, deprived,
> Disdaining all that are caged, or storied, or pictured,
> Through and throughout the true world search
> For their vanished head, for the world
>
> Vanished with the head, the teeth, the quick eyes — .

Like the otter, the wolf seeks his true identity in a place that has denied its existence; but in its search the wolf proves threatening to the human and rational being. Its onrushing feet "siege all thought," and man is powerless to control them. At the end of the poem, a frightened man makes "Wolf-masks," attempting to ward off the evil spirits by tricking them into art, "lest they choose his head" for their own. But, if Walpole is any example, this man will never succeed.

Although Hughes has been accused of celebrating the violence of his predatory animals, in fact fear is the most persistent emotion of his poetic characters confronting the animals in *Lupercal.* In this respect his treatment of man's relationship to the deadly world represented by the animals has changed from the poems in *The Hawk in the Rain,* moving closer to Plath's. In his earlier poems his animals are typically caged, and civilized man appears safe from their fury. Although Hughes's point in these poems is that the safeguards of civilization are a delusion, in his early work he does not explore the dangers of the rampaging animal. As he later turns to confront this force, he examines more fully its dangerous implications for mankind, and, in so doing, he repeats the view Plath expressed in "Pursuit": violence may thrill, but it also terrifies. Although he appears to distance this violence from himself by identifying it clearly in the animal and natural world, it should be noted that these predatory animals come out of his own fantasy world. In "February" he says, "Now it is the dream cries 'Wolf!' " and this dream, like the "dream/ Darkness beneath night's darkness" in "Pike," is "freed" to wander the earth in Hughes's poems. But who dreams these dreams? Wolves cry and the stoat rises from the dead only in poetry. Embedded in Hughes's examination of these stalking spirit-animals is an obsessive fascination with the continual warfare between the predator and its prey. The repressed violence which erupts from what is called a lost legendary world is in fact brought into the twentieth century by the poet who creates it. While this dream has disturbed man throughout history, and a whole world of folklore and magic has arisen to express it, Hughes's poems are literary artifacts, not magical incantations. In them he reveals how his own psyche is divided between powerful dark spirits that attract and threaten, and a sense of extreme vulnerability to them. In this respect the world he creates resembles poems where Plath's poetic persona works through the same conflict, although her emphasis is frequently on the reasonable doubts that cause her to resist the attractions of the great depths. Hughes generally bypasses these doubts and focuses on the watching darkness, the rushing animal.

One poem in *Lupercal* devotes itself directly to the psychology of the predator. In "Hawk Roosting," Hughes pushes to the extreme the darker aspect of his dream world; in the process, by denying all limits to its violence, he curiously reveals that world's limitations. The hawk defines himself: "I hold Creation in my foot," "I kill where I please because it is all mine." Unlike his early hawk in "The Hawk in the Rain," this beast is not vulnerable to the weather. He tyrannizes the entire universe: "My manners are tearing off heads — / The allotment of death." And he concludes, "I am going to keep things like this." All that would deflect him — "Inaction," the "falsifying dream," "sophistry," "arguments" — is cancelled out by this non-reasoning, reasoning bird. Like the pike, this hawk is a life subdued to its instrument. Antihuman, the hawk is the perfect representation of the principle of deadliness in nature, more potent, he imagines, than creation itself or the life principle that produced him. "It took the whole of Creation/ To produce my foot," he boasts, although he falls back on sophistry itself to claim, "Now I hold Creation in my foot." Seeing himself as the pinnacle of creation, he reverts to a falsifying dream to claim his primacy. The trouble with the hawk is his admission that he sits at "the top of the wood, my eyes closed." He is blind to his own vulnerability, imagining only that the trees, the air, the sun "Are of advantage to me," and not an equal advantage to his killer.

The hawk's poem is the apotheosis in Hughes's treatment of the vulturish dream in *Lupercal*. Here, nature red in tooth and claw appears to speak for itself. All the submerged and dispropertied predators in Hughes's dream world may find in the hawk their true representative. But, as the hawk uses human language to deny the human element, disclaims dreams while he enjoys them, attacks arguments yet formulates his own, he becomes not a spokesman for nature but a spokesman for amoral and anti-human instincts in the human psyche. The hawk is a creature that defines himself totally in terms of the human and the rational, as a poetic hawk must. Because he is known to us only through the informing consciousness of his creator, he represents that consciousness at its dead end. He has been forming in Hughes's mind in a number of poems throughout *Lupercal,* and he is the supreme achievement of Hughes's efforts to detail the dark spirits of his underworld: killer, unchanged, the end of Creation. But this creature of violence, unlike the otter or the pike, recalls to us no legendary past or lost world. He is, rather, the result of something that has gone wrong in creation itself, some point at which the creative spirit that produced the hawk (both in nature and in the poet) succumbed to the destruction it had wrought, channeling its powers through the predator. In commenting on this poem Hughes has said, "When Christianity kicked the devil out of Job what they actually kicked out was Nature . . . and Nature became the devil."[9] However, this point is imperfectly realized in the poem, where the hawk-devil appears limited, self-deluded, vulnerable to the first shot from the ground, and not a representative of the dark, fertile powers denied by Christianity. The hawk's manners seem simply designed to outrage the morally righteous, and as such they can represent only the negative aspects of the spirit world.

In "Thrushes," Hughes is more equivocal about the spirit he confronts, although he opens with the familiar reaction: "Terrifying are the attent sleek thrushes on the lawn." What appalls is the bird's remarkable efficiency, its ravening pounce and stab that makes it "More coiled steel than living," "those delicate legs/ Triggered to stirrings beyond sense." The principle behind this murderous machine is what Hughes seeks to discover. He asks,

> Is it their single-mind-sized skulls, or a trained
> Body, or genius, or a nestful of brats
> Gives their days this bullet and automatic
> Purpose?

He answers his own question by claiming ambiguously, "Mozart's brain had it, and the shark's mouth/ That hungers down the blood-smell even to a leak of its own/ Side." Genius and vulturism alike share an "efficiency which/ Strikes too streamlined for any doubt to pluck at it/ Or obstruction deflect." Hughes retreats from this observation in the last stanza, admitting that "With a man it is otherwise." In whatever he does, his heroism as well as his art, man cannot lose consciousness of himself: "his act worships itself." Then, in a puzzling addition, he says that man,

> Though he bends to be blent in the prayer, how loud and above
> what
> Furious spaces of fire do the distracting devils
> Orgy and hosannah, under what wilderness
> Of black silent waters weep.

The devils that distract man from the thrushes' single purpose are morally ambiguous. They appear to be identified with man's "indolent procrastinations," "yawning stares," "sighs or head-scratchings," with human weaknesses; on the other hand, they are part of man's more humane doubts about the thrushes' ravenous appetite. Whatever these devils are, they distract him from the highest purposes of prayer and art, as well as from the lowest instinct, automatic killing. Hughes's average man stands somewhere between these kingdoms, like the otter, tormented by both.

At this point, Hughes appears more fascinated with death and deadliness than does Plath. His attention is directed to predators, to the murderous instinct, to dark, destructive gods. In contrast, Plath turns, in two poems at least, to the creative spirit in man and nature, and there she examines examples of endurance and vitality. In "Snakecharmer," a poem she wrote at the same time as "Lorelei" and "Full Fathom Five," she creates another god of origins, again a man, who is the image of masculine power and creativity. She begins, "As the gods began one world, and man another,/ So the snakecharmer begins a snaky sphere." Significantly, he "Pipes green. Pipes water." He is an image of creative control as "the green river/ Shapes its images around his songs." "He pipes a world of snakes/ Of sways and coilings, from the snake-rooted bottom/ Of his mind." Like God, he creates his world: "let there be snakes!/ And snakes there were." When he "tires of music," he pipes "those green waters back to/ Water, to green, to nothing like a snake./ Puts up his pipe, and lids his moony eye." "Snakecharmer," inspired by a picture of Rousseau, is, Hughes claims, a specific vision revealed to yogis in an advanced stage; but, more than that, it is a clear depiction of the creative power of song, and also it may very well be a portrait of Hughes himself, who had no trouble evoking his imaginative world at this time. Considered against all the ominous water images in her poems, the snakecharmer's water-green world must be judged doubly fertile. This poem about the male snakecharmer is a tribute to masculine prowess and fertility by a woman who saw herself frequently at this time as impotent and sterile. In the poem immediately following "Snakecharmer," "The Hermit at Outermost House," Plath draws another male portrait of strength and endurance that contrasts with her women of this period. "Sky and sea" couldn't "flatten this man out," she says; "The great gods, Stone-Head, Claw-Foot,/ Winded by much rock-bumping/ And claw-threat, realized that." He, too, seems connected with fertility as he "Thumbed no stony, horny pot,/ But a certain meaning green." Here again the indomitable figure is a male, reminiscent of Hughes's tramps and perhaps of Hughes himself. Hughes sees it as "the comic goblin, the tricksterish spirit, the crackling verbal energy, that was the nymph-form — a lot of Caliban in it — of *Ariel.*"[10]

In other poems that came immediately out of Plath's return to America, she turned to her native landscape to detail it with a realism that was new to her work. Hughes has said that she was experimenting with Robert Lowell's style, although she welded Lowell's realism to Hughes's concern with the powers of nature, the absolute otherness of the universe, the relentless rhythm of life. "Mussel Hunter at Rock Harbour," discussed in the first chapter, belongs to this group of poems, as does "Point Shirley," where she reenacts in real life the experience she had recounted in "Dream with Clam-Diggers," once again returning to the seaside of her childhood. She locates the scene with great particularity, identifying landmarks, taking in not only the large vista but also the smallest details. In this place she sets her grandmother, a woman with the endurance of the hermit, who "Kept house against" the sea and "died blessed." The return to this familiar landscape is without reward for the speaker, however:

> I would get from these dry-papped stones
> The milk your love instilled in them.
> The black ducks dive.
> And though your graciousness might stream,
> And I contrive,
> Grandmother, stones are nothing of home
> To that spumiest dove.
> Against both bar and tower the black sea runs.

No ghosts come out of this actual landscape, nor does love; but the speaker in the poem recognizes the elemental power of the sea without the fear that the moors inspired in her. Even when she does endow this particular familiar location with a darker image in "Man in Black," she employs the same specificity of detail ("Where the three magenta/ Breakwaters take the shove/ And suck of the grey sea"). And the man in black who "strode out in your dead/ Black coat" is not a figure that pulls her into its depths, but a point of reference: "Fixed vortex on the far/ Tip, riveting stones, air,/ All of it, together." Unlike the shifting image in "Full Fathom Five" at which she says she "Cannot look much but your form suffers/ Some strange injury/ And seems to die," the man in black is both distant and firm. Between this figure and herself is the shoving, sucking sea, distanced by particular landmarks. The oxymoron "Fixed vortex" is reinforced in the poem's emphasis on fixed points of reference in this constantly changing seascape; but its activity takes place at some remove from the speaker so that its threatening quality is dissipated and rendered enigmatic.

The same specificity of detail is evident in the description of the seaside in "Suicide Off Egg Rock." Against this particularity is posed the man walking into the water to drown himself. He identifies his own body, "A machine to breathe and beat forever," with the inexorable power of life, the public hotdog grills, "Gas tanks, factory stacks" in "that landscape/ Of imperfections his bowels were part of." His blood, "beating the old tattoo/ I am, I am, I am," echoes maddeningly the seaside activity around him. Curiously, this man about to commit suicide does not feel threatened the way Plath's early women walking on the moors did. He feels both removed from this life, "smouldered, as if stone-deaf, blindfold," and curiously assaulted by it as "Flies filing in through a dead skate's eyehole/ Buzzed and assailed the vaulted brainchamber." Like the speaker in Emily Dickinson's poem "I heard a Fly buzz — when I died," the speaker here is distracted at the hour of death by the fly who is both an image of vitality and a reminder of decay. Soon the suicide will be like the dead fish, simply carrion. He leaves nothing behind, and the image of the dead fish recalls to him the source of his suicidal impulse, his creative failure: "The words in his book wormed off the pages./ Everything glittered like blank paper." As he walks into the sea, he hears only "The forgetful surf," the beat of ongoing life that has embittered his existence. "Suicide Off Egg Rock" combines without perfect success a number of issues that concerned Plath during this period: her effort to write realistically about a native landscape, to deal with deeply repressed experience (here, her early suicide attempt), to come to terms with her own sense of creative paralysis. The result is a poem that moves uncertainly from a clearly pictured landscape to the image of self-pity in the forgetful surf.

Two other poems that come out of the experience of this period, but which were not published until *Crossing the Water,* are further attempts to deal realistically with a landscape scene, although this time the territory is new. In "Two Campers in Cloud Country *(Rock Lake, Canada),*" Plath starts out boldly in Hughes's style: "In this country, there is neither measure nor balance/ To redress the dominance of rocks and woods." She continues, "No gesture of yours or mine could catch their attention," "Well, one wearies of the Public Gardens: one wants a vacation," "It is comfortable, for a change, to mean so little." But the old uneasiness over immensity surfaces in the end, and she says, "I lean to you, numb as a fossil. Tell me I'm here." Not a very interesting poem, "Two Campers" nonetheless indicates Plath's search for poetic subjects in actual experience and realistic description. Even here, however, she concludes with an image that has greater significance in her landscape poetry:

> Around our tent the old simplicities sough
> Sleepily as Lethe, trying to get in.
> We'll wake blank-brained as water in the dawn.

The image of a deceptive and encroaching landscape is repeated in "Sleep in the Mojave Desert," where "Noonday acts queerly/ On the mind's eye, erecting a line/ Of poplars in the middle distance"; the trees "recede, untouchable as tomorrow." The tricks played on perception by the landscape will figure more ominously later in "The Moon and the Yew Tree," where she admits despairingly, "I simply cannot see where there is to get to." Here the air is "dangerous," the desert "Comfortless as salt," "Snake and bird/ Doze behind the old masks of fury," and "The day-moon lights up like a sorry mother" (another image to be used again in "The Moon and the Yew Tree"). But the actual dangers are finally only the crickets that "come creeping into our hair/ To fiddle the short night away."

Finally, "Blackberrying," also published in *Crossing the Water,* is another look at a specific landscape. In this poem the view of a blackberry alley is expanded into a vision of "nothing, nothing but blackberries," a "honey-feast" where "The high, green meadows are glowing, as if lit from within." Set against this scene of fecundity and lushness is the sea at the end of the lane where the speaker "looks out on nothing, nothing but a great space/ Of white and pewter lights, and a din like silversmiths/ Beating and beating at an intractable metal." The figures, surfacing out of the sea from Plath's early poems, have disappeared, leaving only a relentless, brutal, beating force, while the land has assumed a new vitality.

This scene, more neutral than the black running sea of "Point Shirley," is the final emptying-out of Plath's seascape. Here she settles on a recognition of Hughes's view of nature.

In the movement from "Lorelei" and "Full Fathom Five" to "Point Shirley" and "Blackberrying," there seems to be a demythologizing of the landscape and a more careful scrutiny of its objective status as a place apart from the visions and terrors that control the psyche of the observer. Actually, one myth has been replaced by another. The sirens and old gods have shaded into a generalized nature principle. The sea is an eater in "Point Shirley," where "The sea in its cold gizzard ground those rounds." The running, beating, sucking, sea is moved by a voracious power. The immensities of desert and wilderness are also infused with primitive strengths, "old simplicities" or "old masks of fury" against which the human and ratiocinative are diminished. In this recognition Plath is closely following Hughes, who says in "Relic": "The deeps are cold:/ In that darkness camaraderie does not hold:/ Nothing touches but, clutching, devours." In such a universe life is threatened.

Different threats to existence are explored in Plath's "Manor Garden" and Hughes's "Crag Jack's Apostasy." Plath addresses an unborn child whose "Head, toe and finger/ Come clear of the shadow." Crag Jack announces his own deliverance from the evil spirits who hovered over him as an infant: "The churches, lord, all the dark churches/ Stooped over my cradle once:/ I came clear, but my god's down/ Under the weight of all that stone." The baby, too, must come clear of "History" that "Nourishes these broken flutings,/ These crowns of acanthus," and of his family heritage, which is not the oppression of institutionalized religion but certain private evils: "Two suicides, the family wolves,/ Hours of blackness." Despite his apostasy, Crag Jack still calls "continually/ On you, god or not god," praying "That I may see more than your eyes/ In an animal's dreamed head," "Keep more than the memory/ Of a wolf's head, of eagles' feet." This memory comes to his "sleeping body"; but his desire is to be

Waking, dragged suddenly
From a choir-shaken height
By the world, lord, and its dayfall —

This dream, reminiscent of the ending of "Pennines in April" with its "still, fiery air, hauling the imagination," is of that explosive vision when the dark gods in the "world under the world" erupt into dayfall, overpower the dark churches, and take command. What the eruption of these gods would bring is not made clear. The only hint of their existence now comes in dreams, in memories of predatory animals, in magic wolf-masks designed to ward off evil spirits.

These evil spirits seem to control Plath's scene. "Incense of death" pervades the manor garden even as the child's "day approaches." It is fall, and the new life forming comes literally into a dying world, but the poem seems also to suggest a larger deadliness. While the child comes clear of the shadow, he enters a world that is itself darkened, and the enigmatic final lines describe what appears to be a world governed by magic:

Some hard stars
Already yellow the heavens.
The spider on its own string

Crosses the lake. The worms
Quit their usual habitations.
The small birds converge, converge
With their gifts to a difficult borning.[11]

This particular combination of signs and omens is frightening. The spider, perhaps an image of fate, appears in Plath's late poem, "Totem," clearly associated with death. And the private associations (Plath's suicide and Hughes's poetic wolves) are themselves treacherous. Neither "The Manor Garden" nor "Crag Jack's Apostasy" is a fully realized poem; but hovering behind each is a world of dark and magic powers that makes "borning" difficult. Hughes wants more than a memory of its deadliness; he seeks some larger vision that will allow him to control it. Plath characteristically recognizes its signs and acknowledges its pervasiveness, but she places the vulnerability of the emerging child against it.

"The Manor Garden" was written at Yaddo, and the actual scene of dry fountains and broken statues, reminiscent also of "The Colossus," is probably drawn from that setting. A quite different rendition of this place is "The Burnt-Out Spa," which develops the image of another ruined colossus, this time a building described as "A monster of wood and rusty teeth." Although the poem opens with a clear sense of death ("An old beast ended in this place"), it is the life force itself that attracts Plath's notice in an image borrowed from "A Bower in the Arsacides, a chapter in Melville's *Moby-Dick*. Using Melville's recognition of the weaver god in nature, where "Life folded Death: Death trellised Life," Plath says, "The small dell eats what ate it once./ And yet the ichor of the spring/ Proceeds clear as it ever did/ From the broken throat, the marshy lip." In this water Plath sees "one/ Blue and improbable person"; but, she claims, "It is not I, it is not I." She draws back from this identity with the natural and significantly female life force that she has recognized, and the poem ends in a peculiar reversal. The speaker, not sustained by the vision she has just evoked, poses her own destiny in contrast:

And we shall never enter there
Where the durable ones keep house.
The stream that hustles us

Neither nourishes nor heals.

This figure, beneath the "toneless water," does not beckon as the Lorelei had, nor does it shift and entice like the old god in "Full Fathom Five," nor does it reclaim decay (as the small dell had done) since "No animal spoils on her green doorstep." This female image is austere and durable but inaccessible to the observer, who lives in a world of change.

Read with Plath's earlier poems about threatening water-spirits to which her observers succumb, this poem appears to be a rejection of the "Drunkenness of the great depths," a refusal of the fatal narcissistic attraction; but implicit in this refusal is also a recognition of the figure's power and endurance. If the stream of time that hustles her neither nourishes nor heals, then the possibility remains that at the depths of this other stream, somewhere in the durable past, is a power that would sustain. Here is Plath's first tentative evocation of the ambiguous female figure who will rise in her *Ariel* poems as a force of destructiveness and vital fury, and here also is her faint recognition, again to be developed more fully later, that nourishment can only be obtained through concourse with this potentially deadly power. She turns from it in "The Burnt-Out Spa," but only after she has established its meaning to her.

"The Manor Garden" and "The Burnt-Out Spa" attempt to combine too much. Starting perhaps as meditations on a particular scene, they move into a vaguely defined area of magic, evil omens and "improbable" spirits which cast a dark shadow over the poems and evoke in the observer certain private fears and associations that are not fully developed. Even as mood pieces the poems are not satisfactory, since the mood changes. The change may be partially attributed to the fact that Plath is working here in new areas, close to Hughes's poems, which she has not fully absorbed. For example, when Plath says, "The small dell eats what ate it once," she echoes Hughes's line in "Relic," "Time in the sea eats its tail, thrives." This recognition casts her into confusion when she tries to unite it with her own condition, and she draws back from it at the end, while Hughes's develops its implications to their grim conclusion by admitting that "None grow rich/ In the sea. This curved jawbone did not laugh/ But gripped, gripped and is now a cenotaph."

In the three years during which Plath wrote most of the poems in *The Colossus*, her efforts to expand the range of her poetry followed three separate, although simultaneous, lines: she began to focus on the non-human world, frequently nature; she drew upon myths and legends; and she started to explore painful areas in her own experience. This movement inward and outward gives her poetry of this period both its depths and its frequent confusion. The first stage of her development beyond her Cambridge poems can be seen in such poems as "Departure," "Hardcastle Crags," "Mussel Hunter at Rock Harbour," and the later "Point Shirley" and "Suicide Off Egg Rock," where Plath looks outward toward a landscape that she describes realistically but against which she always poses an individual whose reaction to it carries the poems into human considerations of fear and uncertainty. When she adds the dimensions of myth and legend in "The Colossus" or "Lorelei," for example, she again retains an individual emphasis so that the "I" in the poem risks becoming simply the private identity of the poet, and not that identity fused with the mythic mask she adopts. This intruding self-consciousness is never fully controlled, even when Plath aims toward a recognition of nature's objectivity in "Two Campers in Cloud Country," "Sleep in the Mojave Desert," "Blackberrying," "The Burnt-Out Spa," or when she attempts to evoke a world of magic in "The Manor Garden." At the same time, these poems do not handle with any thoroughness the troubled consciousness that obtrudes itself in them. The individual in these poems is generally described only as a public person: a walker on the moors, a tender of the idol, a camper. In the last poems Plath wrote during this period, the series she worked on at Yaddo, she began to break into this public person and to explore its depths.

Strangely enough, she started this process by turning away from herself and the human world, taking a topic close at hand — two dead moles that Hughes claims they found at Yaddo — and meditating on it. Part I of "Blue Moles" moves between descriptive images ("Shapeless as flung gloves," "Their corkscrew noses, their white hands/ Uplifted, stiffen in a family pose") and the human emotions they inspire ("pitiable enough," "Blind twins bitten by bad nature," "Difficult to imagine how fury struck — "). Part II develops an identification with the moles: "I enter the soft pelt of the mole." The reservations about "bad nature" and its unimaginable fury are set aside as she follows the moles into their eating world:

> Outsize hands prepare a path,
> They go before: opening the veins,
> Delving for the appendages
> Of beetles, sweetbreads, shards — to be eaten
> Over and over.

Then, in a characteristic gesture, she withdraws from the other in the enigmatic last three lines: "What happens between us/ Happens in darkness, vanishes/ Easy and often as each breath."

In this section, and in other poems like it, Plath attempts to break down the public posture in her poem by simply assuming the public posture of another poet; in this instance, Theodore Roethke, who also identified with the animal and vegetative world. For example, in "The Pit," part 2 of "The Lost Son," he says,

> Who stunned the dirt into noise?
>   Ask the mole, he knows.
> I feel the slime of a wet nest.
>   Beware Mother Mildew.
> Nibble again, fish nerves.

Again, in part 3 of "Where Knock Is Open Wide," Roethke provides this example for Plath:

> I like soft paws.
> Maybe I'm lost,
> Or asleep.
>
> A worm has a mouth.
> Who keeps me last?
> Fish me out.
> Please.

Hughes has admitted that Plath was reading Roethke's poems for the first time during this period; she was also reading Paul Radin's collection of African folktales. In addition, she was engaging in a series of meditations and invocations. Hughes described these exercises to Judith Kroll, claiming that Plath's common procedure was to concentrate on a topic, explore its associations, hand it over to a speaker or persona, then put it aside, and come back to it to write a poem. In this way, preliminary deliberation was combined with spontaneous associations developed in the writing.[12] Considering the extent to which Roethke's strategy and actual images find their way into Plath's poems, the whole process of meditation that Hughes describes apparently failed to free Plath from literary influences. Perhaps she found Roethke a poet so perfectly akin to her own sensibility that she could absorb his insights directly, making his underworld her own; but the later development of her poetry suggests her wide divergence from Roethke's open intertwining of the self and other. He provided her, at this point, with a model she scrupulously followed, and she eventually abandoned that model after it had served its purpose. Roethke's influence is clearly felt in another poem, "Mushrooms," which Plath again developed from an invocation but which may also have come straight out of a close reading of Roethke's poems from which its vocabulary is borrowed. In "Mushrooms" Plath celebrates the life force that nudges and shoves through the earth in the plant's overnight underground growth. The mushrooms with toes and noses "Take hold on the loam,/ Acquire the air." These multipliers work quietly, discreetly; but with one foot in the door they inherit the earth by morning. The same quiet underworld of growing is described also in "The Burnt-Out Spa," where, in a Roethkean image, "little weeds insinuate/ Soft suede tongues" between the charred structure of the spa.

However, "Poem for a Birthday," the final series of poems in the English edition of *The Colossus,* shows Plath's most heavy debt to Roethke. His association of the human and natural world, his search for his own identity through this association, the uncertainty and vulnerability he admits, as well as his poetic confrontation of his own insanity — all these attitudes and interests of Roethke's find expression in Plath's poem. One reason why she found Roethke so useful is that she had herself, in much less startling ways than Roethke, been attempting to express an awareness of the other world of nature and at the same time to understand her own inner world. These two kinds of effort coalesced in his poetry. But "Poem for a Birthday" is a much more fear-ridden series than any Roethke wrote. A reduction to the minimal, for which Roethke felt a special sympathy, did not allow Plath to celebrate unequivocally the life force. There at the roots she felt danger, strange spirits, red tongues, other eaters and thrivers. Also at the roots in her poems another life is forming: that of the child she bears. The reduction to the child, which in Roethke's poems is a strategy for developing his own identity, has a double implication in Plath's series since she is giving birth both to herself and to another being. Images of pregnancy add a different dimension to Plath's poem. Also, it is clear that many of the dense associations in "Poem for a Birthday" derive from her earlier explorations of the life force and from Hughes's poems on that subject. For example, the eating game that has been played from the beginning in the poems of Plath and Hughes is absorbed into Roethke's eating imagery in poems such as "I Need, I Need."

"Who," the first poem in "Poem for a Birthday," starts with this image: "The month of flowering's finished. The fruit's in,/ Eaten or rotten. I am all mouth." Sitting in a potting shed as "fusty as a mummy's stomach," the speaker herself seems to be both the devourer and the fruit that is in storage. The potting shed is a place of decay; the speaker feels "at home here among the dead heads," the "Mouldering heads," the "Cabbageheads." Then her mood shifts, and she says, "Mother of otherness/ Eat me."[13] Her appeal is telluric, an appeal to be consumed by the earth, to return to the roots and grow again. The other world of pure vegetable that survives in storage is the world she seeks. But she is not left alone. At the end she says, "they light me up like an electric bulb." In this very strange poem Plath seems to record the sensations of a highly articulate insane person whose desire to be small and grow again is threatened, both by the decay around her and by her awareness that she will not be allowed either to grow or to decay.

In the next poem, "The Dark House," the speaker has moved more deeply into the underworld. In a more surrealistic version of "Blue Moles," she says, "Moley handed, I eat my way." Again both the eater and the producer, she feels on the verge of some grotesque birthing where she may litter puppies or mother a horse; but here she has evaded those who would light her up and, like the mole, she sees by her own light in the "warm and tolerable" "bowel of the root."[14] "Here's a cuddly mother," she concludes.

In "Maenad," the next poem, the speaker is torn between hopelessness and expectation. "O I am too big to go backward," she despairs; but at the same time she senses a kind of new life forming.[15] She feels "The dead ripen in the grapeleaves" as the grape, the symbol of the god the maenad serves, is taking seed. At the first stirring of new life she says:

> Mother, keep out of my barnyard,
> I am becoming another.
>
> Dog-head, devourer:
> Feed me the berries of dark.
> The lids won't shut. Time
> Unwinds from the great umbilicus of the sun
> Its endless glitter.
>
> I must swallow it all.

Once again the devouring metaphor obtrudes, and her desire to be consumed is thwarted by her sense that she must digest the endless glitter. The attraction to darkness is resisted by the life force, and in this struggle she is exhausted. In the last line she relents and pleads for help, echoing her plea in "Two Campers in Cloud Country": "Tell me my name."

"The Beast" describes another devourer, this time the husband who is a dog, "Mumblepaws," "Fido Littlesoul," "Hogwallow," "Hairtusk." "He won't be got rid of." Married to him, she must "housekeep in Time's gut-end,/ Among emmets and molluscs,/ Duchess of Nothing." But the "bowel's familiar." Although she is down under where the "sky is always falling," she has "married a cupboard of rubbish." Again she seems caught, but now by bridal vows to darkness.

The fifth poem, "Flute Notes from a Reedy Pond," finds the speaker in a more peaceful state: "coldness comes sifting down, layer after layer,/ To our bower at the lily root." There is "little shelter" for the speaker in a world where "frog-mouth and fish-mouth drink/ The liquor of indolence, and all things sink/ Into a soft caul of forgetfulness." "This is not death, it is something safer," the speaker concludes. At last "The wingy myths won't tug at us any more." She seems to have sunk beneath the struggle to eat or be eaten.

From this inert condition she is roused, in "Witch Burning," to a new eating, a consummation by fire where

> Only the devil can eat the devil out.
> In the month of red leaves I climb to a bed of fire.

Finally, "The red tongues will teach the truth." "They've blown my sparkler out," she cries, yet as they turn "the burners up, ring after ring," she is consumed by a new flame.

> Mother of beetles, only unclench your hand:
> I'll fly through the candle's mouth like a singeless moth.
> Give me back my shape. I am ready to construe the days
> I coupled with dust in the shadow of a stone.
> My ankles brighten. Brightness ascends my thighs.
> I am lost, I am lost, in the robes of all this light.

The final poem, "The Stones," takes place in the "city where men are mended"; it is not a greenhouse, but a place where the "grafters are cheerful" and the "storerooms are full of hearts." Falling out of the light into the stomach of indifference, the speaker has been born to an "after-hell." Although this poem owes some apparently realistic details to Plath's first unsuccessful suicide attempt (she buried herself in the cellar and was discovered because of her unconscious moanings), it uses also the imagery of pregnancy as developed in the other poems. But the pregnancy and birth are inverted; it is not the birth track but the "mouth-hole" that gives her a reluctant life. The "Importunate cricket," the lively life-lover, "Drunk as a foetus," alerts those who hunt her out of the "stomach of indifference," her hiding place. In the end she is restored to life not by the throes of birth, but by the tender caresses of medical attention: the "embrace" of the food tubes, the sponges that "kiss" away her lichens, the water that "mollifies" the flint lip. The poem concludes:

> Love is the uniform of my bald nurse.
>
> Love is the bone and sinew of my curse.
> The vase, reconstructed, houses
> The elusive rose.
>
> Ten fingers shape a bowl for shadows.
> My mendings itch. There is nothing to do.
> I shall be good as new.

The association with the earth, the longing for roots, the parallels with the seasons that had been developed in other poems are all cast off. In this city of men, not women, the only production is an artifact, good as new but not new. The life that has come out of the mouth, not the birth track, is a shape, a vessel, a hollow space — a poem, not a baby. The speaker has not grown again, but simply has been mended by what she calls, ironically, love. It is not a personally felt emotion, but something applied to her like the electrical current. Throughout this series, whenever she has felt herself sinking into darkness, someone has applied the electric current to light her up, blow out her sparkler, recharge her, volt upon volt. Persistently the speaker has sought to resist the application of the current by hiding, diminishing, retreating; but in the end she succumbs to it. "I see the light," she says reluctantly and ironically. She is not even mildly grateful for her rescue. Her birth has been forced; she has not been allowed to hibernate and grow again by becoming another. She reappears in the same old shape, repaired and renovated.

In "Poem for a Birthday" Plath has sunk a shaft into her inner life, allowing its turmoil and chaos to erupt at the surface. It is as if the stoat had licked the stylist out of her skull, and what we have is the red unmanageable life spilt onto the page. These poems are, Hughes says, improvisations on set themes, and although it is impossible to detect the themes, it is easy to see how the poems evolve as one image calls forth another. In these poems Plath's manipulating mind seems less active than in anything else that she wrote, although it makes itself felt in odd places where the speaker draws back from a vivid image to comment on it. She took from Roethke's poetry certain images, rhythms, and a general idea of how she might handle madness as a subject for poems; but "Poem for a Birthday" shares neither Roethke's participation in nature nor his driving sincerity and openness. Plath's poems are much less celebratory than Roethke's, as at every point in her effort to go backward she is threatened. "Poem for a Birthday" expresses not an identification with plant and animal life, but a desire to escape human life and her captors by hiding in the potting shed or underground.

Although the last poem, "The Stones," is most obviously drawn from Plath's experience in a mental asylum, every poem in the series except perhaps "The Dark House" depends upon the events of Plath's mental breakdown. The drama that is enacted in these monologues is the fierce battle between life and death in which neither life nor death seems a simple alternative. Something of the confusion of madness obtrudes in these poems: life seems a kind of repulsive force-feeding, and death a tolerable hibernation. Plath's familiar tormentors appear in these poems. The father who has shrunk and the mother who doesn't love her are here to shove her out of the ordinary. The mother is the chief devourer, now turned repellant healer, nosey obtrusive presence whom the speaker would defy by accepting the nourishment of the other. The husband, "Mudstump, happy sty-face," a metamorphosed father, "King of the dish," is also here to tie her in a more oppressive way to the dustbin. The "black-sharded lady" keeps her in a parrot cage.

Running counter to these exterior oppressors is a recurrent image of an inner force that pushes against her. Plath was pregnant when she wrote these poems, and the image of pregnancy takes on a surrealistic aura as it becomes associated both with giving birth and with being born. When she says, in "Who," "I must remember this, being small," she refers both to her own diminishment in the potting shed and to the small life that is nourished within her. The dark house, which she has made herself, similarly becomes both the cells of new life she harbors and the "marrowy tunnels" into which she eats her way toward darkness. Her sense that she is becoming another is also a recognition both that another grows inside her and that she would give herself a new gestation and birth. Sinking into the caul of forgetfulness in "Flute Notes from a Reedy Pond," she seems to accept the birthing, free from the myth that "a god flimsy as a baby's finger/ Shall unhusk himself and steer into the air." And in "Witch Burning" she enacts the fears of the birth throes by claiming that "If I am a little one, I can do no harm," and then by discovering that littleness, like tiny, inert rice grains, is full of starch and hurts when it grows.[16] She finally accepts the pain: "The red tongues will teach the truth."

Plath's pregnancy seems to have opened a precarious psychic space between the tormentors without and the fetus within. Between the mother she would escape and the mother she would become, the battle is often exhausting; it calls forth a desire to be fed by the berries of dark, even as the "hoops of blackberry stems" make her cry. The appetite to eat is also countered by an alien eater, "Dogbody," "Dog-Head," "All-mouth," "a fat sort" who is to blame. At the "bowel of the root," where she would feed, she finds others gnawing away. The desire to clear this space of nourishment so that she may feed and be fed, so that she may sustain the small life within her and return herself to that smallness, is the complex force behind these poems. The poems are frequently obscure, and although individual images stand out with particular brilliance, the poems as a whole and as a series lack the force of their parts. The abrupt shifts of tone between defiance and despair, exultation and complaint, humility and disdain dissipate the impact of individual poems.

As the conclusion of a volume that opens with "The Colossus," "Poem for a Birthday" shows the movement of Plath's poetic persona toward a new identity. The attendant at the ruined statue has become the center of her own attention, and the ruins that are mended are her own. Although she does not attain the oracular and god-like status of the colossus, she has been consumed in flame, reduced to pebble; inadequately revived by mechanical means, she rests uneasily in the "reconstructed" vase into which she has been cast. It is this character who breaks into *Ariel.* The despairing voice of "The Colossus" can be heard throughout "Poem for a Birthday," and it will continue in later poems; but there is also a new defiance and strange exultation in this poem, in such admissions as "I am lost, I am lost, in the robes of all this light." Plath's reading, meditation, and experimental exercises, which make many of these poems derivative and confusing, did finally force her inward to create a spokesman for the rage and drive for dominance at the center of her psyche. For this no model existed; she had to create her own, and she did in *Ariel*.

Hughes was a guide and a partner in the meditations and exercises that released Plath's rush of poems during the Yaddo period. "Mayday on Holderness," mentioned earlier, shows his own experimentation with the Roethkean technique that Plath used in "Poem for a Birthday." Like Plath, he too reverts to the underworld, "Flowerlike, I loved nothing," confronts the vegetative force, recognizes a "motherly summer," hears at the end the call, " 'Mother, Mother!' " But at this point Hughes was not prepared to explore these origins. Although he was to return to this image in *Wodwo* and *Crow*, at this time his poetry remained much more attached to real life, or to natural cycles, than to psychic experiences. "To Paint a Water Lily" is another look at this underworld. Starting from a real plant, he traces the lily on the water's surface, where "the air's dragonfly/ That eats meat" tells of "inaudible" "death-cries everywhere hereabouts." Then he says, "Think what worse/ Is the pond-bed's matter of course," "Prehistoric bedragonned times." And the lily, "deep in both worlds," can be still "Whatever horror nudge her root." Moving toward an identity with this horror and its prehistoric existence in "Fire-Eater," Hughes first describes the stars as "fleshed forebears" of both the "dark hills" and his own blood. Even when the stars or gods, nature, and man separated into distinct divisions, they intermingled to produce gods: in Mary and Semele's fate ("A star fell on her, a sun devoured her"), the old unity between nature and man was restored and out of it Christ and Dionysus were born. The poem then reverses itself, and the speaker assumes that if the stars and sun can devour man, man can also eat them: "My appetite is good/ Now to manage both Orion and Dog." He starts first by taking "a mouthful of earth," "Worm-sort, root-sort, going where it is profitable." In the act, "A star pierces the slug,/ The tree is caught up in the constellations." The union with the earth and the animal brings forth no resurrecting god, however, and the poem ends enigmatically: "My skull burrows among antennae and fronds." The point of the poem is obscured: man, animal, and earth are united by the reversion of the human to the earth without exaltation. In his certainty, defiance, and self-assertion, the speaker in "Fire-Eater" is quite unlike Plath's "all mouth" dependent identity in "Poem for a Birthday," and the mouthful of earth he consumes provides nourishment different from that of the "paps of darkness" which Plath's speaker sucks, even if their endings find him burrowing and her reluctantly mended. The roots Hughes tapped are part of a circular eating process that he imagines goes on throughout the universe. They can provide him only with a sense of his own place in this process, not with a confirmation of his identity.

In general, Hughes's poems do not deal with the search for identity that fascinated Plath. Those that do deal with human beings reveal them not so much in search of themselves as possessed by spirits they cannot control. Some poems in *Lupercal* continue the stylized portraits of *The Hawk in the Rain.* For example, "Witches," written in Hughes's early, almost lilting iambic pentameter (a rhythm that does not seem suitable for the plain truths he speaks), explains that once people believed every woman was a witch, bargaining her body at night, but that such notions are now regarded scientifically as mere sexual fantasies. Not Hughes at his best, "Witches" describes witchcraft as a mere dream-wish of the woman who nightly spraddled under and bridled over men from Ireland to Norway in what Hughes describes, curiously, both as a dance and as the devil "horsing on their every thought." In this day, what goes on in women's heads when they sleep is a matter for "Small psychology," whereas the large world which their bodies travel is the terrain of Hughes's much grander poetic imagination. Sex is, as before in Hughes, the devil; but surely the man who here accedes so readily to his bedevilment and asks mildly, "who's to know," has been hardly less than satisfied by it.

In "Cleopatra to the Asp" he takes another look at sexual fury. Here is a woman to Hughes's liking, tuned to such furious pitch that she speaks with a contemptuousness that Hughes usually reserves for his men. Hughes's Cleopatra is her own "serpent of the Nile," as she says, "I seek myself in a serpent/ My smile is fatal." The same metaphor and boastful recklessness cover both her accounts of former conquests and her present miserable triumph; she says, "Seeming to bring them the waters that make drunk/ Caesar, Pompey, Antony I drank," and in the end to the serpent, "Drink me, now, whole/ With coiled Egypt's past; then from my delta/ Swim like a fish toward Rome." This spiteful Cleopatra is more Hughes's than Shakespeare's, although Hughes takes up Shakespeare's feasting metaphor. Here, feeding the serpent, Cleopatra hopes to make hungry what most she satisfies and to send him off to Rome for other food — not to achieve (like Shakespeare's Cleopatra) a union with Rome in death, but for revenge. It is unlike Hughes to take his subject from literature, but Cleopatra is a native of Hughes's psychological territory. In an uncharacteristic act of imaginative identification, Hughes speaks through this Egyptian queen to describe his own sense of passion's consummative decree: it feeds its victims and is fed by them relentlessly.

Other characters in the poems of *Lupercal* are familiar from *The Hawk in the Rain.* "Dick Straightup" (who fell in the sleet, slept all night and "was chipped out at dawn/ Warm as a pie and snoring") along with the tramp in "Things Present" and the sleeping tramp in "November," are some of Hughes's ancient heroes. "Nicholas Ferrer," one of the "vigorous souls/ That had Englished for Elizabeth," "housekept/ In fire of the martyrs," is another representative of "the fire of God" "under the shut heart, under the grave sod," that Hughes had treated in the early poem "The Martyrdom of Bishop Farrar," although the two are different historical personages.

The poems in *Lupercal* do not represent a significant advance beyond *The Hawk in the Rain,* but they do reveal some important refinements on Hughes's earlier style. The language has eased from his early jammed line to a more even-paced, almost conversational style. The virtuoso performances of rhyme and rhythm in the early volume have given way to serviceable language that does not call attention to its stress or alliterative qualities. Although Hughes seems to have settled on the quatrain as his typical stanza, he writes occasionally in couplets or terza rima, but without the self-consciousness that marked his earlier book. The language is more suited to the sense than earlier. He also takes a closer look at his subject, and even when he does rely on abstractions such as "darkness," "blackness," to define his topic, the surrounding poem provides a fuller inspection of their meaning than he had achieved in his early work. The distance — both in language and in stylization of characters — that had typified his earlier book has been reduced. The rigid split in his early poems between man and animal breaks down in these poems as Hughes begins more fully to explore his subject. Human beings are caricatured less frequently in *Lupercal* than in *The Hawk in the Rain*. The life-deniers, eggheads, and misguided ministers have given way to men open to the horrors in their head, questioning the meaning of their threatened existence, aware of the terrors around them. Although Hughes is still adept at objectifying violence as in "Hawk Roosting" — raising spirits from the dark in "February," for example — he questions his own enterprise in such poems as "Thrushes." Hughes moves in this volume to a deeper exploration of the violence he is certain civilized man must accept, and in identifying it frequently with dreams he creates for himself a subject that he will develop in *Wodwo*. More clearly than his first book, *Lupercal* deals with magic, myths, and folklore in order to locate the dark spirits of Hughes's imagination, and here again in the surrealism of this imagery he finds techniques that he will use more fully in *Wodwo*. In the *Lupercal* poems which do point toward *Wodwo*, Hughes reveals close affinities to Plath's experimentations in free association, surrealistic imagery, psychic explorations. At this point Plath's work was too rudimentary to be a dominant influence on Hughes, but when in *Ariel* she perfected her voice and subject, she was able to point the way for him. In *Ariel* and *Wodwo* their poetic positions reversed once again: Plath flashed posthumously into prominence with *Ariel*, while Hughes's work appeared to halt. The persona of her late poems became the defiant spokesman of uncontrollable violence, and when, after seven years, Hughes published *Wodwo*, his persona was like Plath's early persona — lost, questioning, uncertain.

Notes

[1] A. Alvarez, *The Savage God* (New York: Random House, 1972), p. 6.

[2] Newman, ed., *Art of Sylvia Plath*, p. 190.

[3] See Judith Kroll's discussions of "The Colossus" in *Chapters in a Mythology*, pp. 54, 82, 83, 84.

[4] Plath, *Letters Home*, p. 346.

[5] Ibid., p. 347.

[6] Hughes, *Poetry Is*, pp. 71-72.

[7] Plath *Letters Home*, p. 346.

[8] Newman, ed., *Art of Sylvia Plath*, p. 190.

[9] Hughes, "Ted Hughes and Crow," p. 8.

[10] Newman, ed., *Art of Sylvia Plath*, p. 190.

[11] Plath's imagery in "The Manor Garden" combines some of the same elements evident in Roethke's "Slow Season." The spider, the pears of Plath's first stanza, the birds, and the autumnal decay are combined in Roethke's poem. The opening of his second stanza especially may throw light on Plath's poem, since he gives the spider a more positive function: "The garden spider weaves a silken pear/ To keep inclement weather from its young." His conclusion ("The blood slows trance-like in the altered vein;/ Our vernal wisdom moves through ripe to sere") parallels Plath's, although her image of a new life forming in this season is absent from Roethke's meditation.

[12] Kroll, *Chapters in a Mythology*, p. 222*n*27.

[13] Plath's various calls to the mother are, among other things, echoings of Roethke's poems. Roethke says, "Mother me out of here," "Mother, mother, stir from your cave of sorrow" in "The Shape of the Fire." In "Give Way, Ye Gates," he says, "Mother of blue and the many changes of hay" "I'll risk the winter for you."

[14] The strange birthing parallels Roethke's "Sensibility! O La!" which starts, "I'm the serpent of somebody else."

[15] The desire to be reborn and the sense of its impossibility is again an echoing of Roethke. In "Unfold! Unfold!," he says, "I can't crawl back through those veins,/ I ache for another choice."

[16] Again, see Roethke's "Praise to the End!" for a similar image of swelling and growing: "For whom have I swelled like a seed?/ What a bone-ache I have."

SIX

Ariel

In November, 1959, the Hugheses left Yaddo; by Christmas they were in England, where they intended to settle. Their first child, Frieda Rebecca, was born on April 1, 1960, in a London flat near Primrose Hill and Regent's Park. Although Plath felt that children should be a great impetus to her writing, she actually did not write much during this year, and when she did write, she concentrated not on poems but on women's magazine stories. The next year was no better for poetry. In February, 1961, she had a miscarriage, in March an appendectomy, in September they moved to a new house in Devon, and on January 17, 1962, she gave birth to Nicholas Farrar. Her letters to her mother during these two years report a variety of literary activities: reading poems on the BBC, setting up programs of poetry for broadcasting, editing an American supplement of modern poetry for *Critical Quarterly*, writing a poem on commission for the Cheltenham Festival (for which she won first prize), contacting agents, meeting poets and editors. Although she reports working daily in a study lent to them by W. S. Merwin, she seemed to be concentrating on fiction.

These literary ventures, along with the care of her two small children, diverted her attention from poetry. The few poems that come out of this period reveal Plath turning away from set topics and meditations, instead looking toward particular events in her life — her stay in the hospital, and the experience of giving birth and tending to her children. These poems were not worked up as deliberate exercises; rather, they were written at top speed, according to Hughes, although they are finely crafted and much less obscurely and recklessly associative than the poems of the Yaddo period. Plath seems at this time to be narrowing her focus, directing it once again to her own experience, but now it is her domestic and personal circumstance which mediates a wide range of emotions.

One of the few poems she saved from this period is "Tulips," written in March, 1961, about some flowers she had received when she was in the hospital recovering from her appendectomy. Actually the flowers are only the occasion for a remarkable psychological journey into and out of anaesthesia, the "numbness" the nurse brings her in "bright needles."[1] The poem traces the stages by which the hospital patient sinks reluctantly into an anaesthesized "peacefulness," and equally reluctantly comes out of it, through repeating and reversing the imagery of the first four stanzas in the imagery of the last four so that the poem moves into and out from a central stanza with unusual symmetry.

The "too excitable" tulips and their explosions in the first stanza are what the patient awakes to finally in the last stanza, where she claims that the tulips "should be behind bars like dangerous animals." In the first, she has given her name and day-clothes away; in the last, she reclaims herself: "I am aware of my heart." In the second stanza, as she relinquishes herself to the nurses that "pass and pass," she is propped up "Like an eye between two white lids"; coming back to life in the penultimate stanza, she moves through the same stage where the tulips interrupt the air "Coming and going" and "concentrate" her attention. The nurses' tending in the third stanza is matched by the tulips' watching in the seventh. The sensation that her possessions "Sink out of sight, and the water went over my head" just before she succumbs to the anaesthesia in the fourth stanza is reversed in the sixth, when, awaking, she feels that the tulips "seem to float, though they weigh me down," "A dozen red lead sinkers round my neck." In the middle stanza she attempts, in Emily Dickinson style, to describe the state beyond consciousness: "How free it is, you have no idea how free — / The peacefulness is so big it dazes you."[2]

"Tulips" is an unusual poem for Plath because it does move inward toward a silent center and out again. The fear, shown in many of Plath's early poems, of losing control or the final reluctant relinquishment to unfathomable powers is absent in this process; where she claims, "I am learning peacefulness," "I only wanted/ To lie with my hands turned up and be utterly empty." Even more unusual than this acceptance of self-loss is the process of reversal, where the mind gradually takes hold again after the grim recognition that the tulips' "redness talks to my wound, it corresponds." The common strategy of Plath's poems early and late is for the mind to generate hyperboles that torment itself; but in "Tulips" this generative faculty has a positive as well as a negative function. "Tulips" is not a cheerful poem, but it does move from cold to warmth, from numbness to love, from empty whiteness to vivid redness, in a process manipulated by the associative imagination. The speaker herself seems surprised by her own gifts and ends the poem on a tentative note, moving toward the far-away country of health. Because she has so exaggerated her own emptiness and the tulips' violence and vitality, she must then accept in herself the attributes she has cast onto the tulips, which return to her as correspondences.

If the supersensitive mind can turn tulips into explosions, it can also reverse the process and turn dangerous animals into blooming hearts. The control of "Tulips" — the matching of stanzas, the correspondences developed between the external object and states of consciousness — marks a new stage in Plath's development. Her earlier efforts to train her vision outward, toward the landscape, and to concentrate on realistic details, as well as her very early apprenticeship in set forms combine with the Yaddo exercises in spontaneous associative creation to prepare her for her final poems, of which "Tulips" was the first example. In "Tulips" she develops a new persona. Though she is neither the public persona of Plath's moor-walker or seaside visitor nor the intensely private and fragmented identity of her surrealistic meditations, this speaker shares qualities of both. She is clearly in a hospital, responding to nurses, needles, flowers; but she is just as clearly engaged in an internal drama, reacting to a wild imaginative activity. The tension between outer and inner images is maintained (as it had not been in the early poems) by a tremendous artistic and psychological control.

In this poem Plath reveals what she meant when she said that the manipulative mind must control its most terrifying experiences. The speaker here, responsive to inner and outer compulsions, is able to handle her situation. As the inner tensions intensified in the last months of her own life, Plath was forced to create a persona much more rigid than the speaker of "Tulips." At this point, however, rigidity is what she scorns. She gives the theme a lighthearted treatment in "In Plaster," which develops a conversation between a broken leg and the cast that surrounds it. Unlike the tulips, which correspond, the cast is a totally uncorrespondent entity. It may have the same shape as the leg, but it is "much whiter and unbreakable and with no complaints"; furthermore, it is without personality, stupid, a "dead body" which would not exist without the "ugly and hairy" leg. In contrast, the life encaged in the cast is essential. Transforming an image from "The Stones," the speaker says, "I gave her a soul, I bloomed out of her as a rose/ Blooms out of a vase of not very valuable porcelain." Here, however, the reconstructed speaker of "The Stones" is abandoned in preference for the real life. This faint echoing of Plath's undergraduate essay on the double as a separable soul is not developed in the poem, which goes on to castigate the cast's presumptions of superiority. "Her tidiness and her calmness and her patience" are all contrasts to the speaker's inner itching, blooming, waiting for revenge; but for this speaker the cast's virtues are not appealing. The cast may be a saint, the "superior one," but the speaker says, "she'll soon find out that doesn't matter a bit./ I'm collecting my strength; one day I shall manage without her,/ And she'll perish with emptiness." Too simple to be successful, "In Plaster" is nonetheless prophetic. The speaker in the poem, collecting her strength against external restraints, is the prototype of the rising spirit in Plath's late poems. The reconstructed self imposed from the outside, which was assumed resentfully in "The Stones" and is now parodied in the cast, becomes the target of Plath's imaginative fury in her late poems; but, in order to destroy that self, Plath's late speaker must herself construct a powerful identity.

More typical of this period than the controlled woman in "Tulips" and "In Plaster" is the exhausted speaker, the voice of "Maenad," whose inner energies are not sufficient to organize themselves imaginatively or to confront the forces that bear on them. For example, the insomniac of "Zoo Keeper's Wife" lies awake at night, thinking over her grievances and the particular horrors of her husband's zoo full of "wolf-headed fruit bats" and the "bird-eating spider" — horrors, by the way, that recall Hughes's poems. Her hyperbolic imagination can torment itself, but it cannot control its own inner activity. Although she castigates her "fat pork," "marrowy sweetheart, face-to-the-wall" insensitive husband, she is tortured by his imaginative creatures. She claims, "I can't get it out of my mind," and her only recourse is to "flog apes owls bears sheep/ Over their iron stile" in a futile effort to hypnotize herself into sleep. Again, in "Insomniac," the mind cannot handle memories that "jostle each other for face-room like obsolete film stars." The insomniac's "head is a little interior of grey mirrors./ Each gesture flees immediately down an alley/ Of diminishing perspectives, and its significance/ Drains like water out the hole at the far end." In "An Appearance" the speaker says, "The smile of iceboxes annihilates me," and calls in despair at the end, "O heart, such disorganization!/ The stars are flashing like terrible numerals." "Empty, I echo to the least footfall,/ Museum without statues" states the speaker of "Small Hours"; she imagined herself with a great public, "Mother of a white Nike and several bald-eyed Apollos," but found "Instead, the dead injure me with attentions, and nothing can happen."

Plath turned at this time to her children and her child-bearing experience. This subject provided her with a formula not only for expressing the sense of creative disappointment (the child of "Small Hour" was only a child, and not a Nike or Apollo, just as her poems were without public acclaim) but also for reexamining the correspondence between an inner vitality and its outer form through the relationship between mother and child. This theme, apparent in her poetry since "Poem for a Birthday," involves a new recognition of herself as a creator, rather than as the victim or servant of others' creations. She also displays a new critical awareness that her creativity may not be sufficient to "happen," or great enough to survive.

The final stanzas of the last poem in *The Colossus* announced the bleak achievement of the reconstructed self: "Love is the uniform of my bald nurse./ Love is the bone and sinew of my curse." The opening line of "Morning Song," the first poem in *Ariel,* celebrates a real birth by using the same word: "Love set you going like a fat gold watch." The psychological distance between these two poems is immense, yet both treat love as an impersonal force, applied from the outside. Not my love, our love, their love, but "Love" as an autonomous mover. In "The Stones" the reference is ironic; no love at all went into the electric current, "Volt upon volt" that lighted her up, although she identifies it as the force of "The jewelmaster." In "Morning Song" the jewelmaster love, now a positive image, is aided by the midwife's slap that brings forth the "bald cry" to take "its place among the elements."

This mixture of mechanism and organism, of the elemental and the human, continues in the next stanza. There the baby is a "New statue" in the museum of his parents, a frightening object of the parents' subjectivity, yet also a subject of their concern: "your nakedness/ Shadows our safety." Vulnerable to the "drafty museum" of the world, the baby is still powerfully actual, a solid among drafts. The poem breaks in half after the careful distancing of the child. The imagery turns animate and natural: "All night your moth-breath/ Flickers among the flat pink roses. I wake to listen." The child whom she so effortlessly nurtured in her womb now requires her constant vigilance. Totally responsive to the child, the mother says, "One cry, and I stumble from bed, cow-heavy and floral." In answer, the child turns to the mother, her "mouth opens clean as a cat's." But the baby also has her own separate identity: her "handful of notes;/ The clear vowels rise like balloons."

In moving back and forth between dependence and independence, between solids and drafts, between the gold watch and moth breath, the poem details the frightening objectivity of the child to the mother at birth, the tension between the inner life and its outer form. The child that takes its place among the elements is also a creator whose song, like her mother's, is essential and whose independent existence is both feared and celebrated. The child as the double is confirmed ("Our voices echo, magnifying your arrival") at the same time it is denied ("I'm no more your mother/ Than the cloud that distils a mirror to reflect its own slow/ Effacement") and reconfirmed ("I wake to listen:/ A far sea moves in my ear"). This ojective form, the baby, depends upon the mother's inner life (the milk she produces) for its existence, and the peculiar symbiotic relationship between mother and child allows Plath the most positive expression of the double theme in her poetry.

Although the images and ideas of this poem have been forming in Plath's work, from the pregnancy imagery of "Poem for a Birthday" through her hospital poems about correspondence and the double self, they also can be compared to poems written by Hughes about the birth of Frieda. Such a comparison suggests the imaginative intimacy of the two poets, even on a subject which Plath made her own, but it also brings to light the extent to which they were pulling apart during this period. Hughes's "Lines to a Newborn Baby" start with the same cry that inspired "Morning Song": "Your cries flash anguish and gutter:/ Nothing exists, and you drop through darkness." Using Plath's image from "The Manor Garden," he warns the young baby, "There has been some trouble here, you will find/ A gallery of grisly ancestors," but he concludes, "Soon, you will smile." In this poem Hughes's concern is to console the baby born into "a world tossed into shape/ Like a hatful of twisted lots," "a stalagmite/ Of history under the blood-drip" (an image that Plath will pick up in her later baby poem, "Nick and the Candlestick").

Hughes's speaker recognizes the baby's frightened shock of birthing; instead of trying to comfort her falsely, he tells her dispassionately that her cries are justified, although he thinks she will soon accept life as it is. Plath's poem shows no such concern for the child's place in the universe, although when she came to dwell on this subject in most of her other poems about her children, she could never summon Hughes's assurance that the child would be safe.

In a later poem, "To F. R. at Six Months," Hughes uses Plath's sense of parental loss and gain in the child. "How much is ours when it comes to being born and begetting?" His answer is, "You have dispossessed us./ Some stars glared through. We lean/ Over you like masks hung up unlit/ After the performance." Hughes's unlit masks express a much more intense feeling of depletion than Plath's image of the parent as a drafty museum (curiously enough, his image is close to Plath's plaster-cast reference) to define what is essentially a female experience, the "performance" of birth. The parallels in these poems show how the two poets could penetrate each other's insights, draw on similar images and experiences, cast them in different molds, return again to redevelop hints from the other, and respond poetically to the other.

In "Magi," Plath takes up Hughes's assertion in "To F. R. at Six Months": that "Meltings of the Himalayas, the Congo's/ Load of Africa are among the magi/ That crowd to your crib with their gifts." But Plath identifies quite different magi, a picture of wisemen, "the abstracts," "the Good, the True," "papery godfolk." Her child is safe from these men, who are "Loveless as the multiplication table" because "They want the crib of some lamp-headed Plato." "What girl ever flourished in such company?" she asks. Plath's split between the real child and the abstractions of good or evil (in marked conrast to Hughes's awareness of an original unity now split between nature and human life) becomes another way of handling the theme of inner life and outer control that is her subject in this period. The baby becomes the threatened, vulnerable, weak self surrounded by dark outer forces that would overpower it in "Candles," and the mother is a helpless witness between the "infant still in a birth-drowse" and the shadows that "stoop over like guests at a christening." In a darker treatment of the same theme, "By Candlelight," the baby, "Balled hedgehog," creaks to life, entering an existence endangered by "The sack of black! It is everywhere, tight, tight!"

What is most interesting about these poems is how persistently Plath returns to the same image of the child by candlelight, using it to express concerns that have little to do with candles or with the particular experience of nursing a child. This image allows her to reiterate fears, engendered by the mother in these poems as well as in "Magi," that the baby is threatened from the outside. If the mother in these circumstances does not actually summon the evil fairy to the christening, she does nothing to dispel the dark presence; rather, she evinces the same vulnerability to it that she attributes to the baby. Even the candle she lights is both a "haloey radiance" and a "yellow knife," and she herself becomes the knife-wielder. The Sleeping Beauty motif had a special attraction for Plath, who had used it in "The Disquieting Muses" to define her mother's inadequacies and her own subsequent harrassment by evil spirits. Here, as the mother, she seems to identify herself with the child as an equal victim, powerless as ever. While Plath's poems about her own children appear to deal with a new poetic subject, the concern for the child is another manifestation of the dramatic confrontation between the small life within and forces without that would tighten around it. Plath returns, in "Nick and the Candlestick," to the image of these candle poems, but the defiance of that poem belongs to her late work.

These poems, where the child is a double or an objective image of the mother's vulnerability, lead into "Event," which carries the imagery of "Morning Song" into a darker mode. The subject here — not the child, but the husband as a double — intensifies the woman's fears. She is threatened here not by the darkened world but by the intimate other to whom she is joined. The poem is a reconsideration of love as the fusion of two into one, an idea treated in her first marriage poems. The lovers of "Wreath for a Bridal," whose "stark act all coming double luck joins," now lie "Back to back." "Event" uses the same words that had celebrated the baby's birth in "Morning Song" to express a sense of isolation and eventual dismemberment. The poem first exclaims, "How the elements solidify!" — picking up the line of "Morning Song" where the baby's cry took its place among the elements. The baby's "clear vowels," rising like balloons in the earlier poem, have changed into the owl cry: "Intolerable vowels enter my heart."

The fluidity of "Morning Song," with its echoing voices, flickering breath, and rising songs, has hardened in this poem; moonlight is a "rift," the stars are "ineradicable, hard," the baby's face is "pained, red wood," the speaker walks in "a ring,/ A groove of old faults."[3] Still, the solidity of the scene is threatened by faults: "A black gap discloses itself." The only stirring occurs "On the opposite lip," where "A small white soul is waving, a small white maggot." Encased in her ring, the speaker seems despairingly confident that "Love cannot come here." Seeing the waving maggot, she concludes, "My limbs, also, have left me./ Who has dismembered us?/ The dark is melting. We touch like cripples." The last three stanzas are remarkable for their quick shift from cold assertion to anguished questioning. The speaker seems to have removed herself from love's boundaries by retreating into the deeply grooved ring of her own suffering, yet she notices the other soul waving beyond the gap that separates them, even as that soul immediately becomes a parasite. The force of that image should drive her more deeply inward, yet she remains tormented by it, and her final question is full of agony as well as bitterness.

In "Event," the exhausted voice of "Zoo Keeper's Wife," "Insomniac," and "An Appearance" may be heard, but with a new urgency over physical decay and loss. The possibility of physical violence between man and woman existed in Plath's poetry from the earliest marriage poems of eating and of burning in one fever, and it is not surprising that she should return to this idea to describe any rupture in the relationship. The dismemberment that would leave them both crippled introduces an element that is to dominate Plath's late poetry, its concentration on physical mutilation. These years, packed with child-bearing, her operation, and the physical care of little children, eventually provided a whole range of body imagery for her poetry, which had, up to this time, been generally cerebral and bloodless.

At this point, however, except for some notable exceptions such as "Tulips," she had not brought her immediate experience to full poetic expression. In an attempt to work up poems, she returned to the strategy of her Yaddo period and began again to write on set themes. One such theme was offered by the trees in her front yard at Devon; it became the source of three poems, "Little Fugue," "Elm," and "The Moon and the Yew Tree." According to Hughes, "Little Fugue" came first; its diffuseness reveals the old procedure of concentrating on an object until it evoked a train of spontaneous associations. Plath abandons the particularity of her early landscape poems as well as the Roethkean ploy of penetrating the vegetative world in favor of establishing a natural setting ("The yew's black fingers wag;/ Cold clouds go over") which serves only to focus her meditation. This meditation begins slowly — threatens, in fact, not to begin at all, as the yew and cloud offer no sign language to the poet. She attempts to prime the image by avowing that she likes "black statements," "The featurelessness of that cloud," and a first association arrives: "The eye of the blind pianist," "His fingers had the noses of weasels." It leads nowhere, and the speaker, incorporating her own poetic strategies in the poem, attempts once more to invoke the meanings of the objects by naming them again, "Black yew, white cloud," and the meditation again falters: "The horrific complications./ Finger-traps — a tumult of keys."[4] But the speaker has identified her problem: her fingers are traps that will not let out the sign message, the music, the poem. She starts over, again invoking the muse, "I envy the big noises,/ The yew hedge of the Grosse Fuge."

This first half of the poem has been a finger exercise in which Plath seems willing to engage in the ancient rite of the poet described in *The White Goddess:* " 'When he sees the person or thing before him he makes a verse at once with his finger ends, or in his mind without studying, and composes and repeats at the same time.' "[5] But, up to this point in the poem, the fingers have refused to write automatically; although the speaker keeps claiming her fondness for the black-and-white image and her envy of its noise, her fugal composition never proceeds far beyond a repetition of the original words. Then suddenly the keys under her fingers release their tumult: the black tree becomes arbitrarily "a dark funnel, my father," whose voice she now can "see" "Black and leafy." In Druidic finger language, the little finger is given to Mercury as a Conductor of Dead Souls and is connected with the yew tree, sacred to the death-goddess Hecate. The resistance of the speaker to the yew's sign language can be attributed, then, not merely to a failure in meditation or poetic inspiration, but also to an unwillingness, despite protest to the contrary, to follow where it pointed.

Once recognized however, the yew/ finger/ father assumes a militaristic identity, giving orders, "Gothic and barbarous, pure German." The associations flood; the yew and the you of the father are fused in an image of death: "Dead men cry from it." About the yew, she asks, "Is it not as tortured?" and "you, during the Great War" "Lopping the sausages" that color the speaker's sleep, "Red, mottled, like cut necks." The tree-spirit father is not only a figure from the dead; he is a death-dealer as well. Except for this vivid image, he refuses to come clear. Worse than his bloody legacy of death is his silence, which forces the speaker back to the other aspect of her original image, "the cloud over the yew tree, its featurelessness." The clouds become "vacuous sheets" spreading over the speaker, who asks, "Do you say nothing?" The father mutilator, himself mutilated, recedes.

The whole poetic enterprise to make a poem in the mind without studying, through spontaneous associations, breaks down. "I am lame in the memory," the speaker says, attributing to herself the physical attributes of her father as well as the psychological state of amnesia which he induces. The trance has produced no concourse with the spirits of the dead, and, as she recovers from it, she can claim only that "Death opened, like a black tree, blackly." A return to matter-of-fact existence from this meditation is not a victory, but a falling back into a world of lists: "These are my fingers, this my baby./ The clouds are a marriage dress, of that pallor." Like "The Colossus," where the speaker was married to shadow, the speaker's marriage here is to blankness and poetic silence. The idea that the dead father or some ruined statue held, or rather tantalizingly withheld, knowledge or the magic that would release poetry is persistent in Plath's poems, and every period of creative sterility in her life produced a poem or poems that evoked this dead or ruined but always absent figure. At this point the figure, earlier mythicized, takes on some of the particular attributes of Plath's own father (his physical debility as well as his German ancestry) as well as those of her husband (the silence here, as well as the one-legged father, recall details of "Event").

Any suggestion that Plath was beginning to create a mythic drama in which the father-husband male figure is a particular demon must be qualified, however, by "The Moon and the Yew Tree," which names the real source of creative sterility as the mother-moon. During 1961-62 Plath suffered from a writer's block; she attempted to break out of it by making it the subject of poems. The speaker in these poems attempts to contact correspondent spirits or messengers from the dead which represent both the other and also that part of herself that is silent or dead. The connection between speaker and spirit is often imagined as a marriage or a bond of kinship (father, mother, sister) by the speaker who feels herself fatally incomplete, crippled, deaf, alone in her silent world. Plath's poems are never free from the threat that the other or the spirit may be a predator or parasite, but the open acknowledgment of the other in Plath's tree poems evinces a greater willingness than ever before to risk its dangers.

These tree poems mark a change from the Roethkean methods displayed in "Poem for a Birthday." Here Plath is not reducing herself to the minimal, but attempting to bring into consciousness the magic spirits contained in the other world of which the tree is an emblem. Hughes's influence in this process is obvious. He wrote poems on similar topics; furthermore, he admits that he saw the moon and the yew tree and suggested that Plath write a poem about them.[6] It is clear, too, that without his suggestions Plath might not have written these poems, and it is doubtful that they really helped her overcome a long writing block. With "Tulips" she was not only beginning to find new subjects in her domestic and personal experience, but she was also developing a new poetic immediacy of vivid imagery. She had, as we have noted, discovered her body as a source of poetic images. Now these meditations drew her back into her mind. Their black-and-white images are a temporary abatement of the blood red that bloomed in "Tulips" and would flood the later poems. It is perhaps one of the ironies of Hughes's relationship with Plath that his encouragement of topics from the non-human and non-intellectual world should have driven her into reflective poetry at a time when she was about to take a different exit out of the mind.

"The Moon and the Yew Tree" provides, nonetheless, an interesting companion poem to "Little Fugue" because it treats the same subject — lack of vision — neither by vainly evoking the spirit of the tree nor by identifying it with the dead father but by clearly naming its source in the moon-mother. The yew, so central to the meditation of "Little Fugue," is only a prop in "The Moon and the Yew Tree," a "Gothic shape" (this time neither barbarous nor Germanic but, in its architectural description, connected with the Sunday morning church bells) that points toward the poem's major symbol, the moon. Plath ignores the opportunity to elaborate her family symbolism, the father-yew and mother-moon, and resists the possibility of developing a meditation on the moon. The moon is no object for associative thinking; she states emphatically, "The moon is no door." The poem remains from beginning to end in the location announced in its first line: "This is the light of the mind, cold and planetary." There is no escape from this place, since the landscape perfectly mirrors the mind: "I simply cannot see where there is to get to," "it is quiet/ With the O-gape of complete despair." (These lines may be a direct address to Hughes, who suggested the poem's subject. It led nowhere for her.)

The poem develops another light, the church bells' "tongues affirming the Resurrection" and the church candles recalling the sweetness of Mary, but somehow the oppositions do not work. The Gothic-yew-father associations of "Little Fugue" are ineffective in this poem, which identifies that symbolism with the church and Mary as unbelievable. "The moon is my mother," the speaker claims, "She is bald and wild." While the speaker says she would like to believe in tenderness, in Mary, in the Christian concept of the resurrection, she is, as the child of the moon, the heir to the despair, darkness, and death of this pagan moon-goddess. At the same time, the moon appears to be a much more substantial figure than her opposite, Mary.[7]

Ambivalence toward the moon is part of all Plath's treatments of this central symbol in her poetry. The moon is, Plath wrote in "The Rival," "something beautiful, but annihilating." She loved the beauty and the danger. Even in "The Disquieting Muses," an early work, the consoling and comforting mother is cast off in favor of "dismal-headed/ Godmothers," muses who share many of the evil attributes of the moon-muse yet who also teach the truth. Although the moon here, as in "The Rival," is a "great light borrower," "sees nothing" of "holiness," there is in this poem a suspicion that the sweetness of Mary and the gentleness of the church candles cast an illusory light. The mother-moon image in Plath's poetry would replace the false mother who nurtured illusions. If this mother were a wild witch, she would still be a more dependable other, a more perfect reflection of the poet's own spirit than any sweet and tender intercessor. If the "message of the yew tree is blackness — blackness and silence," the moon's "O-gape of complete despair" is the poet's. If the yew tree is the tree of death, the moon is the goddess that controls it. And finally, if the yew is the father, the moon is the wild mother preferred over both the sweet mother and the black father. The poet need not meditate on the message of the moon; she knows it as part of her own wisdom.

The definition of a female muse or correspondent spirit continues in "Elm," which transposes the spirit of the tree to a feminine voice that takes on many attributes of the moon-goddess. In contrast to the silent yew, this spirit speaks to the poet, but its questions and answers seem to be the poet's own. The poem develops a dialogue that appears first to be directed by a tormenting tree-spirit toward the speaker, although eventually the speaker and the tree seem to merge. It is this, it is that, the tree claims; when the speaker demurs, the tree begins to speak its own secrets. The tree starts out tauntingly: "I know the bottom, she says, I know it with my great tap root:/ It is what you fear." The speaker says, "I do not fear it: I have been there." Again the tree inquires, "Is it the sea you hear in me" "Or the voice of nothing, that was your madness?" Receiving no answer, the tree strikes closer this time: "Love is a shadow./ How you lie and cry after it." As a female tree-spirit, it articulates the woman's fears that love has "gone off, like a horse," that it too will gallop impetuously "Till your head is stone" "Echoing, echoing." "Or shall I bring you the sound of poisons?" it asks.

These death threats force an identification between the tree and the woman, who are both opposed to the sun ("I have suffered the atrocity of sunsets," "My red filaments burn and stand, a hand of wires") and to the wind ("Now I break up in pieces that fly about like clubs"). The final death imagined is, for the female tree, the most terrifying: "The moon, also, is merciless: she would drag me/ Cruelly, being barren./ Her radiance scathes me." "How your bad dreams possess and endow me," she claims. But the tree-spirit-woman is curiously impregnated by this female moon-image, "inhabited by a cry," although she is "terrified by this dark thing," "its soft, feathery turnings, its malignity." It looks "with its hooks, for something to love" and sees only the "pale irretrievables" of clouds. The woman in turmoil gives in: "I am incapable of more knowledge." The faces of love pass, while the face, "So murderous in its strangle of branches," stays to impart "Its snaky acid kiss" that "petrifies the will." The kiss of death seems to be the gift of the female-moon-tree spirit who is also the muse, the source of the woman's cry.

Plath's contact with the female spirit of the elm tree is much more entangled and confused than her meditation over the male yew tree. The blackness and silence of the yew are remote, compared to the dark penetrating and interstrangling of the female spirits in tree and moon. In this poem Plath began to explore the creative-destructive female spirit whose identity she was to assume in her late poems. The obscurity of "Elm" reflects the ambiguous pull of these spirits on her psyche, as it demonstrates Plath's still incomplete knowledge of how they could operate.

Between "Elm" and the creative outpouring of her late poems, which began in October-November of 1962 and continued until her death, Plath's marriage with Hughes broke up. The tremendous personal strain of the separation, the misery of what she imagined (or, rather, knew) to be an abandonment, the rage of jealousy and hatred that it inspired had the immediate effect of arousing her poetic energies. Her letters to her mother reveal a desire to start an independent life; she claimed that once she accepted or, as she said, made the decision to live alone "miraculously, my own life, my wholeness, has been seeping back."[8] The personal situation was obviously much more complicated than that; but in some senses Hughes's departure fired Plath's new drive toward self-identity. As the other half, the competing other, the double, even the colossus, he had in some way stolen part of her whole self. As wife and mother, she had been divided from her whole identity as poet. Now, alone, she no longer had to divide herself; she could be mother-creator-poet, no longer half of a poetic team. Nor did she any longer have a poetic teacher, an exercise-setter or list-maker. She set her own tasks.

The subject on which Plath wrote her last poems is the original one, herself. It is clear that as early as "Tulips" she was beginning to move away from Hughes's poetic topics toward new experiences of her own; she even moves in this direction in "Elm," which attempts to identify female spirits from the world of magic that seemed to be Hughes's private domain. Still, without Hughes's absence the rapid development of her late period might have been delayed. Viewed as a whole, Plath's poetry in 1961 and early 1962 seems full of false starts, potentially fruitful topics not pursued, a blockage of her best impulses. Only when she was left alone, free to develop as she could, was her writing block overcome; then she seemed, in Alvarez's estimation, possessed. The worked-up trances of her meditations appear, in this light, to be mere child's tricks.

After Hughes's departure Plath was admittedly working under the extreme psychological necessity of expressing her own new self. That fact alone could account for the creative breakthrough, but much of the energy of these last poems also seems to erupt like a jet that had been forcibly restrained. The speaker in Plath's poems, who before had typically presented herself as a servant, attendant, victim, exhausted or empty mind, now bursts forth on her own, casting off all bonds to announce her own energy and power.

The preface to this last period is a series of bee poems in which Plath turns to the queen bee as her model. While these poems share some of the obscurity of "Elm" over the female image, they are more realistic than "Elm," and unclear in a different way. In the opening poem, "The Bee Meeting," the speaker herself seems uncertain about what is going on. Some village ritual is in progress, and while the speaker is included in it, she keeps looking for its ominous significance. Her rush of questions reveals her suspicions: "Is it blood clots the tendrils are dragging up that string?" "No, no," she assures herself, "it is scarlet flowers that will one day be edible." Although every detail causes her concern, she claims, "I could not run without having to run forever" — a feeling reiterated in her letters of this period, which detail her desire to face life alone and not to seek help by returning to her mother. Although she realizes that the villagers are hunting the queen bee, she feels somehow that she herself is attacked. She asks, in the end, "why am I cold?" In the next poem, "The Arrival of the Bee Box," she herself, now the owner of bees, loses her fear, decides to be "sweet God" and let them free. In "Stings" the mysterious activity between the bee-seller, the bee, and a third person watching is only the pretext for the speaker's identity with the queen bee, now the "red comet" flying. Finally, in "Wintering" the bee (like the woman in "the time of hanging on," the winter) attests to new life: "The bees are flying. They taste the spring."

The significance of this sequence rests chiefly in its exploration of female identity and experience. Bees had a special importance for Plath, whose father was an authority on the bumble bee and who herself became a keeper of honey bees in Devon. In a poem from *The Colossus,* entitled (significantly) "The Beekeeper's Daughter," she had already developed the strange sexual implications of the male beekeeper. Although the poem is usually discussed as evidence of the daughter's submission to the father, in fact the "maestro of the bees" moves through a lush, erotic, and overpowering female landscape. The "garden of mouthings," the dilating corollas and their encroaching musk, "circle after circle," the "well of scents almost too dense to breathe in" — all are descriptions of an engulfing female sexuality. In this symbolic landscape, the father is "Hieratical," not responsive to the aggressive sexual messages, but fixed like a stone symbol. As a result, his daughter, too, is "sister of a stone," unable to identify with the female eroticism she evokes.

The next stanza describes a landscape in which sexual intercourse is perverted: "Trumpet-throats open to the beaks of birds," not to the fertilizing powers of bees. "The anthers nod their heads, potent as kings/ To father dynasties" — but in this context impotent, unfathering, "a queenship no mother can contest" because there is no queen at all. The father-king does not mate with the daughter-queen. For the male bee, the queen bee's fruit is "death to taste," but this male beekeeper is cut off from that symbolic sexual death by his own death. He has gone underground where the daughter seeks him, setting her eye "to a hole-mouth" in an image that recalls the earlier "garden of mouthings" and female sex organs. In this recognition of her own sexuality (looking into herself, she sees her own "eye/ Round, green, disconsolate"), she identifies "this Easter egg" of new life that the maestro had denied. She threatens, "Father, bridegroom," "The queen bee marries the winter of your year." Such a marriage will be death for the father, bridegroom, and new life for the queen bee in the spring.

The overwhelming Oedipal love for the father that he rejected in the opening, thus making it impossible for the daughter to develop through it her own erotic nature, must be recognized and worked through by tracking down the father, attracting him "Under the coronal of sugar roses" (an artificial symbol of her sexual sweetness), and killing him by marrying him. Hughes says this poem recounts a key event in her *Vita Nuova;* although he does not elaborate on his point, the key event is, at the most literal level, her marriage. Allowing her a new sexual identity, that relationship also allowed her to express her awareness of a thwarted Oedipal impulse.

If "The Beekeeper's Daughter" works through an early sexual awakening, the later bee poems focus on quite different female experience. Gone is the overripe erotic garden of the early poem. In "The Bee Meeting," the scene is a village social; the speaker goes to hunt the queen bee in the company of the rector, the midwife, the sexton — those public agents of marriage, birth, death, the world in which she must now define her identity. The queen bee eludes these searchers. "She is very clever," Plath says. But the villagers are actually helping to preserve the queen bee by moving the virgins who would kill her. Still, not very grateful, the queen rises, "The upflight of the murderess into a heaven that loves her." Left behind, the speaker identifies at this point not with the flying bee, but with the empty box, an emblem of survival ("Pillar of white in a blackout of knives") and a possible coffin.

"The Arrival of the Bee Box" is more positive about this "clean wood box" that would be a coffin except for the "din" within, "the swarmy feeling." The owner wonders what would happen if she freed the bees; "I am no source of honey/ So why should they turn on me?" She resolves to set them free tomorrow. In the box imagery, with its rampant life, Plath begins to develop a familiar situation in her poetry: inner turmoil and outer form. To open the box is to open the possibility of attack by its contents, a warning she seems anxious to ignore. It is in fact this activity that she explores in "Stings," where she and a man in "white smiles" remove the honey cells from the hive. Once again the queen bee does not show herself; if she exists at all, she is old, "Poor and bare and unqueenly and even shameful." All that the speaker recognizes are "winged, unmiraculous women,/ Honey-drudgers," with whom she does not want to identify, although she wonders if "These women who only scurry" will hate her. In control now, she sees "A third person watching," who has nothing to do with the bee-seller and herself. He is "a great scapegoat," the person the bees attack. "They thought death was worth it," but the beekeeper refuses that death. "I/ Have a self to recover, a queen," she admits, although again she does not find her but imagines her as a flying "red comet."

This curious choice between revenge on the man which means death and recovering a self which signifies life introduces a prophetic note into the poem. With this acceptance she is able, in "Wintering," to accept also the activities of women who "have got rid of the men,/ The blunt, clumsy stumblers, the boors." Knitting, tending the cradle, harboring life in her body-bulb, she will survive. The bee sequence tells of the search for a female identity in a world without men, without stings, without knives. It is "the room I have never been in," where the "black" is bunched "like a bat." The speaker now enters with her "torch," lighting "appalling objects," "Black asininity. Decay./ Possession." This open confrontation with the blackness at the center of her own existence, and not associated with some outside threat, is the source of her tentative recognition that she will survive. For once she is totally on her own — a painful recognition which reflects Plath's own situation.

The female identity with which Plath had to cope every day was not that of the virgin honey-drudger or queen bee but that of the mother, and it is not surprising that she began to elaborate this role more fully in her poetry. "Nick and the Candlestick" retains some of the imagery of her early baby poems, but it is more tightly constructed, more cryptic, more defiant. It divides evenly in half: seven stanzas for the candlestick, and seven for Nick. The first part of the poem is a surrealistic picture of what is described as a cave, but it might also be the darkened room in which the mother sits with her child, or the mother herself conceived as a space enclosing the child. In this space things are running down, and the candles demonstrate the process: "Waxy stalactites/ Drip and thicken, tears/ The earthen womb/ Exudes from its dead boredom." Using images from the bee poems, the speaker describes herself: "Black bat airs/ Wrap me, raggy shawls." It again appears to be winter, and the poem develops a series of visual, then metaphorical associations: candles dripping, caves, icicles, echoes, newts, fish, piranha religion. The principle behind these randomly chosen elements eventually becomes clear: they all exist through the reduction of themselves or something else.

In such a setting, then, the baby is a surprise. "O love, how did you get here?" the mother asks. He does not follow the same principle: "The blood blooms clean/ In you, ruby." In identifying the baby with a stone, the mother dissociates him from the process of diminishment. In the end she says, "Let the mercuric/ Atoms that cripple drip/ Into the terrible well,/ You are the one/ Solid the spaces lean on, envious./ You are the baby in the barn." In a world where everything is running down, the child's solidity is prized; but, like the baby in the barn, the child is also connected to that "piranha/ Religion, drinking/ Its first communion out of my live toes." The connection is left unexplored, and in the baby-mother relationship the mother is sustained in her isolated cave which she has hung with "roses" for the baby whom she calls "Love, love." This love, unlike the autonomous love identified with the adult male in "Poem for a Birthday" and "Morning Song," is personal, maternal, self-sustaining, and in the last analysis self-directed. One of the spaces leaning on the baby is the mother, who finds in his solidity an obstruction to all forces that would diminish her.

In a number of poems written at this time, Plath returns to her earlier concern with the dangers of the world which are so easily bypassed in "Nick and the Candlestick." Often these threats to the child are rendered more dangerous by being channeled through the mother herself. In "Mary's Song," Plath becomes the wailing mother, bearing her holy child into an evil world where the Sunday lamb cooking becomes, in quick association, the sacrificial lamb, the victims of the holocaust, and finally the torments of her own life as the heart is itself a holocaust. The poem ends in despair, "O golden child the world will kill and eat."

In "Child," the mother's desire to fill her child with images "grand and classical" is stymied by her own inadequacies, "this troublous/ Wringing of hands, this dark/ Ceiling without a star." The dangers in "Brasilia" are not only to the mother, "nearly extinct" while her baby cuts his tooth in her thumb, but also to the child who may be attacked by the male god, "You who eat/ People like light rays." She prays, "leave/ This one" "unredeemed/ By the dove's annihilation." The male principle in these poems, associated both with Christianity as a predatory religion and with the violence of history, is always destructive — "A death tree" she calls it, in "For a Fatherless Son." "It is good for me." Good to see only her face when she looks into the child's face. While she seems to be aware that this relationship may have its sexual dangers ("One day you may touch what's wrong"), she is explicit about its present sexual rewards as she says, employing a traditional sexual metaphor, "your smiles are found money."

Implicit in her poems about her children is an underlying concern with the violence of history, frequently associated with the male world. In "Brasilia" her prayers seem to be concerned not only with the male God of Christianity but also with the manmade violence of atomic radiation and drugs. In "Thalidomide" she carpenters "A space for the thing I am given," wondering "What leatheriness/ Has protected/ Me from that shadow — / The indelible buds,/ Knuckles at shoulder-blades." In such a world it was difficult to build an existence for herself or to create one for her child. This interest in the destruction of recent history had been forming for a long time.

Although she had no memories of World War I and no legends of ancient heroes to celebrate as Hughes did, she found the events of World War II and the threat of atomic radiation in her own time necessary subjects for poetry. She came to these subjects rather late, and it is difficult to determine what actually inspired her political awareness. Perhaps it was history itself, since the first evidence of her concern with these matters appears in letters to her mother which attack Britain's "incredible and insane bombing of Egypt, and lament the Russian invasion of Hungary.[9] Living in England, closer to the source of political turmoil, may have been another factor in her interest. And Hughes's own concern both for contemporary affairs and for the social studies he was teaching at secondary school when they were first married, as well as the books on Russian history, the Jews, and the Nazis that he read at this time in connection with his teaching, might also have reinforced Plath's response.[10] Whatever the source of her political awareness (and perhaps it dated from much earlier than this period, although neither her letters nor her poems reveal it), she reacted intensely to the events of 1956, feeling shocked and almost physically sick about the Suez crisis and the Hungarian revolution.

Her concern with political issues did not diminish with time. In 1960 she took her newborn baby to watch the Easter weekend "Ban the Bomb" protest. She struck what was to be a constant thematic note in her poems when she wrote, "I felt proud that the baby's first real adventure should be as a protest against the insanity of world-annihilation. Already a certain percentage of unborn children are doomed by fallout and no one knows the cumulative effects of what is already poisoning the air and sea."[11] More than a year later she was worrying about strontium 90 levels in milk, and explaining that she had been so depressed by reading about the terrifying marriage of big business and the military in America, and about the John Birch Society, that she had not been able to write letters. She says, "I began to wonder if there was any point in trying to bring up children in such a mad, self-destructive world. The sad thing is that the power for destruction is real and universal."[12] This worry, a dominant theme in her poems about children, recalls a similar concern, expressed in her apprenticeship poems, that the woman or the lovers would be destroyed by the collapse of the universe.

In the last months of her life, however, Plath began to expand her historical perspective and at the same time to merge her private agony with the whole tradition of destruction she saw running through history. In an interview she admitted to a new interest in reading history. "I am very interested in Napoleon, at the present: I'm very interested in battles, in wars, in Gallipoli, the First World War and so on, and I think that as I age I am becoming more and more historical. I certainly wasn't at all in my early twenties."[13]

Becoming historical, Plath did not become any less subjective. In "The Swarm," a poem quite unrelated to the other bee poems, she conscripts Napoleon into her private world so that the "dull pom, pom in the Sunday street" of her own town, where a swarm of bees is being shot down, becomes an attack not only on the bees but also on Napoleon, as well as on the "furnace of greed" that burns through history. "It is you the knives are out for/ At Waterloo, Waterloo, Napoleon," she says. Like Napoleon and like Ted Hughes, as we see from the imagery, the swarm, which thinks the bullets are "the voice of God/ Condoning the beak, the claw, the grin of the dog," is doomed to be duped by its trust in destruction. Thinking that he plays with chess people while the "mud squirms with throats" which he sees as "Stepping stones for French bootsoles," Napoleon and his army "Walking the plank draped with Mother France's upholstery" march with the bees straight "Into a new mausoleum." "How instructive this is!" the speaker says of the capturing of the bees, and its lesson displays Napoleon with the honey-gatherers, not the bees, as evidence of a universal greed: "O Europe! O ton of honey!"

What is interesting about this poem, despite the confusion of its associations with Napoleon, is Plath's criticism of those who believe in a God that condones the beak. This poem marks a change in her attitude from "I Want, I Want" in *The Colossus,* where she recognized the patriarch that set wolf and shark to work; furthermore, that change places her at odds with Hughes's view of the universe. In fact, "The Swarm" may be an attack on Hughes as well as on Napoleon. Hughes was, as we have seen, fascinated with the kind of God or the powers that fused the universe and engineered the hawk's hooked feet and head, and in poem after poem he examined the evidence of its violence.

Besides being unlike Plath's other bee poems, "The Swarm" is also unlike her historical poems, since the speaker is not implicated in the action except in the most general terms. In "Getting There," however, the speaker actually participates in the violence of history, identifying with all the victims of wars. Again Plath's personal situation feeds into the poem — she saw herself as the victim. The poem is a pastiche of war scenes: from World War II, "The terrible brains/ Of Krupp" and the trains carrying Jews to death camps; from World War I, the boxcars carrying troops and wounded men; from Napoleon's retreat, "It is Russia I have to get across"; from the martyrdom of Joan of Arc, "The body of this woman,/ Charred skirts and deathmask/ Mourned by religious figures." The train that carries the speaker through these scenes and through which she is dragging her body is a metaphor for the violence of history and for the violence of her own life. The train "is dragging itself,/ it is screaming — / An animal/ Insane for the destination,/ The bloodspot," its wheels fixed to the "leash of the will — / Inexorable." Her will, God's will, and the will of history became one. It drags with it "the men the blood still pumps forward," "what is left of the men/ Pumped ahead by these pistons, this blood/ Into the next mile." The life force and the thirst to kill are ironically related; both pump forward with automatic purpose. Hughes will take up this image in "Second Glance at a Jaguar," when he talks of the jaguar's body as "just the engine shoving it forward." Plath's speaker is anxious: "How far is it?/ How far is it now?" "I cannot undo myself." All she seeks from the "gods" that know only "destinations" is how far she must journey through this landscape of thunder and guns, where her feet slip in "Thick, red" mud. As the train nears its destination, which is finally identified as "The face at the end of the flare" or the kill, the "carriages" become "cradles" and the speaker steps "from the black car of Lethe,/ Pure as a baby."

This poem is usually read as a poem about Plath's death wish. The many references to history suggest that she is concerned not simply with the speaker's own death, but with the violence of history. She imagined herself as wounded, bleeding, although still living in a world that kills and thrives. In talking about Napoleon's defeat in "The Swarm," she said, "How instructive this is!" Her point here seems to be the opposite: we are not instructed by history; rather, the train that drags itself through the battlefields of history ultimately becomes the "black car of Lethe," a symbol of the forgetfulness of the past. It becomes a cradle, nurturing a new generation of killers; the pure baby who steps from it will perpetrate murder because she has forgotten the world's past history of murderousness.[14]

In "Totem," the violence of history is domesticated in the eating habits of men. The relationship between one thing and another is a relationship of blood, of killing and eating. The poem opens with the image of the train from "Getting There." Here, "The engine is killing the track"; but the speaker assures us that "It will be eaten nevertheless./ Its running is useless." Then, in a series of associations, the speaker traces the eating process: the field that fed the pig that fed the butcher that fed man that feeds on Christ. This principle at the heart of things does not scare the speaker. She knows that

> The world is blood-hot and personal
>
> Dawn says, with its blood-flush.
> There is no terminus.

But Dawn is obviously wrong; there is a terminus. Like the flies that "buzz like blue children/ In nets of the infinite," we are all "Roped in at the end by the one/ Death with its many sticks." Whether the process is traced horizontally by a train ride through history or vertically by the food chain, the world in Plath's late poems is "blood-hot."

The spilling of blood became for her a symbol of the life force pulsating with a creative violence that outraged destruction. The simplest accident, such as cutting her thumb when chopping onions, becomes cause for "A celebration" of the blood that "rolls/ Straight from the heart." "What a thrill," she says, relishing her own gore when

> The balled
> Pulp of your heart
> Confronts its small
> Mill of silence.

In "Contusion" she concentrates on that moment when "Colour floods to the spot" while "The rest of the body is all washed out." Blood is the evidence of vitality against the blankness and silence of the world. While Dame Kindness in "Kindness" assures her that "Sugar can cure everything," the speaker knows that there is a more "necessary fluid" — "The blood jet is poetry,/ There is no stopping it." Poetry is the creative act by which the heart persists against silence and a kindness that would anaesthetize its fury. The image cuts both ways: the blood jet is evidence both of the heart's persistent life and of its exhaustion of that life in poetry. Kindness would stop such a sacrifice. The blood flood is also simply the menstrual flow, and for the barren women of "The Munich Mannequins" "Unloosing their moons, month after month, to no purpose," it means "no more idols but me." Unlike the creative jet of poetry or the procreation of children, the menstrual bloodletting is simply a form of self-indulgence, the flood of self-love.

Plath's fascination with blood in her late poems is not limited to her own blood pumping out. For her, the world itself was blood-hot. In "Poppies in July," the flowers are "clear red, like the skin of a mouth./ A mouth just bloodied," and her wish is to "bleed, or sleep!" In "Poppies in October" she claims that "Even the sun-clouds this morning cannot manage such skirts," and she asks, "O my God, what am I/ That these late mouths should cry open." In "Letter in November," "the world/ Suddenly turns, turns colour" as she walks, her Wellingtons "Squelching and squelching through the beautiful red." Walking on her property alone, she sees the apple tree's "irreplaceable/ Golds bleed and deepen, the mouths of Thermopylae." These late poems with their bleeding mouths recall the earlier "Tulips," where the flowers brought to the hospital room remind the patient both of her sickness and, paradoxically, of her health.

The particularity of Plath's blood images not only is new but also distinguishes her work at this point from Hughes's. The blood imagery is not mere fantasy, but fantasy riveted to fact. Characteristically she starts with a cut, a bruise, a poppy, an apple tree, and fastens on this concrete image until it changes under her scrutiny into evidence of some larger violence. In contrast, her early poems are fairly bloodless, although when blood is mentioned it is always metaphorical and positive: the pregnant woman is "red fruit" in "Metaphors," the poppies' "petalled blood/ Burns open to sun's blade" in the early "Two Sisters of Persephone," the blood beats "the old tattoo/ I am, I am, I am," for the "Suicide Off Egg Rock." No bleeding here; rather, the blood beat of life.

Much of this affirmative association is evident in the later blood images as well. Blood is a sign of the violent vitality of life, as in "Poppies in October," where the poppies are "a love gift/ Utterly unasked for" that remind the poet of the woman in the ambulance whose "red heart blooms through her coat so astoundingly." However ominous, this image is not so deadly as the contrasting concept of the sky "Igniting its carbon monoxides." Again in "Letter in November," the "gold-ruddy balls" of the apples form a contrast to the "thick grey death-soup" of the atmosphere. Sometimes this vitality is proof against the suffocating surroundings; sometimes, however, it is itself threatening. (In "Poppies in July," the speaker says, "it exhausts me to watch you/ Flickering like that, wrinkly and clear red.") In "Cut" blood, in the image of redcoat soldiers, runs out, causing her to ask, "Whose side are they on?" The nourishing blood in "Medusa" is even more threatening, as the speaker says of a motherly figure:

> You steamed to me over the sea,
> Fat and red, a placenta
>
> Paralyzing the kicking lovers.
> Cobra light
> Squeezing the breath from the blood bells
> Of the fuchsia. I could draw no breath.

The paralyzing placenta is a strange form of murderousness, a surrealistic image of the life-denying nurturer that Plath had developed in different terms in "The Disquieting Muses." Here it seems to be both a life-giver ("Lens of mercies" "Pushing by like hearts") particularly associated with the mother ("Old barnacled umbilicus,") and a life-taker ("your wishes/ Hiss at my sins") associated with the male ("Off, off, eely tentacle!")

In these late poems, then, Plath is working out an image pattern of bloody violence that derives directly from the female situation in which bleeding may be either a normal, healthy issue, evidence of a natural rhythm, or a sign of sterility and wounds. The woman's more numerous blood relationships give these images a peculiar density: blood may be the "red fruit" of the fetus she nurtures or the "blood jet" of poetry she creates, as well as the "mouths of Thermopylae" or the "Kamikaze man." The blood blooms or jets in violent activity, or it floods and drains. The predominance of mouths here, bloodied mouths or mouths of war, is another peculiarly female feature of these poems, a fantasy of the maternal role. The blood relationship between pregnant mother and child is perverted by Plath into the engulfing placenta on the one hand or the blood-sucking object (significantly, a natural object, flower or fruit) on the other.

The violence of these poems is intense, immediate, omnipresent. The creative source of violence is the female body. Unlike the poems she has written that deal directly with birth, miscarriage, or surgery ('Morning Song," "Parliament Hill Fields," "Tulips"), these poems transpose specifically female experiences into a particular perspective on the world. In the turmoil of her last months the psychic wounds she suffered were translated into physical wounds. The blood beating out of her became evidence of her inner energy; to celebrate it, she even reveled in self-inflicted wounds. The "blood-hot" fury that drove her was evidence of her own passion, self-love, and suffering.

Violence erupts in another form when Plath combines the intensity of the blood imagery with her interest in history and a rage which stems, no doubt, from her abandonment by her husband but which finds voice by borrowing some of his strategies. The woman who speaks in "Daddy" resembles Hughes's hawk. She has the streamlined efficiency of the thrush's ravening stab as she goes after her victims.

Hughes's hawk says, "I kill where I please," and finds his echo in the girl in "Daddy" who says, "So daddy, I'm finally through," "If I've killed one man, I've killed two," "Daddy, daddy, you bastard, I'm through." The violence of the hawk is in the girl. But Plath extends Hughes's subject by making it at once more concrete and more universal. For example, Hughes's comment that the hawk's "manners are tearing off heads" is fastidious in comparison to Plath's concrete, bloodthirsty reference not only to the stake that she thrusts into her victim's "fat black heart" but also to the torture she has endured from the man who "Bit my pretty red heart in two" and "drank my blood for a year." Again Plath is much more specific than Hughes about the course of creation as the source of the violence; she locates it in the "black shoe" she has lived in, or the "boot in the face" she has suffered. The specificity of the imagery here is one element separating Plath from Hughes; the references to history are another. While critics have associated Hughes's hawk with Hitler, Hughes himself has been careful to avoid any such direct connection in the poem. In contrast, Plath connects her plight with that of the Jews, claiming she "may well be a Jew." The father-husband figure whom she finally kills is then a "Panzer-man," "A man in black with a Meinkampf look," emblem of all the black men who have loomed as threatening forces in her poetry.

"Daddy" is a poem of revenge, and its violence is a reaction against torture. Whatever its source in Plath's life, its literary source may very well be Hughes's animal poems. Here Plath takes up, with a correspondent fury, the violence celebrated in "Hawk Roosting." The incantatory rhythm, insistent rhyme schemes, and ritualized figure of the woman speaking here (which Hughes will borrow back with all Plath's improvements for *Crow*) suggest a mind as rigid as the hawk's. Plath's poem shows the limitations of the mind that operates only to rehearse the perfect kill. While Hughes may have thought the thrush's ravening stab was like Mozart's genius in entertaining no distractions, Plath's depiction of the monomaniacal daughter-victim-killer suggests she was aware that such a figure was far from a genius. The simplicity of her language matches the simplicity of her thinking; in fact, her violent rage has subsumed all other feelings or thoughts.

In "Daddy" and a number of other late poems, the most difficult problem is the effort to assess the poet's relationship to her speaker. Because "Daddy" calls upon specific incidents in Plath's biography (her suicide attempts, her father's death, her marriage), we are tempted to identify the poet and the speaker directly, although such an identification cannot account for the fact that Plath employs techniques of caricature, hyperbole, and parody that serve to distance the speaker from the poet and at the same time to project onto the speaker a strange version of the poet's own strategies. "Daddy" becomes a demonstration of the mind confronting its own suffering and trying to control what it feels controls it. The speaker's simplistic language, rhyme, and rhythm become one means by which she attempts to charm and hold off the evil spirits. Another means is the extreme facility of her image-making. The images themselves are important for what they tell us of her sense of being victimized and victimizer; but more significant than the actual image is the swift ease with which she can turn it to various uses. For example, she starts out imagining herself as a prisoner living like a foot in the black shoe of her father. Then she casts her father in her own role; he becomes "one grey toe/ Big as a Frisco seal," and then quickly she is looking for his foot, his root. Next he reverts to the original boot identity, and she is the one with "The boot in the face." Immediately she finds "A cleft in your chin instead of your foot." At the end she sees the villagers stamping on him. Thus she moves from booted to booter as her father reverses the direction, and the poem's sympathies for the booted or booter shift accordingly.

The mind that works in this way is neither logical nor psychologically penetrating; it is simply extremely adept at juggling images. And it is caught in its own strategies. The speaker can control her terrors by forcing them into images, but she seems to have no understanding of the confusion her wild image-making betrays. When she identifies herself as a foot, she suggests that she is trapped; but when she calls her father a foot, the associations break down. In the same way, when she caricatures her father as a Fascist and herself as a Jew, she develops associations of torture which are not exactly reversed when she reverses the identification and calls herself the killer of her vampire-father. The speaker here can categorize and manipulate her feelings in name-calling, in rituals, in images — but these are only techniques, and her frenzied use suggests that she employs those methods in the absence of any others. When she says, "Daddy, I have had to kill you," she seems to realize the necessity of the exorcism and to understand the ritual she performs, but the frantic pitch of the language and the swift switches of images do not confirm any self-understanding. The pace of the poem reveals its speaker as one driven by a hysterical need for complete control, a need arising from a fear that without such control she will be destroyed. Her simple, incantatory monologue is the perfect vehicle of expression for the orderly disordered mind.

In talking to A. Alvarez, Plath called her late poems "light verse." "Daddy" does not seem to fall easily into that category, despite its nonsense rhymes and rhythms, its quickly flicking images. It is neither decorous nor playful. On the other hand, considering its subject, it is neither ponderous nor serious. Above all it offers no insight into the speaker, no mitigating evidence, no justification. Perhaps Plath's classification is clear only if we consider her speaker a parodic version of the poet — and, of course, if she were consciously borrowing from Hughes's animal poems, these poems must be read as a comment on his poetic voice as well. Plath's speaker manipulates her terror in singsong language and thus delivers herself in "light verse" that employs its craft in holding off its subject. For all the frankness of this poem, the name-calling and blaming, the dark feeling that pervades it is undefined, held back rather than revealed by the technique. The poet who has created such a speaker knows the speaker's strategies because they are a perverted version of her own, and that is the distinction between the speaker's "light verse" and the poet's serious poem. If this poem comes out of Plath's own emotional experience, as she said her poetry did, it is not an uninformed cry from the heart. Rather, Plath chooses to deal with her experience by creating characters who could not deal with their own experiences and, through their rituals, demonstrate their failure.

Plath's late poems are full of speakers whose rigid identities and violent methods nor only parody their torment but also permit them to control it.[15] The peculiar nature of the speaker in "Lady Lazarus" defies ordinary notions of the suicide. Suicide is not the joyous act she claims it to be in her triumphant assertion that she has done it again. Her confidence, at the moment of recovery, that her sour breath will vanish in a day and that she will soon be a smiling woman is a perverse acceptance of her rescuers' hopes, although she calls her rescuers enemies. The impulse of the speaker is the overwhelming desire to control the situation. She is above all a performer, chiefly remarkable for her manipulation of herself as well as of the effects she wishes to have on those who surround her. She speaks of herself in hyperboles, calling herself a "walking miracle," boasting that she has "nine times to die," exclaiming that dying is an art she does "exceptionally well," asserting that "the theatrical/ Comeback in broad day" knocks her out. Her treatment of suicide in such buoyant terms amounts to a parody of her own act. When she compares her suicide to the victimization of the Jews, and when she later claims there is a charge for a piece of her hair or clothes and thus compares her rescued self to the crucified Christ or martyred saint, she is engaging in self-parody. She employs these techniques partly to defy the crowd, with its "brute/ Amused shout:/ 'A miracle!' " and partly to taunt her rescuers, "Herr Doktor," "Herr Enemy," who regard her as their "opus." She is neither a miracle nor an opus, and she fends off those who would regard her in this way.

The techniques have another function as well: they display the extent to which she can objectify herself, ritualize her fears, manipulate her own terror. Her extreme control is intimately entwined with her suicidal tendencies. If she is not to succumb to her desire to kill herself and thus control her own fate, she must engage in the elaborate ritual which goes on all the time in the mind of the would-be suicide by which she allays her persistent wish to destroy herself. Her control is not sane but hysterical. When the speaker assures the crowd that she is "the same, identical woman" after her rescue, she is in fact telling them her inmost fear that she could (and probably will) do it again. What the crowd takes for a return to health, the speaker sees as a return to the perilous conditions that have driven her three times to suicide. By making a spectacle out of herself and by locating the victimizer in the doctor and the crowd, rather than in herself, she is casting out her terrors so that she can control them. When she boasts at the end that she will rise and eat men, she is projecting her destruction outward. That last stanza of defiance is really a mental effort to triumph over terror, to rise and not to succumb to her own victimization. The poet behind the poem allows Lady Lazarus to caricature herself and thus to demonstrate the way in which the mind turns ritualistic against horror. Although "Lady Lazarus" draws on Plath's own suicide attempt, the poem tells us little of the actual event. It is not a personal confession, but it does reveal Plath's understanding of the way the suicidal person thinks.

The smiling woman of "Lady Lazarus," acquiescent in her female identity, surfaces in a number of late poems. In "The

Tour" the speaker is the agreeable niece who greets her maiden aunt with mock hospitality, "Do step into the hall," "Yes, yes, this is my address./ Not a patch on *your* place, I guess." After apologizing for the mess, she leads her aunt right into it, showing her the frost-box that bites, the furnace that exploded, the sink that ate "seven maids and a plumber." With mock concern she warns, "O I shouldn't put my finger in *that,*" "O I shouldn't dip my hankie in, it *hurts!*" The speaker manipulates the aunt's curiosity, turning it back on itself by maintaining a tone of insistent courtesy and forced intimacy that is designed to protect the aunt from the brazen exhibition of her open house of horrors. The speaker's ability to manipulate her aunt is matched by a more sinister ability to control her terrors by locating them in furnace or stove where they have a separate identity. The poet who felt that the intelligent mind must manipulate its most terrifying experiences also knew that the deranged mind could hold off its terror and separate itself from the agony it suffered, as the speaker here does. Here is the too-inventive mind that exults in self-laceration.

The speaker in "The Applicant" is another person in control, here a comic figure. She provides a burlesque of the marriage contract drawn up between the empty-headed man and the living doll he desires. However, her insistent refrain ("Will you marry it?") suggests that she is, despite her all-knowing pose, very anxious for a positive answer. She is like the applicant herself, willing to make any claim and to accede to any demands in order to strike a bargain, although she couches all her comments in scorn and scoffing both at the characters and at the institution of marriage. Still, she seems trapped by the sexual stereotypes she parodies. The ventriloquism of this poem hides the fact that this is an internal debate. The sexual fear that has driven the "sweetie" into a closet and the boy to his last resort also propels the manipulations of this shrewd and too-agreeable woman.

Another voice in Plath's late poems modulates the shrill hysteria of her female manipulators. It can be heard at the end of "Lady Lazarus" in the promise to rise and eat men, but in that poem its full force is undercut by the jaunty, jeering quality of what has gone before. In "Purdah" it rises naturally at the end from a long series of exclamations, although it needs (and has) no exclamation points itself. The woman speaker who sits "cross-legged," guarding her sexual availability until the bridegroom arrives, reflects his view of her: "So valuable!" "How the sun polishes this shoulder!" Only when the moon rises do her "visibilities hide." The moon with its "cancerous pallors" allows her a kind of safety. When the bridegroom arrives, he penetrates her veil, her body. "I am his," she says simply, aware that her eye reflects in its "concatenation of rainbows" his orgasmic pleasure. But she is not satisfied and begins to utter her repeated threat, "I shall unloose"; then she makes clear that "at his next step," his next sexual approach, she will unloose not the 'Doll he guards like a heart" but "The lioness,/ The shriek in the bath,/ The cloak of holes." She will kill him, as Clytemnestra killed Agammenon, in the bath. The eye veil and mouth veil, the cloak that guards all other bodily holes, will be unloosed in violence. The sexual implications of this imagery are complicated: unloosing the cloak of holes, the woman appears to be offering herself sexually to the bridegroom, although her sexuality, openly revealed, becomes predatory and its victim is the man. In this last stanza the woman is the sexual assaulter, and the fury of her sexual power is much more violent than that of the man who simply "guides/ In among these silk/ Screens." The female sexual assault destroys both the man and the woman he has made into "Jade — / Stone of the side" "of green Adam," an idol to worship and use. The woman's unloosing is "One note/ Shattering/ The chandelier/ Of air," the "jewelled" existence of her purdah.

The lioness unloosed in "Purdah" is the identity for which Plath searched in her bee poems and which she identified with a rising figure: "The upflight of the murderess," the flying "red comet." Her double nature, liberator and destroyer, may be explained by reference to the two lioness-goddesses of Egyptian mythology. One is Sekhmet, the terrible goddess of war and battle, whose name means "the Powerful." Claiming that her heart rejoiced in killing, she attacked men with such fury that the sun-god, fearing the extinction of the human race, appeased her with a magic potion. The other is Bast, whose origin as a lioness-goddess personified the fertilizing warmth of the sun. Goddess of pleasure, she loved music and dance. Plath's conception embraces both goddesses; she might have been especially attracted to Sekhmet, who was beloved of Ptah, the protector of artisans and artists, but the lioness's merger with the sun in "Ariel" suggests that Plath was also interested in the aspect of the lioness as a fertile mother. Reconsidering "Purdah" in this light, we can see that the lioness as a sexual entity has both the terrifying energy of the female predator and a fructifying power that would threaten any man who would turn the object of his desire into stone.

"Ariel" is the name of the horse Plath rode, the "Pivot of heels and knees." Although she admits that she is sister to "The brown arc" of the neck, she also claims she cannot catch it, as if it were not the pivot but something racing out of control. But as "God's lioness," and connected with the "cauldron of morning," Ariel is also a biblical reference to Jerusalem as the scene of a holocaust that burned sacrificial victims.[16] In the process of identifying with the galloping horse ("How one we grow"), Plath converts this animal fury into "Something else" that hauls her through air, the fire that consumes her. Like the shining of the rook in "Black Rook in Rainy Weather," this horse's speed can "seize" her senses, haul her eyelids up; but in this late poem she does not wait, as she had earlier, for the angel's "rare, random descent." Rather, she is part of the radiance ascending from the holocaust. She moves through a landscape of darkness that would cast its hooks into her, hold her, but she emerges: "White/ Godiva, I unpeel — / Dead hands, dead stringencies." Unlike the Godiva who had ridden naked through the streets in order to fill a condition upon which her husband had promised to relieve the town of a tax, this Godiva cancels personal debts. Finally she says,

And I
Am the arrow,

The dew that flies
Suicidal, at one with the drive
Into the red

Eye, the cauldron of morning.

A poem that moves from "Stasis in darkness," "substanceless," to the "cauldron of morning" cannot be adequately described as an expression of suicidal impulses, although Plath's use of that word demands explanation. The arrow and the dew, although in apparent apposition, do not reinforce each other. The arrow kills, the dew is killed; the arrow at one with the red eye is its apotheosis, while the dew is consumed by the sun. The dew, like the child's cry melting and the unpeeling dead hands and even the foaming wheat and "glitter of seas," symbolizes all that will be overcome or sacrificed in this arrow's drive into morning. But the speaker, identifying with the arrow, presents herself as no sacrificial victim on the altar of any god. The arrow, like the horse, "God's lioness," absorbs the power of the avenging God: "at one with the drive/ Into the red/ Eye," it is associated with the fury that lit the holocaust.

The sexual implications of this imagery reinforce this reading and develop as well its use in "Purdah." The female speaker here identifies with the horse, a symbol of masculine sexual potency which, as the arrow, becomes a phallic image that drives into the eye, the circle associated with female sexuality. Far from a desire to transcend the physical, "Ariel" expresses the exultation of a sex act in which the speaker is both the driving arrow and the receiving cauldron. "God's lioness" in "Ariel" calls upon both strands of the female mythological lioness: as an arrow she is associated with battle, and in her merger with the sun she absorbs its fertility. Destroyer-creator, masculine-feminine, the spirit with which the speaker identifies in "Ariel" is whole, entire in itself. The fires that burn in honor of and through this spirit are emblematic of its passion and ecstasy.

It is exactly this passion that the speaker of "Years" finds missing in God, with his "vacuous black," "great Stasis." What she admires is "The piston in motion —", "the hooves of the horses,/ Their merciless churn." She rejects the "Christus,/ The awful/ God-bit in him/ Dying to fly and be done with it." Just as she had rejected for her children the abstractions of the magi in "Magi" and the "dove's annihilation" in "Brasilia," so here she finds unacceptable the Christian idea of transcendence, "Dying to fly." "What is so great in that!" she exclaims. She will have none of it: "The blood berries are themselves, they are very still." Her "soul" dies before the piston in motion, and in her "blue distance," her heaven, "the pistons hiss." Although the figure flying upward in Plath's poems is a positive image of dominance and violent energy, it is in its female associations quite different from the Christian image of a transcendent God. Not the "God-bit" but the goddess-bit, its redness clearly connects it to the "blood berries," to life and not to the life promised through death. This female figure is the pre-Christian goddess celebrated by Robert Graves in *The White Goddess.*

Paradise for this figure will be something other than the heaven imagined by a patriarchal religion. In "Fever 103°" the speaker describes her approach to it. "Pure? What does it mean?" The speaker rejects the idea that "The tongues of hell" can purify her; they are "Incapable/ Of licking clean/ The aguey tendon, the sin, the sin." Plath piles multiple associations into these lines. The Christian concept of purgatory, where sins are purified, is rejected, but so is the classical conception of hell as the abode of the dead, guarded here by a "dull, fat Cerebus," whose "triple/ Tongues" include, along with the lynx and the sow, the lioness. The smoke that rises from these sacrificial fires of hell threatens to suffocate the speaker, just as "Isadora's scarves" made her the victim of her own individuality. The smoke that chokes "the aged and the meek,/ The weak/ Hothouse baby" becomes "Radiation," a symbol from "Brasilia" that connotes both atomic warfare and the fleshly annihilation of Christian transcendence. The idea is reinforced here by the repetition, "the sin, the sin."

The speaker is not one of the weak destroyed; she continues "flickering, off, on, off, on." Like Christ, she continues in this state for "Three days. Three nights," until she becomes "too pure for" the figure she addresses as "Darling." Through this purity, in which the man's body becomes like the "lecher's kiss" of the sheets, she achieves God-like status above the masculine. "Your body/ Hurts me as the world hurts God," she says. She is her own light, "lantern — / My head a moon," "my gold beaten skin." In this state it is her vitality, her "heat," that she imagines will astound the man, her "coming and going, flush on flush," "All by myself," and not in sexual concourse with the man. As she rises, "The beads of hot metal fly," and she becomes her own fireworks. She is "a pure acetylene/ Virgin," not the Virgin Mary but the Light itself, and her attendants are "roses," the image of vitality in Plath's poetry, and "kisses," "cherubim," "whatever these pink things mean." "Not you, nor him" will be the attendants of this female apotheosis in which she casts off the masculine world and her own sexual identity in it, "(My selves dissolving, old whore petticoats)." "Fever 103°" is a rejection of the man and the selves that man created, in favor of a purely female identity in which the light is not the transcendent Light but heat, a flush, a red camellia.

"Edge" may be read as the final statement of the woman perfected in "Fever 103°." "Her dead/ Body wears the smile of accomplishment" as she folds back into it all that she has created — her love, her art, her children. "The illusion of a Greek necessity/ Flows in the scrolls of her toga," uniting the "scrolls" of her death robe and the "scrolls" of her poetry as her final adornment. Into this image she folds each dead child, "a white serpent," and through this identification with Cleopatra she becomes the proud and fated queen who is both destroyer and destroyed. She folds her children into her body, as they have drained her into theirs, and thus she reclaims the self split into lover and mother. The perfected woman closes "as petals/ Of a rose close when the garden/ Stiffens and odours bleed/ From the sweet, deep throats of the night flower." Not a cold Greek statue, but a rose bleeding, the accomplishments of this woman at the end of *Ariel* are far greater than those of the woman who said of herself at the end of *The Colossus*, "The vase, reconstructed, houses/ The elusive rose." She has become that rose, its elusiveness realized in her children, her fatal love, her poetry, all now absorbed into herself. Her valedictory is to the moon-mother-muse: "She is used to this sort of thing./ Her blacks crackle and drag." This poet, the "night flower," the moon's off-spring, speaks to the moon through "sweet, deep throats" that transform the witches' crackles into song. These are the words of the final poem in *Ariel*, "Axes," that make the wood ring and release the sap, echoes which travel "Off from the centre like horses," "The indefatigable hoof-taps." The volume ends with the "piston in motion." The "fixed stars" that "Govern a life" are the center from which the "indefatigable" words run.

Ariel must be read as several chapters of a creative autobiography, written by a woman whose purpose in the last years of her life was to come to terms with the various female roles and identities into which she had been split. It is full of wrong leads, frustrated efforts, obscure and private battles that attest to the difficulties she had to face and to the energy she expended on them. Her final poetic accomplishment was not to transcend these hardships, but to face them directly and to leave a record of that confrontation. In the image of the rising lioness/ Virgin/ red comet, she identified a female figure violent enough to triumph in a world that Plath imagined would reduce the woman to a jade statue — but a female also with creatively violent powers of her own.

Notes

[1] In a letter to her mother written from the hospital, Plath comments on the anaesthetist. See Plath, *Letters Home*, p. 411.

[2] For a discussion of "Tulips," see my comments and those of others in "Sylvia Plath's 'Tulips': A Festival," *Paunch*, XLII-XLIII (December, 1975), pp. 65-122.

[3] In a later poem, "The Couriers," the ring image is used again and becomes simply a symbol of marriage and betrayal unattached to old griefs: "A ring of gold with the sun in it?/ Lies. Lies and a grief." Love's fever that had

burned and sickened in "Event" flares to a new and destructive violence in "The Couriers," where it is "the immaculate/ Cauldon, talking and crackling."

[4] For a discussion of Plath's use of magic in this poem, see Judith Kroll's comments in *Chapters in a Mythology*, pp. 109-115.

[5] Quoted in Robert Graves, *The White Goddess* (New York: American Book-Stratford Press, 1948), p. 165.

[6] Newman, ed., *Art of Sylvia Plath*, pp. 193-194.

[7] For a complete discussion of moon symbolism in Plath's poetry, see "The Central Symbol of the Moon," in Kroll, *Chapters in a Mythology*, pp. 21-79.

[8] Plath, *Letters Home*, p. 462.

[9] Ibid., pp. 282, 284.

[10] Ibid., p. 289.

[11] Ibid., p. 378.

[12] Ibid., p. 438.

[13] Plath, *The Poet Speaks*, p. 169.

[14] Kroll's discussion of the death in this poem as an intermediate step toward rebirth suggests the limitations of her effort to fit all of Plath's poetry into *The White Goddess* mythology. See *Chapters in a Mythology*, pp. 158-165.

[15] For a fuller discussion of this aspect of Plath's poetry, see my article, "Sylvia Plath and Confessional Poetry: A Reconsideration," *Iowa Review*, VIII (Winter, 1977), 104-115.

[16] See Kroll's comments in *Chapters in a Mythology*, pp. 180-182.

SEVEN

Wodwo

The seven years between *Lupercal* (1960) and *Wodwo* (1967) mark a difficult period in Hughes's poetic career. In the year or two immediately following the publication of *Lupercal*, Hughes emerged as a figure of some prominence in literary London. Plath's letters attest to his success: "I wish you could see the mail he gets! Italian translators, asking the British Council to speak to him, American editors over here hoping to meet him, magazines and newspapers panting for his poems and stories. He has already sold his five or six new poems several times over."[1] In 1960 and 1961 Hughes tried a variety of literary activities. He attempted to write a successful play. He also put together a children's book, *Meet My Folks!;* began to write short stories, some of which are included in *Wodwo;* and prepared programs and wrote radio plays for the BBC. Although he never wrote the one play that would ensure their financial future, Hughes did manage to support the family by these money-making ventures. The few poems that he published between 1960 and 1963 show him rehearsing old themes, attempting nothing new. This relatively barren poetic period may be explained in a variety of ways: he was devoting his major energies to other efforts; he had succumbed to public demands on his time; his attempt to raise money left him little time for poetry. It is also clear that Hughes had written himself out. Although the poems in *Lupercal* are a refinement of his earlier style and a slightly more thorough examination of his earlier themes, they do not mark a significant advance in his work. The enthusiastic reception of *The Hawk in the Rain* and then *Lupercal* did not encourage him to develop; but with *Lupercal* he had essentially exhausted his original subject, the violence of the universe. He could intensify its message in poems like "Hawk Roosting," or he could question its significance in "Thrushes," but he could not at this point explore its implications more fully. In the years between 1957 and 1961, when Plath was attempting to develop her own voice and to break through a series of writing blocks, Hughes seems to have enjoyed an almost unbroken period of productivity. Such a long visitation from the muse was not to last, nor was it without hazards. Continuing to write, Hughes began to repeat himself. Unchecked by any fallow periods, he never needed to explore new poetic techniques, expand his vision, reexamine his ideas. There is a uniformity about *Lupercal* that is disturbing. When Hughes turned to other forms of writing immediately after the publication of *Lupercal,* the insights he might have gained from the plays and stories he wrote then were not carried over into his poetry, which continued mainly in the same vein as his earlier work.

How much his own poetry was affected by what he recognized correctly as a new stage in Plath's development, beginning with "Tulips" in March, 1961, cannot be adequately assessed. He wrote very few poems during this time, just as Plath had written very few during 1957-60 when he had been very productive. If, as Alvarez said, that period was Hughes's, then this time was certainly Plath's. It would be easy to make too much of this point. Hughes had many personal reasons for not writing poems, and of course when Plath began her last period of intense productivity in October–November, 1962, she and Hughes were separated, so he could not have been immediately affected by that stage at all. Whatever the effect of her poetry, her suicide in February, 1963, drove him into an almost complete poetic silence for about three years. When he began to write again in 1966, his poetic style and subject matter had changed.

Wodwo, which includes poems published as early as 1960, must be read with this background in mind. It is the chart of a spiritual and creative quest, and its dominant voice is that of the quester, asking, with the figure in "Wodwo," "What am I?" Although Hughes's headnote to the volume suggests that the "stories and the play in this book may be read as notes, appendix and unversified episodes of the events behind the poems, or as chapters of a single adventure to which the poems are commentary and amplification," in fact *Wodwo* is not a unified work. Whatever the relationship between the stories, the play, and the poems, the poems themselves do not form chapters of a single adventure; rather, they encompass several visions, different purposes, disparate voices. The poems move from the stark landscapes that have dominated Hughes's poetry since *The Hawk in the Rain* to the beginnings of a mythic vision that would be more fully developed in *Crow*. They start with the distanced observer of the "bored" sea in "Pibroch" and develop to the agonized speaker in "Skylarks" who cries, "O lark/ O song, incomprehensibly both ways — / Joy! Help!" The poems in *Wodwo*, read in the order of their publication, suggest the nature of Hughes's development during these seven years — from a poet of Olympian assurance about the stony universe in which he lives, to a poet painfully open to the terrors of death and meaninglessness. Where Hughes's early poetry had celebrated the hawk, the wolf, the fox, his later poems in *Wodwo* turn to more humble animals, singing the song of the rat, the psalm of the gnat. The shift in focus forces a change in poetic style, evident in the differences between the opening poem, "Thistles," a hard look at the physical world in Hughes's old style, and the surrealism of such later poems as "New Moon in January" and the last two parts of "Gog," or the allegorical style of "Logos" or the simple, repetitive rhythms of "Gnat-Psalm." *Wodwo* is a volume more varied in technique and subject than either of Hughes's earlier collections; this variety marks it as an important transitional work in his career.

The poems in *Wodwo*, first published in magazines in 1961 and 1962, generally fall into two predictable categories: landscape poems and war poems. In neither does Hughes say much that is new. Nature is (here, as before in Hughes's poetry) that bleak territory, uncongenial to human beings, where the elements collide and "Nothing lets up or develops." To express his sense of such a universe in "Pibroch," "Thistles," "Sugar Loaf," "Still Life," Hughes depends upon the peculiar strategy of personification. The thistles are "splintered weapons" of a "decayed Viking"; the stone in "Still Life" has fingers; the hill is a "dull, trusting giant" in "Sugar Loaf"; and in "Pibroch" the sea is "bored," the stone has a mind, the tree is like a deranged old woman.

The impulse to personify nature is an old poetic strategy by which man makes himself at home in the universe, but Hughes's use of it here is unusual, since his purpose is to show an essentially impersonal universe. For example, when he says, in "Pibroch," "The sea cries with its meaningless voice," he seems to be saying that the sea's voice is meaningless to its human auditors. Yet, as the next few lines prove, Hughes is saying that the sea's voice is meaningless *to itself*, which is "Without purpose, without self-deception" — although the first suggestion is not entirely ruled out, since the presence of the human observer can be heard in the third line's admission that the sea is "Probably bored with the appearance of heaven." We must ask, how would the sea be aware of heaven? The fading in and out of the human perspective is evident in the second stanza, where it is announced that "A pebble is imprisoned/ Like nothing in the Universe," an apparently human observation, and then the focus shifts to the stone which is "growing/ Conscious of the sun's red spot," "dreaming it is the foetus of God." The wind of the third stanza, "Able to mingle with nothing," and the tree of the fourth, "Unprepared for these conditions," are, in their personified conditions, identified with the human place in nature; but also as part of nature, they are almost too anxious, too human, to make sense in a meaningless universe.

These irresolutions are not improved by the ending, which appears to return to the human world as if the nature scene of "Pibroch" had been instructive: "This is where the staring angels go through./ This is where all the stars bow down."

Where these particular events take place or what they signify is nowhere clear in the poem. If the world is completely meaningless, then man's efforts to endow it with significance are futile. But by allowing the sea, the stone, and the tree to have a mind, a voice, a dream, Hughes has in fact endowed them with purpose, with reactions to heaven and God — in short, with all that he claims they lack. The problem here, as in "Hawk Roosting," is that Hughes allows nature to speak in human language in order to prove that nature does *not* speak in human language. It does not work. He cannot have it both ways.

In these nature poems Hughes seems to be reexamining the voracious eating habits of the sea, first explored in "Relic" and "Mayday on Holderness." The situation has not changed since these poems. The "maker of the sea" is still recovering itself in "Still Life," which seems to depict a scene much like Plath's seaside in "Departure." The "penury" Plath had noted is evident in "Still Life," where the stone "thinks it pays no rent"; but Hughes goes on to elaborate a greater penury, that of the sea which reclaims itself in the "veins" of the "harebell" where it "sleeps, recovering" in order eventually to break the rock. The efficiency of the life cycle in nature attracts Hughes's admiration, as it did in his earlier work.

The war poems also rehearse familiar themes. In "The Warriors of the North" Hughes once more pays tribute to the ancient heroes, whose murderous instinct is the last evidence of English vitality before the great Puritan suppression: "A cash-down, beforehand revenge, with extra,/ For the grueling relapse and prolongeur of their blood/ Into the iron arteries of Calvin." Again Hughes goes over his father's memories of World War I in "Out," which opens with his father recovering from "the four-year mastication by gunfire and mud" and ends with the son's valedictory: "Goodbye to all the remaindered charms of my father's survival./ Let England close. Let the green sea-anemone close." This poem's third part, titled "Remembrance Day," opens with a startling image of the poppies sold to commemorate the war dead: "The poppy is a wound, the poppy is the mouth/ Of the grave, maybe of the womb searching," "Today whoring everywhere." Plath picked up this image in "Poppies in October" and "Poppies in July" and seemed to develop a potential for horror that Hughes bypasses in his more realistic poem. The image reappears in "Gog III," where the connection between womb and grave is elaborated.

Certainly the most interesting early poem in *Wodwo* is the title poem. The wodwo, the creature with which Sir Gawain fought, is identified as a wood-dweller, a troll, the wild man of the woods, either beast or monster. Hughes's wodwo asks, "What am I?" He sees other creatures and the world itself and still does not know what he is or what relationship he has to anything outside himself. He wonders why he drinks water, why the frogs interest him, whether the weeds know him and name him. Trying to connect himself with something, he says of the weeds, "do I fit in their world?" But he doubts that he is a plant: "I seem/ separate from the ground and not rooted but dropped/ out of nothing casually." Finally he says, "I suppose I am the exact centre"; but even this assumption does not tell him much about what surrounds him. The wodwo's questions are exactly the questions of man and beast in such later poems as "Skylarks" and "Song of a Rat." In "Wodwo," Hughes tries for the first time the voice of the quester. In contrast to the hawk's certainty, the thrush's automatic purpose, the pike's murderous nature, this animal-monster-man is not a life subdued to its instrument, but a life tormented by its ignorance of its own nature, asking, "am I the first/ have I an owner." Receiving no answers, the wodwo concludes, "again very queer but I'll go on looking."

Some of the wodwo's questioning persists in "Gog I," first published in 1961 and included in *Wodwo* with two more parts written much later. Gog is the dragon of Revelation 12:4 who "stood before the woman who was about to bear a child, that he might devour the child when she brought it forth." When the woman escapes, Gog pursues her; unable to capture her, he grows angry and goes off to make war on the rest of her offspring. In Hughes's version he says, "I woke to a shout: 'I am Alpha and Omega,' " and in such a world he seems out of place. "I ran and an absence bounded beside me," he claims. His is the world of the animal, where the "dog's god is a scrap dropped from the table," "The mouse's saviour is a ripe wheat grain" — not the Word, Alpha and Omega. He asks, "What was my error?" He is displaced and frightened: "I do not look at the rocks and stones, I am frightened of what they see." Even his pursuit of the woman who bore the child seems to lack the purpose of the biblical Gog. He says, "My feetbones beat on the earth/ Over the sounds of motherly weeping." Finally he concludes, "I lie down. I become darkness./ Darkness that all night sings and circles stamping." Only the circling darkness testifies to his powers.

Hughes has claimed that "Gog," like his jaguar poem, is an invocation of a body of elemental, demonic force that so alarmed him that he wrote another part to keep it under control.[2] Actually, "Gog I" concentrates on the demon Gog's confusion in a world governed by the voice of God. The poem takes a much darker turn in its other two loosely related parts, which were written later and belong to a different stage in Hughes's development. Perhaps more indicative of work to come is "Theology," also published in 1961 as part of "Dully Gumption's College Courses"; that poem says of the creation story in Genesis, "All that's simply/ Corruption of facts." Drawing on Graves's *White Goddess,* Hughes explains that Adam ate the apple, Eve ate Adam, and the serpent ate Eve. The serpent, now sleeping his meal off in Paradise, smiles to hear "God's querulous calling." Here is the beginning of *Crow* — but a number of years and several poems separate "Theology" from *Crow.*

One such transitional poem is "Full Moon and Little Frieda," unique in Hughes's work for its openness to the child's views of the wonders of nature. It is a "cool small evening" as the poem opens, yet there is a sense that the evening is small not because the universe has diminished, but because it has contracted its force and beauty to the child's view. A small evening for a small child who is "listening./ A spider's web, tense for the dew's touch," "mirror/ To tempt a first star to a tremor." This give-and-take between the child and nature, so unlike anything Hughes ever described in the adult world, is delicately balanced by the realistic picture of cows coming home for milking, their "dark river of blood," "Balancing unspilled milk." Then the child cries, " 'Moon!' " " 'Moon! Moon!' " And the poem concludes, "The moon has stepped back like an artist gazing amazed at a work/ That points at him amazed."

When we consider that at about this time Plath was writing such poems as "The Moon and the Yew Tree" and "The Rival," in which she was trying to depict the female witch-muse moon, "Full Moon and Little Frieda" takes on a new significance. The little girl's first recognition of the image that was to haunt her mother (although here it is the man in the moon, not the woman in the moon) seems innocent enough. Yet, if the moon is an artist amazed at a work that points at him, then the little girl may be that work, another daughter of the moon, and, as such, heir to all the evils it contains which now seem to be contracted in amazement. "Full Moon and Little Frieda" does not develop this possibility, although the balance maintained here in the spider's web, the dew's touch, the tremoring star is so delicate that it seems destined to be upset. It is a strange poem for Hughes, since its affirmation of wonder seems to contradict almost everything else he ever wrote about nature. It seems hardly possible that this poem was written by the author of "Pibroch."

Hughes had a number of different poetic moods in this period. A contrast to "Full Moon and Little Frieda" is "Her Husband," a poem of domestic bitterness that seems to come directly out of the novels of D. H. Lawrence. The husband comes home "To grime the sink and foul towels and let her/ Learn" "The stubborn character of money." "The fried, woody chips, kept warm two hours in the oven/ Are only part of her answer." Like Plath's "Event," this poem is Hughes's reconsideration of that state that, in "Incompatibilities," he imagined "Cold-chisels two selfs single as it welds hot/ Iron of their separates to one." The man and woman are permanently separated. The drinking, singing, wife-baiting collier and his proud, clean, dutiful, hateful wife are stock characters, and their relationship, where both "will have their rights," is part of the standard love story of poverty in its peculiar English form. Here is a poem that attempts to deal with the same social class that Hughes was treating in his stories.

In the few poems published in 1963 and 1964, and in others written at that time, Hughes's vision darkens, his images intensify, his focus contracts to the concrete and human; yet at the same time these poems are dense and seem to deal with more than their announced subject. For example, "Kreutzer Sonata" draws on Tolstoy's story of the jealous Pozdynshev, who stabs his wife once he has discovered her with her fiddler, Trukachevsky. However, in Tolstoy the story is told by Pozdynshev, who relives the event as he recounts it to someone else. His monstrous monologue on the horrors and defilement of marriage that lead up to the murder is mitigated by his own abuse of himself and his refusal to show anything but the bad side of his character. In Hughes's poem the speaker is not Pozdynshev, but someone who stands back from him and judges: "Say goodbye, for your wife's sweet flesh goes off,/ Booty of the envious spirit's assault." Tolstoy's character claims that, because the Russian gentry eat too much, they have excess sexual drives that force them into the corruption of marriage. Hughes's speaker sees it from a different angle: it is not the excess of sexuality that torments the husband, but the fear of sex, the husband's idea that sex is the "excellent devil" which must be sacrificed. Hughes's point is stated clearly enough in the final stanza:

> Rest in peace, Tolstoy!
> It must have taken supernatural greed
> To need to corner all the meat in the world,
> Even from your own hunger.

This simple moral conclusion about Tolstoy's excessive moralizing does not really develop from the poem's concrete images, which draw attention to the sexuality of the murder. The poem opens with a powerful image right out of late Plath:

> Now you have stabbed her good
> A flower of unknown colour appallingly
> Blackened by your surplus of bile
> Blooms wetly on her dress.

The flower of her wound "Drinks its roots" in her vitality and "breathes them to nothing." It is "A sacrifice, not a murder," and the enraged husband becomes another manifestation of Hughes's Puritan who, denying his sexuality, becomes a murderer. His "dagger has outdone everybody's," especially "That fiddling, leering penis," Trukachevsky. The murder becomes a castration as "Trukachevsky is cut off/ From any further operation on you." The speaker asks, "Yet why should you castrate yourself/ To be rid of them both?" The "supernatural greed," the "envious spirit's assault," the sacrifice "for God" force simple judgments on the cuckolded husband, whose wife's blooming flower and sweet flesh celebrate what appears to be her innocent sexuality. Hughes ignores the husband's hatred, whipped up in Tolstoy's story, and his comment on the situation (why castrate yourself? why corner all the meat?) completely denies the rage infidelity inspires. While not exactly a defense of infidelity, Hughes's "Kreutzer Sonata" is an easy attack on the sexual repression of the injured partner.

The musical motif of "Kreutzer Sonata" continues in a much more oblique poem, "Cadenza," which shifts from realistic details to a series of surrealistic images. Framed by the violinist's shadow that vanishes in the first line and his crashing return in the final line, "Cadenza" develops through images of destruction and death. The rising grasshopper sucking a "remote cyclone" and the "full, bared throat of a woman walking water,/ The loaded estuary of the dead," suggest the domination of death and a death goddess. The speaker is both "the cargo/ Of a coffin attended by swallows" and "the water/ Bearing the coffin," an emblem of the dead and the world of death. But the coffin "escapes — as a black diamond,/ A ruby brimming blood,/ An emerald beating its shores." This curious combination of jewels, suggesting the death, vitality, and new life of a ritual sea burial, is obliterated in the final destruction that overtakes the world as "the whole sky dives shut like a burned land back to its spark — / A bat with a ghost in its mouth."

Echoes of Plath's poetry appear in the water images and blood-brimming ruby and bat ghost, in the general sense of undefined spirits hovering over this landscape, and in its surrealistic associations. The violinist, "Blue with sweat" at the end, seems to be haunted by the voices of the dead, the "coffin that will not be silent," "the bat with a ghost in its mouth," as if he were trying to escape from a terror he describes as overpowering. The poem, too private in its associations, never comes clear of the shadow it evokes, although its images are haunting. Whereas Hughes's poetry had been almost totally without human characters, now suddenly they enter, tormented by death.

The color symbolism of "Cadenza" reappears in "The Green Wolf," which moves from the opening more or less realistic description of the death of a paralyzed "neighbour" to the surrealism of folklore. The title refers to *The Golden Bough*'s account of the actual burning of a man clad in green (the Green Wolf) in the midsummer fire festivals in Normandy, in order to purify the community of witches and insure the return of vegetation. In Hughes's poem the sacrifice of the green wolf in the death of the paralyzed man takes place in a world dominated by the powers of the White Goddess, queen of the underworld, whom Plath had treated in her late poems. The "warn hawthorn blossoms," "Their palls of deathly perfume," are her emblems, as is the "beanflower" whose "living mouth" contains the spirits of the dead, contriving to be reborn as human beings by being eaten by women. In "the scarves of dew, the wet hair of nightfall," this witch-goddess snares the souls of the dead and absorbs the red of the "dark bloodclot," the green of the wolf-man, the black jet of the beanflower.

Without reference to Graves's myth, however, "The Green Wolf" would be almost completely obscure. Read with Graves in mind, the poem appears to be a bitter recognition of the death goddess. The hawthorn and the beanflower "Unmake and remake you," the speaker says. "You watch it approaching but you cannot fear it," although he sees its approach as "worse," "worst of all." Another poem of this period, "New Moon in January," pays tribute to the deathly demands of the moon-witch, "O sail of death!/ Frozen/ In ether." It is as if Hughes attempted to aproach the subject of Plath's death by addressing the moon-muse-witch whom she served; but he can only cry out in anguish to this image.

"New Moon in January" was published in 1963 and "Cadenza" in 1964, a period of very few poems and a time of extreme personal stress for Hughes. Their inchoate quality reveals his own difficulties with the subject of death. His tough guy pose collapses. Keith Sagar tells us that, in the month of Plath's suicide, Hughes wrote "The Howling of Wolves"; it was followed in March by "Song of a Rat," and from then until 1966 by nothing except a long play from which "Ghost Crabs" and Part III of "Gog" were salvaged.[3] Hughes seems to have turned back to the world of the animal as an escape from his private suffering, although the wolves' howling and the rat's song are cries of confusion and pain through which Hughes transmits his own anguish. The wolf, which had surged through "February" in pursuit of the "true world," has been reduced in "The Howling of Wolves" to a wodwo-like creature that does not know its own nature: "The eyes that never learn how it has come about/ That they must live like this,/ That they must live/ Innocence crept into minerals." "It howls you cannot say whether out of agony or joy." The "dead weight of darkness" that the wolves' howling drags up has lost the fecund and terrible potential it possessed in "The Bull Moses" or "Pike"; here the wolf "goes to and fro, trailing its haunches and whimpering horribly." Hughes contracts his entire bestiary in that image of the whimpering wolf. The demonic fury that he had so boldly evoked as a counterpoint to civilization in his early animal poems loses its force as he begins to search it for its ultimate source. Is it the joy he had earlier imagined, or the agony of never learning its own nature, he asks. This wolf is "small, it comprehends little," reflecting at this point the poet who creates it.

The same ignorance is in the song of the rat, another small creature which cannot deal with the meaninglessness of the universe. "Song of a Rat I" is entitled "The Rat's Dance" — the dance of death, which evokes from the rat "in the trap" only endless "screeching." The rat "cannot think," as man does, " 'This has no face, it must be God.' " Ultimately it can only die, "bow" and be still "With a little beseeching of blood on its nose-end." "The Rat's Vision" of Part II is of that purposeless life-force that fused the wolves' howling in a world of death and darkness. As the rat screeches, the dandelions, the yard cinders, and the trough by the gate all cry, " 'Do not go,' "although they too have "no future, only their infernal aftermath," and are "fatalist of starlight and zero." Part III, "The Rat's Flight," is without song as the "Shadow of the Rat/ Crossing into power/ Never to be buried," "supplants Hell." In "The Rat's Dance," the "Iron jaws" of death had been "stealing" the rat's "backbone" "For supplanting every human brain inside its skull with a rat-body that knots and unknots." The rat's flight is finally to cross into power through death, and in that peculiar word, "supplant," to become the hell in the human brain, which cannot confront its destiny. The rat's song, "Trying to uproot itself into each escaping screech," "threatening the constellations" "to keep off" "While it works this out," is like all songs, a futile effort to make sense out of a senseless universe. In the rat's accession to death and his failure to work out his torment, the galaxy is rocked: heaven shudders, the stars jolt, the "sleep-souls of eggs" wince. The harmony of the spheres in Part II had been "Forcing the rat's head down into godhead," forcing the rat to "Stay" in its life-death trap, to continue its disharmonious screeching, to accept it all as the work of the gods. When the rat passes into the power of the dark shadow, it refuses "the arrangement of stars," instead choosing Hell, where it reigns in threatening silence.

As Hughes's immediate poetic reaction to Plath's death, "Song of a Rat" is a painful effort to confront the agony of her life and poetry, the misery of his own suffering and guilt, the source of song in pain. The screeching of the rat in the trap, threatening the constellations to keep off, echoes the shrieks in Plath's late poems in which she tries to "work out" her terror; furthermore, it reflects her own demand that oppressive elements keep out of her way ("Off, off, eely tentacle!' in "Medusa," or "Step off!" in "Gulliver"). The stars in

Hughes's poem, "glitterers in the black," are transformations of one of Plath's images: the death figure in "Death & Co" "Bastard/ Masturbating a glitter," or the "black phones on hooks/ Glittering/ Glittering and digesting/ Voicelessness" in "The Munich Mannequins." The world Hughes now faces in "The Rat's Vision" is the landscape of his own grief: "The widowed land/ With its trees that know how to cry." The "Shadow of the Rat" "Never to be buried" is the shadow of death that will dominate Hughes's vision from this point onward.

"Gnat-Psalm," one of the first poems Hughes wrote when he began again in 1966, takes up where "Song of a Rat" left off. Although the gnats are "Dancing/ Dancing" and "Singing/ Singing," their message like the "rat-body that knots and unknots" inside the human brain is runic: "Scrambling their crazy lexicon,/ Shuffling their dumb Cabala," "Writing on the air, rubbing out everything they write," "Jerking their letters into knots, into tangles." They are "Immense magnets fighting around a centre," which eventually they locate in themselves. Their singing admits the presence of death: they are the nails in the still-dancing hands and feet of the crucified "gnat-god"; they witness the graveyards, the wind "bowing with long cat-gut cries"; yet still they sing and continue "A dance never to be altered," riding their bodies to death. But the speaker of the poem is not taken in by their optimism. He calls them "little Hasids," identifying them with the eighteenth-century sect that stressed the mystical element of religion and encouraged piety and optimism. "You are the angels of the only heaven!/ And God is an Almighty Gnat!/ You are the greatest of all the galaxies!" the speaker exclaims sardonically. He concludes by admitting that their dancing "Rolls my staring skull slowly away into outer space." For the gnats' lexicon is crazy, and the Cabala, an oral tradition, is "dumb." The spaces toward which the speaker stares are as empty as ever once the gnats have danced themselves to death; their song, unlike the rat's screeching, is a blind reconcilement to the unbearable facts of the universe.

Some of these facts are the subject of "The Bear," evidently part of a longer narrative poem which may explain its symbolic significance. As it appears here, the bear is "the gleam in the pupil" of the "huge, wide-open, sleeping eye of the mountain" — a genius loci, perhaps the she-bear to the Goddess of the Mill, or the Moon as Bear-Goddess, described by Graves. This bear seems to belong to that identification of the White Goddess as the spirit that turns the mill of the universe and, like Janus, rules beginnings and endings, since here the bear "is glueing/ Beginning to end/ With glue from people's bones." However, the bear is more clearly associated with endings as the poem develops. "The bear is a well/ Too deep to glitter/ Where your shout/ Is being digested," or the bear is "a river/ Where people bending to drink/ See their dead selves." These images connect the bear with the double, which Plath had employed in similar ways in "Mirror"; there a woman bends over a lake, "She comes and goes,/ Each morning it is her face that replaces the darkness." Hughes identifies his bear at the end: "He is the ferryman/ To dead land." As such, the bear is representative of the creator-destroyer who glues beginning to end to close the circle of creation. The surrealism of this poem passes through the animal world to some obscure activity behind it.

Through the howling of the wolves, the screechings of the rats, even the centrifugal psalm of the gnats, and the activity of the bear, Hughes begins to break out of the rational structures of his earlier poems, to evoke animal noises different from the ones that had sounded defiant in his early work, to retreat from the fixed position of the observer and to open himself to what he now confesses is bewildering. In this process he seems to move toward the position of the Plath persona who had always been uncertain and bewildered by what she could learn from the universe, and who (like Hughes's persona here) tended in her late poems to see the world in images of her own nightmares.

Hughes's early certainty about the animal world and his assurance that the animal runs beneath our consciousness, threatening any effort at ratiocination, are abandoned in these poems where the animal is itself a victim of blind force: the wolf does not know how it came to be, the rat is caught in a trap it cannot escape or understand, the gnats' mindless dancing to death is just a weaving and bobbing on "the nothing." The blank spaces and shivering heavens of Hughes's expanded but empty universe draw upon Plath's view of the "great Stasis," God "In your vacuous black,/ Stars stuck all over" in "Years," or on her depiction of "the big God" in "Lyonnesse," where "The white gape of his mind was the real Tabula Rasa." Her admission in "The Moon and the Yew Tree" that "I simply cannot see where there is to get to" seems shared by Hughes. Embedded in these poems in which Hughes puzzles over the meaninglessness of the universe, the pointless life force that rushes through a death-ridden world, is a concern with the meaning of language itself, the possibility of singing at all in such a world. Only the gnats seem able to keep going, although they scramble their words and shuffle their interpretations; their activity suggests the difficulty of their effort. The lines will not be read except haltingly ("Scribbling on the air, sparring sparely") or jarringly ("Jerking their letters into knots, into tangles") in a mimetic form of their song. The rat, trying to uproot itself in every screech, is a symbol of the poet Hughes felt himself to be: his lines abandon traditional rhythms, his language turns to disharmony, and his speaker attempts to drag his meaning up from the depths.

Two poems that Hughes wrote during this time appear to hark back to his earlier preoccupations with a predatory animal spirit, as if he were trying to rediscover by repetitive incantations the spirits with which he seems to have lost contact. "Ghost Crabs" is a nightmare invasion by giant ghost crabs; they come out of the sea at nightfall when the sea darkens and "A depth darkness thickens," the same subterranean world of the pike. The poem opens slowly, as in a meditation. The crabs come, first appearing to be rocks, "mangling their pallor"; then they are identified as crabs, giant crabs, ghost crabs, in an attenuated process of recognition, reminiscent of "The Thought-Fox." They "emerge/ An invisible disgorging of the sea's cold," "spill inland," "Gliding like shocks through water," "Press through our nothingness where we sprawl on our beds." But these spirits do not come after men: "They stalk each other, they fasten on to each other,/ They mount each other, they tear each other to pieces." "They are the powers of this world," "the turmoil of history," "the convulsion/ In the roots of blood, in the cycles of concurrence," "God's only toys." They only ruffle our dreams, although we awake "With a gasp, in a sweat burst, brains jamming blind/ Into the bulb-light," as if they had attacked us. Man appears totally insignificant in the world of the giant crabs: for them "our cluttered countries are empty battleground." If they are in fact God's only toys, they absolve man of that tormenting possibility; but their presence opens the greater horror that man is the ghost, that "nothingness," without any substance to the powers of the world. The turmoil of history, the convulsion of the blood root refers, then, not to human history or to human life, but to some primeval force in which man does not even figure.

While the crabs were ghosts, the jaguar in "Second Glance at a Jaguar" is an actual animal, again the jaguar at the zoo from *The Hawk in the Rain,* although here described in much more elaborate physical detail. His motion is perfectly captured in the clear description of "The hip going in and out of joint, dropping the spine/ With the urgency of his hurry." He is described in a series of similes: "Like a thick Aztec disemboweller," "Showing his belly like a butterfly," "His head/ Is like the worn down stump of another whole jaguar,/ His body is just the engine shoving it forward." The jaguar is "Muttering some mantrah, some drum-song of murder/ To keep his rage brightening," "Wearing the spots off from the inside,/ Rounding some revenge," "Hurrying through the underworld, soundless." Here is an animal out of Hughes's earlier period, although described with a new intensity. The present participles of the verbs keep pace with the jaguar, "Going like a prayer-wheel," never stopping, building up image after image of ferocity. The poet's mantra keeps beating until the spirit of the underworld, emblematized in the jaguar, arises "soundless" at the poem's end.

More typical of this period is "Skylarks," which begins with a description of the properties of the skylarks ("Barrel-chested," "whippet head," "leaden/ With muscle") that serve them "For the struggle/ Against/ Earth's centre," the effort "To supplant/ Life from its centre." In Part II the birds, too, become symbols of some driving force; their command is "Not die/ But climb/ Climb/ Sing/ Obedient as to death a dead thing." The rapture of Shelley's "blithe spirit" has become Hughes's "song, incomprehensibly both ways — / Joy! Help! Joy! Help!" Like the howling of the wolves, the skylarks' song may be for either agony or joy. They seem first to be "like a hunting arrow," "Like a bullet," flying directly upward to a sure target. Yet in another view the larks are "Scrambling/ In a nightmare difficulty/ Up through the nothing." The command to "Not die/ But climb" seems to arise from an energy that is automatic ("its heart drumming like a motor") and, on the other hand, from an imperative to struggle against the odds. The skylarks in Part V are "Like sacrifices set floating/ The cruel earth's offerings/ The mad earth's missionaries." Like the gnats dancing their bodies to death, the larks are "Battering and battering their last sparks out at the limit." All this energy expended toward nothing forces the observer of the skylarks to admit, "So it's a relief" "When they've had enough, when they're burned out/ And the sun's sucked them empty." Then they dip and float and stoop, and the speaker says "maybe the whole agony was for this/ The plummeting dead drop." But the drop to earth is no more a suicide drive than their battering through the ether, because just before they plunge into the earth they glide off, land on a wall-top, like plucky survivors, "Weightless,/ Paid-up,/ Alert,/ Conscience perfect." The poem about the skylarks' climb and drop is, on one level, simply an accurate description of their flight; but the presence of an observer, who supposes that the skylarks just let their gaspings rip in and out through their voicebox yet exclaims that their song is "incomprehensibly both ways," who feels his "idleness curdles/ Seeing the lark labour" and senses a relief when they stop, forces the skylarks' flight into some human significance. The bird which lands on the wall, "crest up," mocking such efforts, is a progenitor of crow; but at this point the speaker's concerns have been too intrusive to fade completely away. What does the bird's flight signify?, the speaker asks again and again, and the "alert" bird offers no answer. In *Selected Poems* Hughes added two new sections to "Skylarks," underscoring its death theme and the bird's agony. However, those sections are not successfully grafted onto the original poem, and they leave open two possibilities: the birds may be obedient to death, or simply frolicking in the heavens.

The skylarks' cry is heard from a different source in "A Wind Flashes the Grass," where the wind's "incomprehensible cry/From the boughs" "Sets us listening for below words,/ Meanings that will not part from the rock." This poem measures the distance Hughes has traveled from the certainty of "Still Life," where he announced the presence of the "maker of the sea" in the harebell's veins. In the later poem the wind in the trees is "the oracle of the earth," which will not divulge its meaning. Even the trees "too are afraid they too are momentary/ Streams rivers of shadow."

The predominance of darkness, fear, and incomprehension in these poems is concentrated in "You Drive in a Circle," in "the swamped moor-wallows, the mist-gulfs of no-thinking" where the sheep, "rooted like sponges," are undeterred. But the speaker asks, "What could they lose, however utterly they drowned?/ Already sodden as they are with the world, like fossils." Turning his question on himself, he says, "Where are you heading? Everything is already here," "Your destination waits where you left it." In "Heptonstall," the village in the Pennines where Plath was buried, Hughes locates his own destination in "Black village of gravestones" "Whose dreams die back/ Where they were born." His conclusion is a simple trick of letter reversal that swerves from meaning: "Life tries./ Death tries./ The stone tries./ Only the rain never tires." Out of this same dark valley in "Ballad from a Fairy Tale" he sees in a dream the vision of a swan, "A slow, colossal power/ Far too heavy for the air/ Writhing slowly upwards/ It came beating towards me." He inquires, " 'Mother,' " " 'O Mother,' " " 'Will it be a blessing?' " But the mother's answer he dares not write. The "enormous beauty" passes opposite the house where his father was born, where his grandmother died, and leaves the valley dark. This swan with its "bare, lovely feet" and long dress fluttering seems to be a figure out of Plath's poetry, although Graves's identification of the White Swan with the goddess of poetry may be significant here. That her presence strikes this speaker with terror and silence is evident in the darkness she casts over the valley and her confirmation, as the speaker says, of "all I had dreaded/ But with its meaning doubled," although never stated. This terrifying female spirit, as well as the mother figure, will appear in "Gog III" in much more ominous form. The ambivalent awe and fright she instills makes her one of Hughes's private demons.

This spirit hovers over "Stations," which starts, like "The Green Wolf," with death. The speaker here claims he can understand the "haggard eyes/ Of the old/ Dry wrecks"; but by implicit contrast it is this other, "wild look — out of an egg/ Laid by your absence" that he cannot understand, although he says, "In the great Emptiness you sit complacent,/ Blackbird in wet snow." Again Hughes draws on Plath's images: the wild looks of her later poems, and her claim in "Paralytic" that "Dead egg, I lie/ Whole/ On a whole world I cannot touch." The blackbird, like the bat of "Cadenza," is the spirit of death, her image. What torments him is the "surrender to total Emptiness." This is as close as Hughes ever comes to a direct poetic recognition of Plath's death:

> Absence. It is your own
> Absence
>
> Weeps its respite through your accomplished music,
> Wraps its cloak dark about your feeding.

The poem concludes with the assurance that "Whether you say it, think it, know it," "it happens" — death happens, leaving "The head with its vocabulary useless."

A number of poems in *Wodwo* which were written late in the seven-year cycle of its creation reveal Hughes's attempts to discover the origins of the death principle which he had handled in a variety of the earlier, more private poems. Although his searching for an underlying plot that would make his mental vocabulary useful shows him moving toward the grim mythological world of *Crow,* these poems engage the agony of the human predicament more directly than *Crow.* They are only tentative gropings toward the stripped-down version of the world in *Crow,* and they draw heavily on *The White Goddess.* Graves's explanation of the displacement of the universal Goddess, whose devotees accepted pleasure and pain, by the Universal God of pure Meditation, the Logos, whose devotees divided the true spiritual Creation from a false material one, provides the background for Hughes's "Logos." It opens, "God gives the blinding pentagram of His power/ For the frail mantle of a person." In Graves, God's pentagram of power consists of the five heavenly bodies that symbolize the five material senses (Moon, Mars, Mercury, Jupiter, Venus), regarded as sources of error by spiritually minded servants of the God of pure Logos. By molding this power onto the flesh, the God of spirit made its survival "unlikely" and against the odds — but, if it did survive, it would be evidence of his own "perfect strength." Birth and procreation became by "God's leave" a "doomed bid/ To grapple to everlasting/ Their freehold of life." In such a system "Creation convulses in nightmare." The material world, the maternal aspect of creativity, the power of the Universal Goddess will not be reduced so easily to pure spirit. "God's first cry" is not the Logos, but a response to the persistence of the material, creative world, this "nightmare moving/ Still in its mouth." God's first cry is also the cry of the female destroyer-creator goddess, who now is known chiefly for her destructiveness and in the sea is "pulling everything to pieces/ Except its killers." Her cry precedes both the "Logos" and the male spirit God who created the "Logos." She is God's mother, and "God is a good fellow, but His mother's against him." Hughes's poem glosses Graves's comment that "What ails Christianity is that the old Mother-Goddess religious theme and the new Almighty-God theme are fundamentally irreconcilable."[4] Because the Logos would be identified as pure spirit, it puts itself in eternal opposition to the material and maternal world, and the powers of creativity turn destructive, nurturing only killers.[5]

"Reveille" turns to the biblical creation myth, reading it more carefully than orthodox Christianity has. Sounding like *Crow*, "Reveille" opens with a deceptively simple admission: "No, the serpent was not/ One of God's ordinary creatures." As a "legless land-swimmer" creeping "with a purpose," he seems to come out of the sea (that territory of the Mother-Goddess) not to test Eve's faith, but to awaken in Adam and Eve (created by the God of pure spirit to be "Each the ever-lasting/ Holy One of the other") the awareness that, in such a paradise of spirit, their flesh will cause them pain. Graves describes the Orphic creation myth in which a benign serpent god had coupled with the White Goddess in the form of a female serpent. This serpent was not one of God's ordinary creatures, but a manifestation of the Mother-Goddess that the male God of Christianity ousted. Her return in the Christian version of creation as a male serpent not only "crushed all Eden's orchards" but stretched out beyond Eden, "The black, thickening river of his body" "Over the ashes of the future." The female creator-destroyer again becomes, in the male myth of Christianity, only a destroyer.

The fate of a world that represses the goddess is eternal destruction in "Karma." The whole history of wars from Zion to Buchenwald is "a hundred and fifty million years of hunger" in which "the heart, a gulping mask, demands, demands/ Appeasement/ For its bloody possessor." The newborn baby, lamenting that it ever lived in "Logos," appears in "Karma" with its "cry for milk/ From the breast/ Of the mother/ Of the God/ Of the world/ Made of Blood." The poem ends with the claim that "they" (perhaps the years of human destruction) "have gone into dumber service," "fatten/ Under the haddock's thumb," "have melted like my childhood under earth's motherly curve," have so permeated the world with destruction that they cannot be dissociated from life itself, cannot be identified even by the poulterer's "hare hanging/ Upside down above the pavement/ Staring into a bloody bag," or by "eyes from the depths/ Of the mirror's seamless sand."

In "Gog II and III" Hughes develops this plot most fully. Gog of Part I, as we have seen, belongs to the category of the wodwo, a creature uncertain of his own identity but rendered more ignorant because he is out of place in a world governed by the spirit which announces that he is Alpha and Omega. From Hughes's attacks on the Christian concept of Logos, pure spirit, in "Logos" and "Reveille," we can place Gog in a larger mythical framework. The song "jarring" his mouth is the nightmare moving in the mouth of God, evidence of the powers of darkness that the God of pure spirit would deny. "Gog II" begins with the announcement that "The sun erupts. The moon is deader than a skull" — the apparent victory of the spiritual creation represented by the sun over the material creation represented by the moon, the male sun over the female moon, again images drawn from Graves. In this world the "creatures of earth/ Are mere rainfall rivulets"; the material world is denied, while "the atoms of saints' brains are swollen with the vast bubble of nothing," the emptiness of spirit. But the speaker asks, "Then whose/ Are these/ Eyes?" "Sun and moon, death and death," "Death and death and death — / Her mirrors." The section ends in a chant to the moon goddess who, "deader than a skull," "mirrors" only death, death, death. The moon of Plath's "The Moon and the Yew Tree" or of "Elm" or the "immaculate/ Cauldron, talking and crackling," "A disturbance of mirrors" in "The Couriers" seems to have contributed itself to this section. However, in "Gog II" Gog is nowhere present, and the female is associated not with the "motherly weeping" of "Gog I" but with the principle of death itself, seeming to confuse the story of the monster Gog.

"Gog III" introduces the "hooded horseman of iron" who, coming out of "the wound-gash in the earth," "Out of the blood-dark womb," seems to be both the representation of the female destructive creator and the "Holy Warrior" of the patriarchal Christian God, seeking revenge on the female, searching for "the softness of the throat, the navel, the armpit, the groin." His eyes "have found the helm of the enemy, the grail,/ The womb-wall of the dream that crouches there, greedier than a foetus,/ Suckling at the root-blood of the origins, the salt-milk drug of the mothers." The monster iron horseman seeks to free himself from the monstrous mother who has created and nurtured him. The poem pleads,

"Shield him from the dipped glance," "The groved kiss," "Lift him/ Out of the octopus maw and the eight lunatic limbs/ Of the rocking, sinking cradle." Yet in the end he rides effortlessly on "the horse shod with vaginas of iron" and "Gallops over the womb that makes no claim."[6] The "fanged grail" and glittering "lance-blade, the gunsight," show him to be a nightmarish version of the Grail Knight seeking the meaning of the Holy Mysteries — mysteries now perverted not only from their pagan identity with male and female sexuality, but also from their Christian connections with the crucifixion. What he seeks is within himself: the "fanged grail" "Whose coil is under his ribs," as well as "in the belly of woman," and "Whose satiation is in the grave."

Hughes's poem draws upon the conception of English history that he had elaborated as Shakespeare's myth in the introduction to his selection of Shakespeare's poems. There he talks of the drastic consequences of the Reformation in which the goddess of medieval and pre-Christian England, who was the goddess of natural law, of love, of all sensation and organic life, was drawn into court by the Puritan Jehovah, a contest clearly drawn from Graves's view of the battle between the pagan Goddess and the Christian God. Hughes says, "When this suppressed nature goddess erupts, possessing the man who denied her, and creating this king-killing man of chaos, Shakespeare has conducted what is essentially an erotic poetry into an all-inclusive body of political action — especially that action in which a rightful ruler is supplanted by a half-crazed figure who bears in some form the mark of the beast."[7] The iron horseman of "Gog III" is that half-crazed figure, trying to kill not the king but the woman who has herself become a monster.

He, too, is a death principle. His iron purpose is in contrast to the monster in "Gog I," who wanders confused, "massive on earth," his feet beating "Over the wounds of motherly weeping." Hughes presents these characters again in his children's book, *The Iron Man,* where two monsters, a space-bat-angel-dragon which eats people, and an iron man who eats iron, battle each other until the iron man wins. The space-bat-angel-dragon becomes his slave in heaven, singing the music of the spheres which fascinates the world's people. Between the massive dragon of "Gog I" and the knight of "Gog III" there is little to choose: one is frightened and uncertain of himself, but probably not dangerous; the other is resolute, stalwart, and a killer. The one's purpose keeps the other's confusion in balance. The horseman of iron has something of the mechanical about him, while the massive figure is attuned to the terrors of the earth. There emerge in these two figures the skeletons of two opposing centers of power, the nature monster and the principle monster, that have a long history in Hughes's poetry. Behind the horseman of iron is the Puritan, and behind the massive figure is nature. In his children's story the iron man wins when these two forces oppose each other, but the space-bat-angel-dragon enjoys a glorious transmutation and becomes a kind of victor in his defeat. Hughes performs no such redeeming ritual in "Gog." The massive figure feels himself hunted and watched by eyes that mirror death.

The plot of "Gog" is essentially obscure. There is evidence in "Logos," "Reveille," and "Karma" that the principle of creativity has been repressed by a patriarchal religion for so long that it has erupted into its violent opposite; such evidence would lead us to identify the monster, whether horseman or Gog with that Puritan repression. The horseman of iron recalls the iron arteries of Calvin in "The Warriors of the North." But the goddess of creativity, love, and organic life is nowhere present in the poem, which devotes its chief verbal energies to a depiction of the vengeful male warrior hunting down the insatiable power that crouches at the womb wall. "Gog" may be Hughes's expression of the violence that evolves from the suppression of the nature goddess; but in the triumph of the iron horseman there is an element of finality, even glee, which suggests that he is the ultimate victor.

When the poet cries, "Bring him clear of the flung web," "Shield him," "Lift him," he may be repeating the Puritan Jehovah's desperate desires, or he may be expressing an equally desperate identification with this figure of force.

The nature goddess appears here only as the threatening monster she has become in a male-dominated world — "the coil that vaults from the dust," the kiss "that swamps the eyes with darkness," "the octopus maw." Although, in his comments on Shakespeare and in his attacks on the Logos, Hughes posits the higher claims of the original Mother-Goddess, he was never able to write a poem in which he celebrated her. She appears always as a monster, giving him (as in "Ballad from a Fairy Tale") answers he dares not write, messages through which he sees all he had dreaded. The dread is partly the death dream of "Gog," but it is also dread of being engulfed: "The unborn child beats on the womb-wall./ He will need to be strong/ To follow his weapons toward the light." The fear of not escaping from the womb wall is a fear of woman — not the fear that her creativity has been suppressed, but the fear that it might not be overcome.

If the stories and play in *Wodwo* may be taken as "unversified episodes of the events behind the poems," then they, too, reveal the male's fear that he will be engulfed. In "The Rain Horse," a man returns after twelve years to a hill he had remembered. While he is waiting for the "right feeling" to arise in him, he is attacked by a rain horse, the spirit of the place, which he tries unsuccessfully to fend off with stones. When he gets free, the "ordeal with the horse" "hung under the surface of his mind, an obscure confusion of fright and shame." In "Sunday," the boy Michael goes to watch Billy Red, the rat-catcher, kill rats with his teeth, but Michael is sickened by the grotesque spectacle and runs away, unable to speak. The presence of a girl who ignores him at first but speaks to him afterward, as he is escaping from the male rat-killing world, suggests that part of Michael's fear is of the flesh and sex.

The protagonist of "Snow" is lost in a snowstorm, trying to figure out where he had come from and where he can go in a world that frustrates his every effort, although he is confident that "so long as I keep control, keep my mind firm," "I have nothing to do but endure." Grooby in "The Harvesting" is another man trying to endure, hunting a hare as he fades in and out of consciousness, the victim of a sunstroke.

Finally he fires at the hare and "blackness struck him," this time permanently. "The enormous white dog's head opened beside him," and the actual collier's dog becomes a surrealistic image of engulfing death. The boy in "The Suitor" stands outside the dark house of the girl whom he scarcely knows, although he thinks she seems to smile at him in school. He discovers there another suitor, a watcher in the dark who plays the flute in her garden. Somehow the presence of this rival drives the bewildered boy to "a slow, skin-stretching grimace, a contorting leopard-mask," as he abandons his sexual innocence and assumes the grin of the predator.[8] The wounded Ripley in the play "The Wound" wanders through a surrealistic landscape of death and destruction, presided over by ominous female figures. When he gets to his camp, the soldier who takes him in says only, "That's animal instinct for you." Ripley has survived the temptations of death, symbolized by the women who threaten always to deter him from his effort to get back to his camp.

The presence of destructive forces and death in these works, along with the persistence of an animal instinct for survival, bind them together and tie them to the poems of *Wodwo*. Much more than the poems, however, these pieces evoke the fear of the male against which his animal instincts struggle but which also arises from those same instincts. The fear of the physical in "Sunday" and the adoption of the leopard mask to cover it in "The Suitor" reveal the boy's confused response to his emerging sexuality; but the rain horse that attacks the man returning to the landscape of his youth also carries a sexually frightening connotation, more clearly expressed in the seductiveness of the female death figures in "The Wound." Certainly these prose pieces provide a much more sensitive treatment of sexuality than any of Hughes's previous work. His earlier poems, where love is the "slavering rush" for the competing breath of two wolves, or "fierce/ Hammer-blows" that weld two to one, look crude and easy from this perspective. But the more difficult and complex vision of *Wodwo* is not without its own obscurity.

The tendency in Hughes's poetry has always been to simplify. His earliest vision was of a world split into two parts, one symbolized by the civilized, repressed zoo-goer and the other by the animal image of vitality and fury that threatened and tantalized him. Exploring this animal nature as he developed, Hughes could evoke its intense rage, its nightmare terrors, its streamlined efficiency, but never its potential for vital energy or creative force. He attempted to cover this aspect of his poetry by saying, "Poetry only records these movements in the general life . . . it doesn't instigate them. . . . Every society has its dream that has to be dreamed. . . . We are dreaming a perpetual massacre."[9] The fact is, however, that in his invocations of demonic fury, in his poems of jaguars and hawks and the heart's bloody demands, he is instigating these movements, deliberately calling them up to poetic expression.

Perhaps only in *Wodwo* does he begin to express his own bafflement at his persistent poetic effort. The violent energy that invades the poems of this volume force from him, as from the skylarks, the scream, "Joy! Help!" Is it from agony or joy, the howling of the wolves, the song of this poet? The point at which he uttered this question is the moment of the most naked self-revelation for Hughes, whose powers of control are dangerously repressive, quick to shut off the agony. The role of the quester was a difficult one for him to assume because, if he did not know all the answers, he certainly was fascinated by those creatures (like the hawk and the jaguar) who did. In "Wodwo" and "Gog I," as in "The Howling of Wolves" and "Song of a Rat," he speaks through a different identity and adopts a new voice. In the later poems of *Wodwo,* turning to Graves's myths, Hughes was able to regain control of the questing spirit by structuring a new plot for creation. Again, an all-knowing speaker expresses himself with defiant conviction. But the forces he was repressing emerge again in the ambivalence toward the female in "Gog II and III," where she appears to be a monster that the monster must kill.[10] The strategy of Hughes's poems is to blame the man of iron, the Puritan half-crazed representative, for the perversion of the pagan goddess of fertility; but as the female figure emerges in his own poetry, she comes only as the symbol of death. Even if she has been shoved down into our deepest memory and so offers no positive evidence of her existence for the modern poet who would serve her, can he in fact posit her as a counterpoint to male destructiveness? When Hughes evokes the goddess, he evokes fears of engulfment that perhaps express his own psychic terror in the face of female power. To control this feeling of helplessness he turns, in *Crow*, to a myth that will contain her.

In these poems of *Wodwo*, and later in the simplicity of *Crow*, Hughes seems to return to his original subject, violence, with new attention. What interests him now is not killer animals, but an unkillable life force that persists against all odds. The turbulent energy that Plath had celebrated in "Ariel" and "Lady Lazarus" becomes Hughes's subject, but while she dramatizes it, he typically meditates upon it. Whereas the exclamation point is Plath's characteristic mark of punctuation, Hughes's is the question mark: "What are they dragging up and out on their long leashes of sound?" "What am I?" "What was my error?" He is baffled by the violence that exhilarated Plath. On that point the two seem to reverse their original positions — it was Hughes who located the fulcrum of violence in the hawk early in his career, when Plath was still meditating on the light that might shine out of the rook in rainy weather. As they developed, Plath came to locate herself at the fulcrum, while Hughes stood back to explore the nature of the universe.

Both Hughes's language and his stance are more general and remote than Plath's. Even when he talks about blood, he distances it with his terminology: "the gruelling relapse and prolonguer of their blood," for example. Something of the concreteness of Plath's blood imagery is evident in "Gog III," with its insistence on "the wound-gash in the earth," "the blood-dark womb," "The blood-crossed Knight," "the root-blood of the origins"; but even here Hughes seems to repeat the word without evoking an image. He tries to maintain the positive and negative associations that blood imagery has in Plath's poetry, but the abstractions of the poem work against him. Not until *Crow* does Hughes succeed in using Plath's concrete images of violence.

Notes

[1] Plath, *Letters Home,* p. 392.

[2] Hughes, "Ted Hughes and Crow," pp. 8-9.

[3] Sagar, *Art of Ted Hughes,* p. 61.

[4] Graves, *White Goddess,* p. 390.

[5] "Logos" provides an interesting background for Plath's "Fever 103°," which also attacks the idea of purity associated with a patriarchal religion. The "tongues of hell" cannot lick clean the "aguey tendon." When the woman rises at the end of that poem, she casts off the male world in which female flesh is "whorey" and achieves a paradise in which she is the light, the heat, the flush, a pure image of female vitality.

[6] This horseman is reminiscent of the monster in Plath's early poem, "The Snowman on the Moor," who appears with "Ladies' sheaved skulls," "dangling from that spoke-studded belt."

[7] Hughes, *With Fairest Flower While Summer Lasts,* p. xviii.

[8] Sagar says that Hughes wrote "The Suitor" on the day after the birth of his son, Nicholas. When he read the story to Plath, she said, "That is your best story. But the girl is me, and the flute player is death." See Sagar, *Art of Ted Hughes,* p. 165*n*6.

[9] Hughes, "Ted Hughes and Crow," pp. 6-7.

[10] For a discussion of the difference between Plath's and Hughes's treatment of this female goddess, see Anthony Libby, "God's Lioness and the Priest of Sycorax: Plath and Hughes," *Contemporary Literature,* XV (Summer, 1974), 386-405.

EIGHT

Crow

Crow marks a new stage in Hughes's career and is, despite its flaws, a significant accomplishment. To examine it here, at the end of a study of Plath and Hughes, is to look at it from a particular perspective, but not one which distorts its achievement. *Crow* shares with Plath's late poems not only a tone and style, but also certain thematic concerns that are quite new to Hughes's work. At the same time, *Crow* is the most elaborate exploration of issues that have concerned Hughes from the beginning of his career. A consideration of the book in this double context should enrich, rather than diminish, our appreciation of it.

To begin where Hughes himself has admitted beginning, we may consider his discovery of a new voice and, with that voice, a means of expressing a vision more directly, concretely, and forcefully.

> The first idea of *Crow* was really an idea of style. . . . The idea was originally just to write his songs, the songs that a Crow would sing. In other words, songs with no music whatsoever, in a super-simple and super-ugly language which would in a way shed everything except just what he wanted to say without any other consideration and that's the basis of the style of the whole thing.[1]

This stylistic breakthrough, similar to the one Plath made in *Ariel*, freed Hughes from the conventional rhythms of his early work — an important departure, since he has said that "the very sound of metre calls up the ghosts of the past and it is difficult to sing one's own tune against that choir." Although *Crow* is not without its musical echoes, its style or styles allow Hughes to sing a tune that has aroused a critical fury similar to that which *Ariel* aroused, and for somewhat the same reason: Hughes had simply gone too far.

Of course, going too far is exactly what Hughes was attempting. He has said that the poems were something of a shock to write, and that some arrived with a sense of having done something taboo. However, an important rhetorical strategy in *Crow* (and much less a matter of inspiration than Hughes would have us believe) is the deliberate invasion of taboo or prohibited ground through the comic inversion of sacred texts, the mischievous deflation of a grand style, the parodic language of the unheroic but super-bird Crow.[2] Hughes's new style tunes itself against the choirs of convention, but the super-ugly language of Crow frequently depends on our knowledge of the stuctures it subjects to outrageous abuse. Crow's songs sometimes are nothing more than the naughty schoolboy's facile blasphemy, just as Plath's women occasionally sound like petulant children. But in the best poems Hughes hones his style to a flat, brutal plainness that drives straight into taboo areas with what he described in "Thrushes" as "An efficiency which/ Strikes too streamlined for any doubt to pluck at it/ Or obstruction deflect."

Hughes had been working toward this efficiency for years. Although some of the poems in *Wodwo* announce it, too many of them are weighted with doubts and rerouted by deflections. Like the monster in "Wodwo," Hughes seems to be searching in that volume for answers to vital questions, but the process itself is, of necessity, bumbling and inefficient. *Crow* goes straight to the point, shedding all but the precise words he wanted to say. Yet Crow's style is not so much a matter of stripped-down language as of a bold and defiant posture. In this he resembles no one more than the speakers of Plath's late poems who never flinch in their attacks. The sheer will of the speaker propels Plath's poems, just as Crow's bravado drives his song. The language and the stance admit no qualifications either in Plath or in Hughes, whose every line is a stab against rational expectations and the conventionally prohibited. Both Plath's women and Crow speak as if in a trance, and the force of their declamations derives from the simple, repeated, incantatory style and imperturbable stance of the spellbound. Hughes would have us believe that he himself was spellbound when he wrote them, and that the poems simply erupted on the page from that deep level of psychic experience shared by the poet and the conjurer. He has also claimed that Plath's late poems were messages from the same depth, written at top speed — statements from the power in control of her life. Whatever their source, these poems share certain rhetorical strategies which may provide us with a greater insight into their effectiveness than any rumination on the way they were written.

Much of the verbal power of Crow and of Plath's women derives from skill at caricature. A highly self-conscious device in its skeletal exposures, caricature may also express the simplifications of the total unself-consciousness of the possessed. In Plath, ordinary human beings are turned into grotesque stick figures. The flat-hatted auntie in "The Tour," the "Sad hag" of "Lesbos," the empty-headed boy and sweetie in "The Applicant," as well as the Fascist "Daddy" and "Herr Enemy" of "Lady Lazarus," all are creatures stripped naked as they enter Plath's range of vision. Normal human relations are reduced here to stylized and sinister actions: love becomes a hook, a kitchen conversation turns into the sucking of the "blood-loving bat," and the baby is a nail driven in. Crow's imagination is equally reductive. Although the weird and gloomy drawings of Leonard Baskin were the supposed impetus for *Crow*, in fact Hughes's poems have more in common with a hard-edged cartoon image than with Baskin's sprawling, ragged figures.[3] Like Plath's characters, Crow revels in caricature; in his version St. George hacks away at the monster with "A ceremonial Japanese decapitator," Oedipus turns into a "howling brat," the sphynx into a "Dickey-bird," the Fall into a new game, God into a bungler.

Crow clearly relishes not only the cartoon caricature, but also the effects of the animated comic strip. The action of "Crow and Mama" is straight out of the preposterous antics of something like the "Road Runner," using its every cliché.

For example, Crow "jumped into the car the towrope/ Was around her neck he jumped out./ He jumped into the plane but her body was jammed in the jet — " then "He jumped into the rocket and its trajectory/ Drilled clean through her heart" but, crashing on the moon, he "awoke and crawled out/ Under his mother's buttocks." The unkillable and indefatigable Crow has the tenacity and the frustrations of the cartoon figure. Somewhat like Plath's speakers, although more raucous, he is a survivor. In "Truth Kills Everybody" he holds on not only to "a naked powerline, 2000 volts" but also to "A gone steering wheel bouncing towards a cliff edge," and finally to the "earth, shrunk to the size of a hand grenade" which, as every cartoon addict would expect, explodes and "BANG!/ He was blasted to nothing." Again, like the cartoon figure and also like Plath's speakers, Crow inhabits a rapidly shifting reality so that atrocities flick by with astounding speed. He is able to recount the most violent events, one after the other, without pause. Just as Plath's speaker can call her father God, Fascist, vampire, bastard, shifting identities without reflection, so Crow can change shape to deal with anything his imagination casts up to him.

Closely allied to the caricatures of Crow's songs is his penchant for the double tactic of hyperbole and understatement. Plath uses the same combination, but while her poems begin with understatement and often end in hyperbolic threats, Crow's songs typically recount wildly exaggerated events and conclude with the deflating punch line of the tough guy. For example, Crow's incredible feats in "Oedipus Crow," where "Mummies stormed his torn insides" yet "He contorted clear," and where "A gravestone fell on his foot/ And took root" but still he bit through the bone and fled, conclude with Crow 'One-legged, gutless and brainless, the rag of himself" and "Death tripped him easy." Crow's tight-lipped comment on this situation: "Crow dangled from his one claw — corrected./ A warning." Again, in "Crow's Song of Himself," the hyperbole of the repeated claims builds from the first statement that "When God hammered Crow/ He made gold" to the final boast that "When God said: 'You win, Crow,'/ He made the Redeemer"; but they are superbly blasted by the final lines: "When God went off in despair/ Crow stropped his beak and started in on the two thieves." Crow's typical strategy is to endure fantastic struggles and then give up, or turn his back, or lie cataleptic or speechless with admiration.

Behind these tactics is simply Crow's tough-minded will to endure, but his are also the techniques of the prankster who makes trouble and then retreats behind a bush to watch it work. In "A Childish Prank," for example, Crow steps in while God falls asleep pondering the problem of the soulless Adam and Eve he has created. Crow invents sexuality by biting the "Worm, God's only son,/ Into two writhing halves" and stuffing the tail end into the man and the head half into woman, where it peers "out through her eyes/ Calling its tail-half to join up quickly, quickly." Crow's final comment: "God went on sleeping./ Crow went on laughing." In "Crow Blacker than ever," the prankster Crow nails the separating heaven and earth together "So man cried, but with God's voice./ And God bled, but with man's blood." It was "A horror beyond redemption," but as the agony grew Crow grinned, "Crying: 'This is my Creation,'/ Flying the black flag of himself." In these guises Crow is a modern version of the trickster, the double agent from ancient legends who works in constant opposition to the well-wishing creator. He spreads disorder and strife, and at the same time can operate (usually unintentionally) against evil forces and for the benefit of mankind.[4] In "A Horrible Religious Error" Crow acts in this latter capacity. He confronts the serpent, and while God's "grimace writhed" and men and women collapsed into whispers of " 'Your will is our peace,' " Crow fronts the fact without flinching, "took a step or two forward,/ Grabbed this creature by the slackskin nape,/ Beat the hell out of it, and ate it."

Crow the trickster, meddling with creation, seems far removed from the world of Plath's poetry, yet Hughes himself, commenting on "The Hermit at Outermost House," points to this aspect in her work. He says Plath's early poem "has the comic goblin, the tricksterish spirit, the crackling verbal energy";[5] in that poem, we find Plath's hermit sporting with the gods. And in "Years" of *Ariel*, Plath contrasts God in his "vacuous black" to her own violent energy — a contrast comparable to the one between the sleeping God and the flying, grinning Crow.

Crow the trickster shades into parody in such poems as "Crow Communes," where Crow actually attempts to talk to God, who, "exhausted with Creation, snored." So while "God lay, agape, a great carcase,/ Crow tore off a mouthful and swallowed." He asks himself, " 'Will this cipher divulge itself in digestion/ Under hearing and beyond understanding?' " and offers an aside: "(That was the first jest.)" Here is Crow, participating in a parodic Holy Communion which (surprisingly) makes him feel much stronger, although he remains "Half-illumined. Speechless./ (Appalled.)" Crow, who has asked of God, " 'What first?' " has been greeted with silence and forced to find his own answers. Although he eats of the body, he is not made one with God because Crow is superbly "impenetrable." Plath has also parodied the rite of Holy Communion, imagining it in "Tulips" as "what the dead close on" "Shutting their mouths on it, like a Communion tablet" or, in "Medusa," exclaiming to the "God-ball" that hounds her, "What do you think you are?/ A Communion wafer?" "I shall take no bite of your body."

Crow's parody takes another tack in "Crow's Theology." There he realizes God loved him, but he cannot understand who loves the stone until he concludes that "there were two Gods — / One of them much bigger than the other/ Loving his enemies/ And having all the weapons." In this version he is willing to claim that "God spoke Crow," but he wants to know who spoke other things. If the trickster is archetypally Crow's bigger God, then here Crow himself is neither the trickster nor his offspring (although the Raven in Northwest American and Eskimo folklore is a trickster) but just a shrewd observer. When Crow himself tries his luck at creation in "Crow's Playmates," he suffers the torments of the begetter as he makes "God after god — and each tore from him/ Its lodging place and its power" until Crow was "his own leftover." Crow's version of the Fall shifts from parody to farce in "Apple Tragedy," as God turns the apple into cider from which Adam and Eve and the serpent become drunk and, as a result, begin their troubles. Crow's God says of the show, " 'I am well pleased,' " and Crow concludes merrily, "And everything goes to hell." As Crow plays with Christian myths, he does not seek to do away with their contents; rather, he offers a more suitable explanation for them. Love thine enemies, Crow would counsel — but be sure to have all the weapons.

Crow's pranks and tough-guy tactics put him on the side of disorder. His joy is in seeing everything go to hell. In a number of poems, however, Crow himself is not the spreader of strife but a misfit, the victim of a power that refuses to allow a place for Crow in its universe. His birth is "A Kill," and when he alights he shivers "with the horror of Creation"; but he knows he is stuck there where "Nothing escapes him. (Nothing could escape.)" It is a world in which he knew "he was the wrong listener unwanted," but the "utmost gaping of brain in his tiny skull" was just enough to wonder "What could be hurting so much?" In this guise Crow seems to be suffering from the ontological insecurity that hounded Plath's women. In "Crow's Nerve Fails," he wonders if he is "the archive of their accusations," "their pining vengeance," "their unforgiven prisoner," and he concludes that "His prison is the earth." In this prison, he admits in "Crow Frowns," "He is the long waiting for something/ To use him." In "Magical Dangers," when he tries to think himself out of this trap, he is choked, blindfolded, "gangplanked" "into a volcano" until he "Never again moved." Still he does not give up, and in "Crow Sickened" he dived, journeyed, challenging, "Where is this somebody who has me under?" — only to discover that when he struck with all his strength at fear, it was he himself who felt the blow and fell horrified. But he is back a few poems later, in "Crow's Last Stand," to boast that his eye pupil is the final obstacle that the burning, burning, burning sun cannot burn but rages against. And in one of the seven poems added to the second edition of *Crow*,

"Crow Hears Fate Knocking on the Door," the prophecy inside Crow is "I WILL MEASURE IT ALL AND OWN IT ALL/ AND I WILL BE INSIDE IT/ AS INSIDE MY OWN LAUGHTER/ AND NOT STARING OUT AT IT THROUGH WALLS."

Crow's identity as a misfit and an outsider is a unifying theme in the volume of his songs, and while the progression of the poems just traced seems to place Crow in the position of the tormented seeker, it also underscores his primeval energy and anarchical power. Crow's paradoxical nature combines forces that the divisive habits of reason seek to separate, so Crow is both tricked and trickster, bungling and shrewd, wondering and convinced, deadly and vital. His nature is not so much double as unitary. He includes multitudes, as he himself realizes in parodying Walt Whitman in "Crow's Song of Himself." If Crow's own identity defies categories, it also resists definition by outside references. Crow is not simply the destructive anti-force to the Creator: he is both a creator in his own right, making gods for playmates, and also the one who beats hell out of the snake. He is not the mindless counterforce to civilization, either, since he witnesses and muses while the "word" poisons seas, burns whole lands, and drinks out all the people. In fact, he resists such destruction himself when words attack him with "the glottal bomb," "guerrilla labials," "consonantal masses" so that his subhuman status becomes actually a source of superhuman strength. Crow's unitary nature is the secret of his fascination. As demon or as dark god, he may be dismissed as willfully perverse; but in his defiance of opposing categories he represents that mysterious nature that is both repulsive and strangely fertile. Here again Crow is like the trickster-divinity of folklore, and like many of the speakers in Plath's poems as well. Mean and perverse they may be, but they are also uncontainable and lively.

Crow's nature is most clearly exposed in the laughter that echoes through his songs. From one angle it appears merely diabolical, an expression of his relish for violence and antihuman predilections. Car accidents, meteorites crashing on baby prams, patients writhing in pain — all are merely sidesplitting jokes to Crow. But laughter serves another purpose as well. For the man in Crow's "Criminal Ballad" who cannot hear his children for the machine guns and screaming, laughter is a release from weeping. At the same time, it is not easy to laugh in this world, and the grin that seeks a permanent home cannot find it in the faces of pain or suffering or violence, where mankind is too involved in its torment to laugh. The grin is forced to retreat to the skull which, as the emblem of death, wears its permanent feature. The anarchical energies of laughter erupt with fantastic powers; just how this works is evident in "In Laughter." The poem starts out with a realistic account of catastrophes that all occur against its background, but it shifts quickly into surrealism, where "Only the teeth work on/ And the heart, dancing on in its open cave/ Helpless on the strings of laughter." What begins as a black comedy on the violence of modern life moves straight out of social commentary into an unreal dimension where only laughter survives. Sadistic it may be, but laughter also has a vitality of its own. "The Smile," like laughter looking for its occasion, is a different manifestation of this energy. It shares laughter's delight in violence and its source in pain, but it arrives at the instant of death "for a moment/ Mending everything." It does not promise understanding, and it leaves as soon as it comes — but for an instant it works. Laughing, grinning, smiling, Crow and the characters of his songs confront their dark destinies with an equally dark power.

Behind the laughter are Crow's persistent jokes, another time-honored means of invading taboo ground. His jests with God have been amply discussed, but Crow has an equal fondness for the sexual joke. His Oedipus complex is so thoroughly abused in a number of poems that Hughes seems to be not only imitating but also parodying Plath's "Daddy." "Mama Mama" echoes through his poems, just as "Daddy, daddy" resounded through hers. Openly flaunting forbidden love, Crow's jokes also reveal, just beneath their surface, an intense fear of sex that comes through when he appears most candid. Even when Crow invents sexuality from the worm, the phallus is "the wounded end hanging out" while the woman-seducer's sex is safely buried deep within her. The title of

"Crow's Undersong" reveals his view of man's place against the woman who insatiably comes and comes and comes, even while Crow attempts to fend her off by claiming she cannot manage anything but coming. And in "Lovesong," although both man and woman are engaged in sucking each other into themselves, the woman plays a dirtier game. Her smiles are "spider bites," while his are "the garrets of a fairy palace." Her laughs are "assassin's attempts"; his are "occupying armies." Her kisses are "lawyers steadily writing"; his, "the last hooks of a castaway."

If the woman in these poems is the eternal female principle, she is both threatening and fertile, bringing in "Crow's Undersong" her appetites as well as her song, "Petals," "an animal rainbow," and even hope itself.[6] Her double nature is the subject of "Fragment of an Ancient Tablet," where she is split in two: "Above — the well-known lips, delicately downed./ Below — beard between thighs" and "Above, the face, shaped like a perfect heart./ Below — the heart's torn face." As the mother figure in Crow's poems, she represents the nurturer who threatens but without whom there is no life. When the man in "Revenge Fable" kills her with the rational weapons he calls truth, she dies, and with her dies the natural world she symbolizes. But he also destroys himself. Again, in "Song for a Phallus," when Crow "split his Mammy like a melon/ He was drenched with gore/ He found himself curled up inside her." The mother, seducer, lover all contain the double powers of life and death. Cut off from her, man is removed from his own life; tied to her, he is joined with death.

Although Hughes is more overtly mythological in his evocation of this female principle, he treats here the same creator-destroyer figure that Plath portrayed in "Lady Lazarus," "Ariel," and in her poems about bees and the moon. Sometimes she identifies with her energies, as in "Lady Lazarus"; at other times she feels overpowered by them, as in "The Moon and the Yew Tree," where the moon is her mother, "bald and wild," or in "Medusa," where the "barnacled umbilicus" and the fat, red placenta squeeze the breath from the "blood bells." In this last poem Plath's fear of the mother is a strange inversion of the Oedipal, a fear that the mother will replace her in the marriage bed. While Plath does not share Hughes's fondness for sexual jokes, her poems touch the same areas of sexual fear and violence, albeit from a female perspective. She inverts the sex act by stabbing the father-lover in revenge for his attacks in "Daddy" and ordering him to "lie back now." When she rises to eat men in "Lady Lazarus," she is the same woman who smiles now with a new glee. As she becomes one with the horse in "Ariel," she is the "arrow" that flies into the cauldron. In "Stings" the queen is a "red comet" flying over the wax house. The frequency with which Plath describes her victory in phallic terms reveals her suppressed rage and fear. Her identification with the vengeful female principle who, in her attacks, turns male is less ambiguous than Hughes's treatment of the same figure for obvious sexual reasons; but in *Crow* he moves beyond the questionings of *Wodwo* to a more forceful handling of the image.

In *Crow*, too, Hughes takes another look at death, the subject that haunted *Wodwo* and consumed Plath's interest in her later poems. *"Death"* as the answer to all the questions posed in the "Examination at the Womb-Door" is the sole owner of the universe, stronger than hope, will, love, or life. When asked who is stronger than death, Crow answers *"Me evidently"* — however, he still confronts death in every song. He is himself the black man, death's emissary, but he is also subject to its fury, always trying to escape the power that would blast him to ash. Crow's view of Creation is "the hallucination of the horror" of waste and desecration and death. Death is the essence of the world in "Crow Tyrannosaurus," where creation "was a cortege/ Of mourning and lament" and man is "a walking/ Abattoir." In trying to account for this world, Crow looks for "The Black Beast" that cannot be found although he is everywhere. This brooding spirit that hovers over *Crow* is introduced in his first song, "Two Legends." In one legend it is "the huge stammer/ Of the cry that, swelling, could not/ Pronounce its sun," and in another the "black rainbow/ Bent in emptiness/ Over emptiness/ But flying." And that spirit is there at the end in "Littleblood" "Grown so wise grown so terrible/ Sucking death's moulty tits." Despite the violence and murderousness of his early poetry, Hughes has never treated death itself with such directness and force. In *Crow* he details again and again not only the living death of the post-holocaust world, the violent deaths of battles and disasters, but also the pervasive deathliness of existence beyond the womb door.

Crow is entirely new, yet in many ways its concerns are completely familiar ones in Hughes's work. Hughes's interest in folklore and myths, his extensive knowledge of shamanism, his particular awareness of the non-human cosmos all find their fullest expression here. But alongside these concerns are a variety of lessons he learned with and from Plath. Like her, he began to break his poetic line, sometimes chopping the four-stressed line in two or into single words, other times expanding it to Whitmanesque lengths. He abandoned also the rigid structures of his early verse and began in *Crow* to organize his poems around incremental repetitions, catalogues, refrains. In *Crow* he shares with Plath a new colloquialism which, like hers, is not a relaxation but a stiffening of diction. The literary techniques of caricature, parody, and hyperbole, new to Hughes, were employed by Plath from the beginning. Behind these rhetorical parallels, certain common thematic obsessions unite their work. The achievement of *Crow* testifies to the importance of the creative relationship between Hughes and Plath, and to the energies it unleashed.

Notes

[1] Hughes, "Ted Hughes and Crow," p. 20.

[2] For an interesting discussion of *Crow* as slapstick rhetorical comedy, see Jonathan Raban, *The Society of the Poem* (London: George G. Harrap, 1971), pp. 165-171.

[3] David Lodge discusses this aspect of *Crow* in " 'Crow' and the Cartoons," *Critical Quarterly*, XIII (Spring, 1971), 37-42.

[4] Keith Sagar comments on Crow as a trickster in *Art of Ted Hughes*, pp. 113-115.

[5] Newman, ed., *Art of Sylvia Plath*, p. 190.

[6] See Sagar's interesting note on this subject in *Art of Ted Hughes*, pp. 167-168.

NINE

Conclusion

Plath's suicide has been used quite simply to explain her work. Even Robert Lowell is driven to assert that "her art's immortality is life's disintegration."[1] And, in a perverse way, Hughes's continuing life enters into an assessment of his career. Alan Bold asks at the conclusion of his study of Hughes and Thom Gunn, "How long can he continue to be? That is the question."[2] Such comments are neither useful in understanding the poems nor accurate in estimating the development of the poets. Art and death are no more inevitable links in Plath's career than life and creative exhaustion are in Hughes's. Plath's poems are death-defying acts, and the expansion of Hughes's work after Plath's death suggests an important growth, not stagnation.

Of more significance in understanding their poetry is the working relationship Plath and Hughes established early in their careers. It was the center of their creative lives, and, if each poet traveled off from it, nonetheless that center's echoes reverberate throughout their work. Only by examining this center is it possible to fully appreciate and comprehend those echoes, those extreme responses which were far from sourceless. Few poets have one constant associate with whom they share daily the common enterprise of writing. Plath and Hughes provide an unusual example of how such a relationship can nourish and sustain (and, it should be admitted, deflect and hinder) individual talents. "Influence" is perhaps not the right word to use to define the interchange between them. They influenced each other, certainly; but, more than that, they were directed and encouraged by their association.

The general course of their poetic collaboration which emerges here from the individual readings of their poems suggests that Hughes's impact on Plath was immediate and wide ranging, and that it was tempered only very late in her life. In contrast, Plath's effect on Hughes was delayed, but in some ways more profound. Always receptive to new influences, Plath was particularly open to Hughes's work and interests. Within weeks of meeting him she was writing poems about him, celebrating him as the nature spirit she imagined him to be. She turned immediately to his subjects: animals, nature, magic. While this phase did not last long or produce any important poems, it did broaden her poetic range. It took her out of her own psyche, forced her to look outside herself for subjects, and at the same time presented her with certain obstacles. The title of her early poem, "On the Difficulty of Conjuring Up a Dryad," summarizes perfectly her trouble in dealing with what she imagined to be Hughes's subjects. If Hughes himself never conjured up a dryad, he nonetheless made Plath conscious of that possibility. She was much more successful and psychologically penetrating when she combined Hughes's fascination with the spirit world and her own recognition of the evil spirits that haunted her. In "The Lady and the Earthenware Head," for example, she had no difficulty in conjuring up "its basilisk-look of love."

As she continued to write the poems that eventually formed *The Colossus,* Plath developed on two fronts. Responding to Hughes's advice and example, she moved inward and began to explore her own background and its mythic associations, and at the same time turned outward to describe the natural world. Her interest in her own background was nurtured (as it has been for so many American writers) by living abroad, and probably that interest was also aroused by her sense of Hughes's roots in quite a different country. She told her mother, "I suppose as one grows older one has a desire to learn all about one's roots, family, and country. I feel extremely moved by memories of my Austrian and German background."[3] This search for what she called "the foundation of my consciousness" was narrowly focused on herself and on what her psyche had absorbed of roots and family. It was encouraged, no doubt, by her early psychotherapy, as well as by her thesis reading of Freud and Jung and Frazer while she was a student at Smith, but it surfaced when she and Hughes were trying to elicit subjects for poems by meditating over the Ouija board. Plath had, from her apprentice period, been engaged in writing poems about what went on inside her head; the poems of this later period, such as "Lorelei," probe the area beneath the rational or conscious, differing from her early work in their mythic dimension. She began to see her own story not as peculiar and private, but as universal. Judith Kroll has surveyed this important aspect of Plath's work, emphasizing the unified mythic vision of her poetry and underscoring debts to Frazer and Graves particularly. Here it is necessary to remember that Hughes also was heavily influenced by Frazer and Graves, and that through them he directed Plath's attention to the archetypal quality of her experience.

During this period Plath was also writing poems about nature; again Hughes's example was helpful. She started writing about landscapes both literally and metaphorically foreign, and the feeling expressed in poems such as "Hardcastle Crags" and "Wuthering Heights" has been interpreted as an expression of deeply rooted fears. Her landscape poems are also accurate descriptions that draw on the subjects of Hughes's contemporaneous poems. " 'Wuthering Heights,' " Hughes has said quite sensibly, "is a description of walking on the moors above Wuthering Heights, in West Yorkshire, towards nightfall. Not a description of the moors, as I say, but of what it feels like to be walking over them."[4] Plath added to Hughes's subject — the moors — a psychological accuracy that he lacked, but she was still attempting his kind of poetry. She moved from these foreign landscapes to poems about her own native shoreline when she returned to Massachusetts in 1957. In these poems, there is a new factuality and a new attempt to see the landscape as a world endowed with her own bad spirits. Many of the poems continue the effort to probe the foundation of her consciousness by examining her native landscape.

The next change in her poetry came during the exercises in meditation and invocation that she practiced with Hughes at Yaddo. Like the earlier meditations over the Ouija board, these efforts were aimed at breaking a writing block and attempting to locate new subjects for poems in submerged areas of her consciousness. "Poem for a Birthday," the series that concludes the English edition of *The Colossus,* reveals the extent to which these exercises failed Plath. Hughes, who supported this development, has said, "She had never in her life improvised. The powers that compelled her to write so slowly had always been stronger than she was. But quite suddenly she found herself free to let herself drop, rather than inch over bridges of concepts."[5] "Poem for a Birthday" demonstrates both how far Plath dropped and what little freedom she enjoyed. Hughes has called these poems "a deliberate exercise in experimental improvisation on set themes"; but the emphasis here must be placed on the adjectives "deliberate" and "set." Although she was consciously trying to write spontaneously, in fact she succeeded chiefly in repeating lines and images from Roethke, whose work she was reading at the time. Paradoxically, whatever forced her to write slowly also allowed her to screen out the influence of other poets. She had a receptive sensibility, and all her powers of concentration were required for her to get behind her easily assimilated influences and to discover her own voice. Abandoning that control in "Poem for a Birthday," she came perilously close to mere imitation.

Insofar as Hughes encouraged these efforts at improvisation, he forced her to work against the grain of her genius. She did have a richly endowed consciousness and direct access to psychic depths, as he was the first to recognize; but deliberate efforts to conjure up those visions were no more successful than her attempts to locate dryads. Even in the eruption of her late poems, when she wrote with great speed, she evinced a kind of control that checked the flaccid associations of "Poem for a Birthday." Hughes has admitted that his own poetic gift was unobliging — at the moment of writing, he was simply possessed by it. Certainly this observation is likewise true of Plath: her best poems came in spurts, without artificial invocations. That she suffered a number of very serious writing blocks, and that she had always deliberately worked up her poems cannot be denied; but her attempt at free association was not at this time a successful alternative to her usual slow method of composition.

The beginning of Plath's final period came with "Tulips," where she did move with extreme control from an actual experience to a vivid evocation of a psychological state. Unlike "Poem for a Birthday," "Tulips" is a highly original poem, developing a system of unique and personal images that have their source not in other poems but in Plath's own life. Soon after "Tulips," however, Plath again found herself without a subject, and, as before, she returned to improvisation on set themes. The poems she wrote at this time, "Little Fugue," "The Moon and the Yew Tree," and "Elm," are enigmatic efforts to write spontaneously; while they are in some ways more powerful and moving than "Poem for a Birthday," they also veer toward the incoherent. They return to Hughes's nature spirits, to the magic of automatic writing, to mythological identities. Not until such late poems as the bee sequence, "Lady Lazarus," "Daddy," and "Ariel," among others, was Plath able to break clear of all influences and to make everything she knew work for her.

These poems are the fulfillment of her long training. They return to her first subject — herself — and to a controlled and high-pitched tone that is evident as early as her Cambridge period. Added to her early concerns are a mythic identity as the rising female, which she had begun to formulate in *The Colossus* and enlarged through her absorption of *The White Goddess,* and a new fund of female imagery with its emphasis on birthing, bleeding, triumphant violence. Although many of these poems read as if they were delivered by

Hughes's hawk, and in some ways echo and mock its stridency and self-centeredness, there is in them a psychological density as well as an almost playful manipulation which Hughes's poems of this period lack. The mask of the female victim assumed in *The Colossus* is reformed, and the agonizingly intellectualized effort to write about the other world of nature and animal is redirected. The persona, if victimized, achieves her freedom by outdoing the furious energy of her oppressors. As she flies into the cauldron of morning, she absorbs the powers in nature and the animal that had overwhelmed her in her early works. The creative-destructive female figure who emerges in Plath's late poems is glorified. The antagonist who always haunted Plath's poetry — the rival, the death-dealer — is accepted in the late poems; she is the other fused with the self, a unified identity which Plath had been seeking throughout her career. In creating this figure, Plath broke the restraints imposed by her own uncertainties and by her long acquiesence to Hughes's guidance. The worrying woman, the insomniac, the troubled wife and mother in her earlier poems are all so unsure of themselves that their sensitivity, love, and creative powers are thwarted and turned inward to self-torment. In these later poems female power is accepted and celebrated. Plath had profited from Hughes's interests in myth and the spirit world, but often his suggestions of poetic topics and his encouragement of free association forced Plath to strain after poetic effects. Alone, at the end, she was able to hear only her own voice, to write of the topic that interested her most — her self — and to use everything she had learned.

Hughes's development, if not quite so spectacular, was similar to Plath's, in the sense that he also had to outgrow certain influences, overcome the rigid formalism of his early poems, move closer to his stereotyped subjects, and open himself more fully to the darkness he celebrated. Plath's influence on his development was important, although it is easier to detect in his later work. When *The Hawk in the Rain* won first prize from the Poetry Center of the Young Men's and Young Women's Hebrew Association of New York, Plath wrote to her mother, "I am more happy than if it was my book published! I have worked so closely on these poems of Ted's and typed them so many countless times through revision after revision that I feel ecstatic about it all."[6] Just what Plath means by her involvement in Hughes's poems is difficult to specify. The revisions she mentions may have been partially the result of her comments. Hughes himself has boasted that his poems arrived in a flash, and, from what he has said of the slow process of Plath's early writing habits, we may assume that his own practice was much more speedy. However, the poems of *The Hawk in the Rain,* all finely crafted in conventional forms, appear to be more the result of deliberate and careful revision than the work of instantaneous inspiration.

The number of love poems and the emergence in them of a powerful female lover suggest that Plath's presence was an important element affecting Hughes's choice of subjects. At the same time, his castigation of the sexually frightened woman in "Secretary" or "Macaw and Little Miss," as well as his disdain for the "Egg-Head," may be read as a treatment of the sexual and intellectual dangers he felt must be escaped not only by the woman but also by the academic that Plath then was. Occasionally he gives Plath's subjects his own assured treatment. The clock that persists in her very early poems is the central image of his "September"; Hughes offers the assurance that "No clock now needs/ Tell we have only what we remember." The sense of impending catastrophe, evident in Plath's apprentice work, is evoked and neatly contained in "Parlour-Piece" and openly celebrated in "Vampire." Although Hughes seems to play closer within the range of what he calls "His terror's touchy dynamite" than Plath did at this time, his stance is so controlled that the full fury of the danger is seldom realized — as it is sometimes in Plath.

Although *Lupercal* continues the distance and the formalism of many poems in *The Hawk in the Rain,* it also offers some evidence of Hughes's advance into the submerged, instinctual life to which he merely alluded in his first volume. Plath's efforts to plumb this depth may have been useful to Hughes.

The animals that had been caged in his earlier poems are now released to wander destructively through the world, or investigated in their subterranean depths in an effort to evoke their horror. The concentrated attention on these symbols of violent energy produces, in Hughes's persona, a mixture of fear and fascination — a response that, in its openness, is still more tautly controlled and less interesting psychologically than the reactions of Plath's personae. At times (in "Pike," for example) he begins to question the meaning of the powers he evokes, but even there he is too quick to distance his subject.

He does, however, start to develop the bare outlines of the myth (borrowed from *The White Goddess*) of the creative-destructive female ruler of the underworld, a figure which loomed in Plath's late poems and forms the basis of his later poems. The old Mediterranean serpent goddess with her tail in her mouth is the image behind the sea in "Relic." She figures again in "Witches," "Snowdrop," "The Voyage," and "Fire-Eater," and in "Mayday on Holderness" he addresses her directly: " 'Mother, Mother!' " In other poems he focuses on the murderous impulse that has been nurtured by the suppression of this pagan goddess. While these poems may be read as Hughes's first efforts to formulate a mythic vision, without his later elaboration of this myth in *Crow* we might not be able to see them as crucial parts of a unified system. The poems are distinct creations, each one offering unique problems of interpretation. In part, the difficulty of identifying the coherence of his vision stems from the variety of discrete and objective subjects he treats. He is still riveted to real objects: the otter, the pike, the wolf, the particular landscapes called "Crow Hill" or "Pennines in April," the witch, the acrobat, the "Mafeking stereotype." Although the experiments in improvisation that he practiced with Plath allowed him to try out surrealistic images, his habit of focusing on an object as a starting point for a poem frequently limited him to that fixed point. His thrushes, for example, are too real and too accurately described to be more than mere birds. In these poems Hughes also tends toward rhetorical questions or general summaries of his position. Despite his condemnation of rationality, the poems of *Lupercal* remain within the bounds of rational discourse. In addition, some take their subjects from literature — a new departure for Hughes, and perhaps one influenced by Plath. "Cleopatra to the Asp," for example, not only treats Plath's subject, suicide, but even uses her imagery — water, the mirror, the moon.[7]

In *Wodwo* Hughes broke through the fixed focus of his earlier volumes, assumed a new poetic tone of questioning, developed a more colloquial style, and revealed the full impact of Plath's influence. Many of these poems were written after Plath's suicide and clearly take death as their subject. The village where she is buried is memorialized in "Heptonstall." Coffins, funeral services, dark heaven, the death mask, all are the images of *Wodwo*. Along with these emblems of finality is the persistent question, Why? And the pain of the response is evident in the title, "The Howling of Wolves," and in the skylarks' cries of "Joy! Help!"

The controlled assurance of Hughes's early personae is abandoned as he openly adopts the wodwo's pose: "What am I?" "What am I doing here in mid-air?" Even the animals that he treats are small, pitiful creatures: the gnat, the rat, rain-soaked sheep. Hughes abandons the quatrain that had been his most persistent form, reducing his line sometimes to a single word, as Plath had done in *Ariel*, and at other times expanding it across the page. The jammed lines of his early work are relaxed, and the language spreads out in colloquial phrasing. Repetition and anaphora mark the poems. They incorporate blankness, with single lines serving for stanzas. The open form that characterizes most of the poems is a perfect vehicle for the questions they formulate. The assurance of Hughes's early stance has been seriously weakened, and his speakers seem more like Plath's early questioners. What emerges in this important volume is a fuller acceptance of the meaninglessness of the human condition.

Wodwo contains a voice in addition to that of the questioner. In it can be heard not only the grimness of Hughes's early poetry, but also the defiance of Plath's late poems, as well as the black humor that will dominate *Crow*. A contrast to the open agony of many poems, it is tough, certain, closed, although not without its inner confusions. In poems such as "Logos," "Reveille," "Theology," and "Karma," Hughes attempts to rewrite the creation story along lines laid down by Robert Graves. Two of the poems start out with "No"; Hughes is denying the biblical version of Adam and Eve and asserting that it must be replaced with the true story of God's mother, the old pagan goddess, the world's creator, long suppressed by Christianity's patriarchal system. In addition to these allegorical treatments, the mother goddess surfaces in various poems as the "white angel" and the mother who reads her message in "Ballad from a Fairy Tale," and as the figure to whom the speaker prays for love in "Wings III." But she is also the devourer and at the same time "the root-blood of the origins" in "Gog," the She-Bear Goddess in "The Bear," Hecate in "The Green Wolf." Hughes's admiration for this double-featured pagan deity could never be expressed without fear of her engulfing power. While Plath incorporated the triumph and destruction of this goddess into her own final mythic identity, Hughes was torn between his desire to celebrate her power and the equally fierce fear of the "grooved kiss that swamps the eyes with darkness." "Gog" is his most ambivalent treatment of this goddess-dragon who is finally overcome — but only by the enigmatic "rider of iron, on the horse shod with vaginas of iron" who "Gallops over the womb that makes no claim."

These poems in which Hughes tries to formulate a mythic framework are efforts to regain the control of his early poems that is so openly shattered in the *Wodwo* poems about death, and are at the same time attempts to engage more fully the dark powers which he imagined fused the universe. The poems are a curious mixture of allegory and surrealism. Much of the imagery is straight out of Plath, and the tone is a combination of her defiant voice and his own earlier assurance.

Crow is a more elaborate treatment of the myth begun in *Wodwo*. The female figure is the central presence from which

Crow cannot escape, although he sees her more clearly than the personae of *Wodwo*. She is part of himself, and at the same time his destroyer. The strategies that Crow employs to survive in the world she dominates are similar to Plath's: sardonic humor, caricature, hyperbole, parody. The nursery rhyme quality of many of Crow's songs echoes Plath in its effort to hold off and charm this spirit. Hughes turned in these poems to what he called the surrealism of folklore, although it has many affinities with Plath's more sophisticated surrealistic techniques.

Hughes has said that the super-ugly songs of Crow would shed everything but precisely what he wanted to say. In *Crow* Hughes did pare his style, but in the process he gained an intensity and a purity of expression that allowed him to penetrate more deeply the world submerged in his consciousness — there to discover, as Plath had done, the universal patterns of an ancient mythology. Also like Plath, he had already read the outlines of this myth in *The White Goddess* and other books on folklore, and he had been treating it in poems since *Lupercal*. Not until after the poems of *Wodwo* that express the fear and agony aroused by Plath's suicide did Hughes begin to explore the myth more fully. In returning to the animal as a subject in *Crow*, Hughes was perhaps trying to escape the personal turmoil he was suffering; but he also brought to the beast fable the insights his misery had offered. Despite its origin in folklore and myth, *Crow* is more deeply rooted in Hughes's psyche than anything he had written before.

While in their late work Plath and Hughes rely on the same myth of the creative-destructive goddess, their responses to it are quite different. For Plath, this goddess is a figure of power and fecundity — destructive and threatening, but in the end an identity to be celebrated and assumed. For Hughes, of course, she was always the other, sometimes the life-affirming spirit battling against the deadening powers of civilization and rationality, but frequently the overpowering and threatening mother, the spirit of death and the underworld, the demon lover. The fears which the goddess unleashed in Hughes produced some of his best poetry, but it is poetry that reveals regressive fantasies, the threat of impotence, ontological insecurity. In these late poems Hughes and Plath seem to have reversed their earlier positions: Plath is now triumphant, and Hughes, if not defeated, is at least fully aware of that possibility. Crow's "Lovesong" summarizes their story: "In their entwined sleep they exchanged arms and legs/ In their dreams their brains took each other hostage/ In the morning they wore each other's face."

Notes

[1] Robert Lowell, "Foreword" for Plath's *Ariel,* p. viii.

[2] Alan Bold, *Thom Gunn and Ted Hughes* (New York: Harper & Row, 1976), p. 132.

[3] Plath, *Letters Home,* p. 346.

[4] Hughes, *Poetry Is,* p. 77.

[5] Newman, ed., *Art of Sylvia Plath,* p. 192.

[6] Plath, *Letters Home,* p. 297.

[7] See Anthony Libby's discussion of this interchange in "God's Lioness and the Priest of Sycorax: Plath and Hughes."

Selected Bibliography

Selected Works by Sylvia Plath

Ariel. London: Faber and Faber, 1965; New York: Harper & Row, 1966.

The Bell Jar. London: Heinemann, 1963; Faber and Faber, 1966; New York: Harper & Row, 1971.

The Colossus and Other Poems. London: Heinemann, 1960; New York: Alfred A. Knopf, 1962; London: Faber and Faber, 1967.

"Context." *London Magazine*, n.s. I (February, 1962), 45-46.

Crossing the Water. London: Faber and Faber, 1971; New York: Harper & Row, 1972.

Crystal Gazer. London: Rainbow Press, 1971.

Letters Home. Ed. Aurelia Schober Plath. New York: Harper & Row, 1975.

Lyonnesse. London: Rainbow Press, 1971.

"Ocean 1212-W." *The Listener*, LXX (August 29, 1963), 312-313. Also in *Writers on Themselves*. Ed. Herbert Read. London: British Broadcasting Corporation, 1964. Pp. 102-110.

"Sylvia Plath." *The Poet Speaks*. Ed. Peter Orr. London: Routledge & Kegan Paul, 1966. Pp. 167-172.

Uncollected Poems. London: Turret Press, 1965.

Winter Trees. London: Faber and Faber, 1971; New York: Harper & Row, 1972.

Wreath for a Bridal. Frensham: Sceptre Press, 1970.

Selected Works by Ted Hughes

A Choice of Shakespeare's Verse. London: Faber and Faber, 1971. Selected, with an introduction by Ted Hughes. American edition entitled *With Fairest Flowers While Summer Lasts*. New York: Doubleday, 1971.

"Context." *London Magazine*, n.s. I (February, 1962), 44-45.

Crow. London: Faber and Faber, 1970; New York: Harper & Row, 1971. (American edition contains seven poems not in the first British edition.)

The Hawk in the Rain. London: Faber and Faber, 1957; New York: Harper & Row, 1957.

"Introduction." *Selected Poems of Keith Douglas*. Ed. with an introduction by Ted Hughes. London: Faber and Faber, 1964.

Lupercal. London: Faber and Faber, 1960; New York: Harper & Row, 1960.

Poetry in the Making. An Anthology of Poems and Programmes from "Listening and Writing." London: Faber and Faber, 1967. American edition entitled *Poetry Is*. New York: Doubleday, 1970.

Recklings. London: Turret Books, 1966. (Limited edition, 150, signed.)

Review of *Folktales of Japan*, ed. Keigo Seki, and *Folktales of Israel*, ed. Dov Noy. *The Listener*, LXX (December 12, 1963), p. 999.

Review of *Imitations* by Robert Lowell. *The Listener*, LXVIII (August 2, 1962), p. 185.

Review of *Myths and Religions of the North* by E. O. G. Turville-Petre. *The Listener*, LXXI (March 19, 1964), pp. 484-485.

Review of *Primitive Song*, by C. M. Bowra. *The Listener*, LXVII (May 3, 1962), p. 781.

Review of *Shamanism* by Mircea Eliade and *The Sufis* by Indries Shah. *The Listener*, LXXII (October 29, 1964), p. 678.

"The Rock." *Writers on Themselves*. Ed. Herbert Read. London: British Broadcasting Corporation, 1964. Pp. 86-92.

Selected Poems, 1957-1967. London: Faber and Faber, 1972; New York: Harper & Row, 1974.

Selected Poems, Thom Gunn and Ted Hughes. London: Faber and Faber, 1962.

"Ted Hughes and Crow," an interview with Egbert Faas. *London Magazine*, X (January, 1971), 5-20.

Wodwo. London: Faber and Faber, 1967. (Contains one poem, "Logos," not in the American edition.) New York: Harper & Row, 1967. (Contains two poems, "Root, Stem, Leaf" and "Scapegoats and Rabies," not in the British edition.)

Studies of Sylvia Plath

Aird, Eileen. *Sylvia Plath*. New York: Harper & Row, 1973.

Alvarez, A. *The Savage God*. London: Weidenfield and Nicholson, 1971; New York: Random House, 1972. Pp. 5-34.

———. "Sylvia Plath: The Cambridge Collection." *Cambridge Review*, XC (February 7, 1969), 246-247.

Butscher, Edward. *Sylvia Plath: Method and Madness*. New York: Seabury Press, 1976.

Hardwick, Elizabeth. "On Sylvia Plath." *New York Review of Books*, XVII, August 12, 1971, 3-4, 6.

Hobsbaum, Philip, "The Temptations of Giant Despair." *Hudson Review*, XXV (Winter, 1972-73), 597-612.

Holbrook, David. "R. D. Laing and the Death Circuit." *Encounter*, XXXI (August, 1968), 35-45.

———. "Sylvia Plath and the Problem of Violence in Art." *Cambridge Review*, XC (February 7, 1969), 249-250.

———. *Sylvia Plath: Poetry and Existence*. London: Athlone, 1976.

Homberger, Eric. *A Chronological Checklist of the Periodical Publications of Sylvia Plath*. Exeter: University of Exeter, 1970.

———. "I Am I." *Cambridge Review*, XC (February 7, 1969), 251-253.

Hughes, Ted. "Notes on the Chronological Order of Sylvia Plath's Poems." *Tri-Quarterly*, VII (Fall, 1966), 81-88. Reprinted in *The Art of Sylvia Plath*.

———. "Sylvia Plath." *Poetry Book Society Bulletin*, no. 44 (February, 1965).

Kroll, Judith. *Chapters in a Mythology: The Poetry of Sylvia Plath*. New York: Harper & Row, 1976.

Libby, Anthony. "God's Lioness and the Priest of Sycorax: Plath and Hughes." *Contemporary Literature*, XV (Summer, 1974), 386-405.

Melander, Ingrid. *The Poetry of Sylvia Plath: A Study of Themes*. Gothenberg Studies in English, no. 25. Stockholm: Almqvist & Wiksell, 1972.

Newman, Charles, ed. *The Art of Sylvia Plath: A Symposium*. London: Faber and Faber, 1970; Bloomington: Indiana University Press, 1970.

Oates, Joyce Carol. "The Death Throes of Romanticism: The Poems of Sylvia Plath." *Southern Review*, IX (July, 1973), 501-522.

Ostriker, Alicia. " 'Fact' as Style: The Americanization of Sylvia." *Language and Style*, I (Summer, 1968), 201-212.

Perloff, Marjorie. "Angst and Animism in the Poetry of Sylvia Plath." *Journal of Modern Literature*, I (1970), 57-74.

———. "On the Road to Ariel: The 'Transitional' Poetry of Sylvia Plath." *Iowa Review*, IV (Spring, 1973), 94-110.

———. *The Poetic Art of Robert Lowell*. Ithaca: Cornell University Press, 1973.

Rosenstein, Harriet. "Reconsidering Sylvia Plath." *Ms. Magazine*, I, September, 1972, pp. 45-51, 96-99.

Schwartz, Murray M., and Christopher Bollas. "The Absence at the Center: Sylvia Plath and Suicide." *Criticism*, XVIII (Spring, 1976), 147-172.

Smith, Pamela. "Architectonics: Sylvia Plath's *Colossus*." *Ariel*, IV (January, 1973), 4-21.

———. "The Unitive Urge in the Poetry of Sylvia Plath." *New England Quarterly*, XLV (Septermber, 1972), 323-339.

Steiner, George. "In Extremis." *Cambridge Review*, XC (February 7, 1969), 247-249.

Sylvia Plath and Anne Sexton: A Reference Guide. Ed. Cameron Northhouse and Thomas P. Walsh. Boston: G. K. Hall, 1974.

"Sylvia Plath's 'Tulips': A Festival." *Paunch*, XLII-XLIII (December, 1975), 65-122.

Uroff, M. D. "Sylvia Plath and Confessional Poetry: A Reconsideration." *Iowa Review*, VIII (Winter, 1977), 104-115.

Studies of Ted Hughes

Bedient, Calvin. "On Ted Hughes." *Critical Quarterly*, XIV (Summer, 1972), 103-121. Reprinted in *Eight Contemporary Poets*. London: Oxford University Press, 1974.

Bold, Alan. *Thom Gunn and Ted Hughes*. New York: Harper & Row, 1976.

Dyson, A. E. "Ted Hughes." *Critical Quarterly*, I (Autumn, 1959), 219-226.

Gitzen, Julian. "Ted Hughes and the Triumph of Energy." *Southern Humanities Review*, VII (Winter, 1973), 67-73.

Grubb, Frederick. *A Vision of Reality: A Study of Liberalism in Twentieth-Century Verse*. London: Chatto and Windus, 1965.

Harrison, Tony. "Crow Magnon." *London Magazine*, X (January, 1971), 86-88.

Hoffman, Daniel. "Talking Beasts: The 'Single Adventure' in the Poems of Ted Hughes." *Shenandoah*, XIX (Summer, 1968), 49-68.

Holbrook, David. "The Cult of Hughes and Gunn: The Dangers of Poetical Fashion." *Poetry Review*, LIV (Summer, 1963), 167-183.

James, G. Ingli. "The Animal Poems of Ted Hughes: A Devaluation." *Southern Review*, II (1967), 93-203.

John, Brian. "Ted Hughes: Poet at the Master-Fulcrum of Violence." *Arizona Quarterly*, XXIII (Spring, 1967), 5-15.

Libby, Anthony. "Fire and Light: Four Poets to the End and Beyond." *Iowa Review*, IV (Spring, 1973), 111-126.

Lodge, David. " 'Crow' and the Cartoons." *Critical Quarterly*, XIII (Spring, 1971), 37-42, 68.

Lucie-Smith, Edward. "The Tortured Yearned as Well." *Critical Quarterly*, IV (Spring, 1962), 34-43.

Miller, Karl. "Fear and Fang." *New York Review of Books*, XXI, March 7, 1974, 3-6.

Newton, J. M. "Some Notes on Crow by Ted Hughes." *Cambridge Quarterly*, V (Autumn, 1971), 376-384.

———. "Ted Hughes's Metaphysical Poems." *Cambridge Quarterly*, II (Autumn, 1967), 395-402.

Press, John. *Rule and Energy: Trends in British Poetry since the Second World War*. London: Oxford University Press, 1963.

Raban, Jonathan. *The Society of the Poem*. London: George G. Harrap, 1971.

Rawson, C. J. "Some Sources or Parallels to Poems by Ted Hughes." *Notes & Queries*, XV (February, 1968), 62-63.

———. "Ted Hughes: A Reappraisal." *Essays in Criticism*, XV (January, 1965), 77-94.

———. "Ted Hughes and Violence." *Essays in Criticism*, XVI (January, 1966), 124-129.

Roberts, Neil. "The Spirit of Crow." *Delta*, L (Spring, 1972), 3-15.

Rosenthal, M. L. *The New Poets*. New York: Oxford University Press, 1967.

Sagar, Keith. *The Art of Ted Hughes*. Cambridge: Cambridge University Press, 1975.

Index